THE ENCYCLOPEDIA
OF MILITANT ISLAM

THE ENCYCLOPEDIA OF MILITANT ISLAM

By Bryan Griffin

With Herb London and Jed Babbin

LONDONCENTER
FOR POLICY RESEARCH

The London Center for Policy Research
New York, New York
www.londoncenter.org

© 2016 The London Center for Policy Research

Designed by Kristina Phillips

ISBN-13: 978-1530333622
ISBN-10: 1530333628

To Frank, Leslie, Jill, Jessica, my whole family, and my dear friends: thank you for the support and encouragement to complete this book.

CONTENTS

PROLOGUE

IN MANY RESPECTS 2015 RESEMBLES 1848, a time when all of the assumptions of the past were called into question. This is a parlous time, a period of possible worldwide conflagration. Islamic extremism is on the rise and with it the belief that history is moving inexorably in its direction.

The West is confused. On the one hand, it is appalled by the level of violence; yet on the other hand, it is not sure of what to do. A viewpoint on how to approach the battle against fundamentalist ideology is spelled out in Jed Babbin's evocative essay at the end of this book, albeit this is an introduction to a topic that requires a full-blown investigation.

What follows this introductory piece is different. So often, I hear people express confusion about militant Islamic organizations—names that are in the news and out of the news. As a consequence, through the leadership of Bryan Griffin, we have attempted to differentiate the major Islamic militant organizations, spelling out who they represent, where they are located, their relative strength and influence, the nature of their leadership, and the degree of cooperation between them.

Tactics among these organizations vary, but the ultimate goal of a global caliphate remains consistent.

Understanding that stage and the actors on it is the overarching premise of this enterprise.

At the very least, our hope is that the reader will gain a better understanding of these militant Islamic groups. As many have suggested, one cannot defeat an enemy that one cannot define. The definitions lie ahead of you.

—Herb London

INTRODUCTION

MILITANT ISLAMIC GROUPS in every corner of the world contend that they must kill infidels and give their lives for their faith. Global jihad organizations from al-Shabaab to the Taliban, from Hamas to the Islamic State, from Boko Haram to Al Qaeda share the same ideology: imposing fundamentalist Islamic rule on the world. Tactics may vary from one group to the next, but the strategy is consistent and cooperation abounds.

Islamic State (IS) leader Abu Bakr al-Baghdadi has said the plan is to conquer Rome. Why Rome? "Because it is the capital of the Catholics, or the Crusaders."[1] The war is not merely one against Catholics, other Christians, and Jews, but a war against infidels, including Muslims who do not share this militant philosophical position. The Islamic State and Al Qaeda have killed as many Muslims as Westerners.

While it has been said many times, it should be repeated that most Muslims are not supporters of this type of jihad. That said, *everyone* who values the Western ideals of freedom, democracy, and the rule of law has the duty to denounce the fundamentalism behind militant Islam.

Islamization, meaning the forced, coerced, or unexamined application of fundamentalist Islam, is in full swing in many parts of the globe, notably throughout Europe. There are at least 20 million Muslims in Europe, comprising 15 percent of the European population. Most are observant, as worshippers who descend on mosques in major cities would suggest. Occasionally, the imams preach against the "Crusaders," code for European Christians. The Europeans, in their naiveté,

3

believe that their democratic principles will ultimately stave off the threat of Sharia. But very few realize that democracy and its accompanying individual rights are what hard-line Sharia forbids. For many extremists, the Koran offers all the wisdom one would require to lead a productive life; all other fields of study are redundant.

When President al Sisi of Egypt said at al Azur Academy, the leading center of Islamic scholarship, that it is time to recognize "the violent dimensions of our religion and address this matter through a revolution from within," his words were largely ignored, in part because they radically departed from Koranic doctrine.

In *The River War*, Winston Churchill noted this fanaticism of what he called "Mohammedanism." He contended that death is as appealing as life for jihadists. By their own words, militant Islamic groups have confirmed this supposition. Hassan Nasrallah, the leader of Hezbollah, has said, "You [the West] value life; we [Islamists] value death. That is our advantage."

Despite comments of this kind, the general Western response is to deny any link between Islam and the motivation behind these militant Islamic groups. Such an attitude harms our ability to adequately face militant Islam, because it fails to recognize the cooperative potential of these groups acting under the same guiding ideology, one that interprets Islamic doctrine as prescribing a violent jihad.

The lack of understanding does not stop at ideological ties. Allow me to pose a pertinent example. Even with evidence that Al Qaeda has tentacles all over the world, President Obama consistently has described it as either defanged or controlled. The incident of terrorism in Benghazi on September 9, 2012, is a perfect example of this pattern. The president's erroneous description of the Benghazi attackers persisted long after 2012. In a speech at the National Defense University on May 23, 2013, the president described the Benghazi attackers as "localized threats," as "local operatives" who may have had a "loose affiliation with regional networks." President Obama gave no hint that many of the attackers belonged to Al Qaeda's international terrorist network. Administration spokesmen have even created an artificial distinction between core Al Qaeda and non-core Al Qaeda. Conversely, a House

Intelligence Committee report confirms that Al Qaeda operates in the Maghreb, the Arabian Peninsula, Iraq, Syria, and the West Bank. It has offices in Europe and even the United States under a variety of front organizations. There is nothing "local" about these groups, nor are they as loosely affiliated as the president suggests. Collectively, these organizations have a presence that stretches from North and West Africa through the heart of Arabia and the Levant into Iraq. They have ties to Ansar al Sharia in East Libya, Boko Haram in Nigeria, and even the Shia rebels in Yemen.

The nations with the highest rate of terrorist attacks are majority Muslim societies. According to a University of Michigan study, the nations with the most attacks and fatalities are Iraq, Pakistan, Afghanistan, Yemen, Nigeria, Somalia, and Egypt. Nations that have a sizable Muslim minority face terrorism from extremists within this minority; e.g., India, Thailand, and the Philippines.

The highest concentration of terrorist attacks is in areas of Islamist conflict. The war in Syria and Iraq fomented by the Islamic State, battles between Hamas and Hezbollah and Israel, the Yemeni civil war, the Taliban insurgency in Afghanistan, and the atrocities of Boko Haram all have active participation by Islamist extremist factions.

Major terrorist attacks worldwide tend to be committed by Islamic extremists. Whether they're the attacks on the World Trade Center and the Pentagon, the Boston Marathon bombings, or the heinous Woolwich beheading, the overwhelming majority of deadly terrorist attacks to date were perpetrated by those subscribing to Islamism, a University of Maryland database shows.

The surge in global terrorism is fueled by Islamist extremism. Despite the false equivalencies and the apologetic rationalizations, all the evidence points to the conclusion that Islamic extremism is one of the deadliest sources of terror in the world. Clearly, terrorism carried out by extremists can lead to the broad generalization that all Muslims support terrorism, a contention already repudiated. But it is the case that Islam has been successfully meshed with prescriptions for violence. Varying cross sections of the 1.6 billion Muslims worldwide, in a Pew Research report, support imposing some form of Sharia by force, including "honor killings" of women accused of infidelity, and even death for those who abandon the Islamic religion.

However, it is important to note that militant Islamic groups share more than just a guiding ideology. They share a methodology.

Relying on a strategy adopted by the Muslim Brotherhood, created in Egypt in 1928, a concerted effort has begun to use social welfare programs to curry favor and then actively recruit unwary citizens for membership. Similarly, as the Holy Land Foundation case pointed out, Islamic charities and educational organizations, many of them active in the U.S. and Great Britain, are front groups to support and finance terror organizations such as Hamas.

The mission of these social organizations, like the mission of their militant counterparts, is to set the stage for an Islamic caliphate, or a country ruled by Sharia and dominated by Islam. From this staging platform, a jihadist offensive can be launched against others. There are more terrorist groups operating now than ever before. Moreover, the availability of weapons of mass destruction and advances in technology only highlight the threat. Social media is yet another facile way to organize and recruit adherents, and is now utilized by these groups.

For years, Saudi Arabia and Qatar funded Sunni militant groups through money obtained from oil revenue. Now that both nations are being targeted by Shia revolutionaries, there is an apparent sobering effect. Nonetheless, Wahhabi ideology, developed in Saudi Arabia, has had a profound influence on radical sentiment. In many madrassas worldwide, the ideology persists along with its first cousins, Salafism and Deobandi. The majority of militant Islamic groups ascribe to one of the aforementioned three sects of Islam.

Militant Islamic groups recruit young and impressionable children. Often, these children come from impoverished backgrounds and are promised food, money, or safety for their families. In their madrassas, which are run by the organizations, the teachers indoctrinate a hatred of the West and a call for war under the banner of Islam. "One Ummah without the West. Until Islam rules, there will be no rest." These words are uttered by six- to 13-year-olds around the globe in a solidarity ceremony with the Islamic State. From Sydney to Rotterdam, from Mali to Jakarta, children are being guided by militant Islamists to adopt this chant.

It should also be noted that lawless regions, not administered by state governments, serve as global sanctuaries for terrorism. In Pakistan's FATA region, areas of northern Afghanistan, and the Sinai Peninsula, training and recruitment occur outside the eyes and ears of government officials.

Notwithstanding all of the challenges on the world stage, philosophically the West doesn't speak a language acceptable under these militants' Sharia, and vice versa. From *"Liberté, egalité, fraternité"* to the Federalist Papers, the West has been repudiating absolute authority in favor of some form of self-government and the recognition of individual rights. Whether it is in Holland or in Somalia, this Western orientation is precisely what Islamists oppose. As they see it, there is no possible reconciliation between the absolutist position implicit in the Koran and Western foundations. Conflict exists, and the West will surrender, Muslims—through internal pressure—will modify the stance of the religion, or militant Islam will be defeated unconditionally. These are stark choices, but as I see it, realistic ones.

In the pages that follow, there are descriptions of 44 of the most prominent militant Islamic organizations. They are located in different places, and each has its own idiosyncratic approach. Yet there is a common thread: they are all committed to international jihad and the ultimate creation of a global caliphate. For all of them, violence is the method, religious zeal the inspiration, and the belief that they represent the will of Allah the motivation. A globally concerted effort on behalf of fundamentalist-inspired conquest is not only possible, it is already happening. If militant Islam is to be defeated, the level of cooperation between these groups, and their common origins and ideologies, must be understood.

—HERBERT LONDON

NOTES

1 "From Sydney to Rome, Until Islam Rules the World." Ynetnews.com. 16 Dec. 2014.

AUTHOR'S NOTE

EACH ENTRY IN THIS BOOK details a different militant Islamic group, with five sub-components: founding, leadership, violence, ties, and funding. The entries read as narrative stories to aid in understanding the origins and history of each organization. Many of these groups share a common parent group or spiritual leader. The majority were formed by mujahideen fighters who shared a common banner in the 1980s. It is notable that, despite any differences in these groups now, at one time most of them fought side by side as mujahideen to repel Soviet forces in Afghanistan during the Soviet-Afghan war.

I end each section with an examination of the ties between the groups and the sources of their funding. If the threat of militant Islam is to be truly appreciated, the cooperation between these groups on behalf of a global jihad must be understood.

References within an entry to other militant Islamic groups are in **bold**, to make the cross references stand out. Almost every group is tied to at least two other militant Islamic groups listed in this book. This underscores the case that cooperation between the groups either is plausible, is likely, or already exists.

Not only do these groups share common roots and cooperate with one another, but their tactics are noticeably similar.

Many groups use social welfare programs to create a dependency among impoverished populations. While each group has its ideological masterminds, many of the foot soldiers owe their role within militant Islam to poverty. The senior ideologues use food, money, and the promise of a better life to lure recruits and quell dissent. Welfare is used strategically to create obligation. In addition, the recruits are typically young, impressionable men, and indoctrination is always a part of the training process.

Islamic charities, many of which operate in the U.S. and Britain, are frequently used as front groups for money schemes that finance the militant groups. Many donors to such groups are likely unaware of the true causes they are funding.

The typical objective of these groups is to create an Islamic caliphate, or a country completely ruled by hard-line Sharia and dominated by Islam, that can then be a staging platform for a jihadist offensive against the rest of the world. To consolidate ultimate power and marginalize opposition, many of the groups' militant elites embrace Marxist political ideology. Should they be successful in establishing a caliphate, a centralized theocratic nation as a sovereign actor on the global stage would allow these groups to grow unchecked and stockpile for a worldwide offensive. In Pakistan's FATA region, which is lawless and informally administered, many groups operate off of official radars and in a jurisdictional gray area to regroup, gain recruits, and avoid Pakistani or international punishment. This region is a dangerous advantage to these groups, and an illuminating example of the power of militant Islamic control of a territory without reprisal. The ability of each modern country to withstand these groups' separatist objectives is within the purview of the security of every nation on Earth.

As groups continue to form, they also continue to create spin-off groups, which grow in size, recruitment capacities, and militant capabilities. There are more militant Islamic groups now than ever before in history. These groups are growing, spreading, and multiplying.

Attacks are becoming deadlier with improvements to weapon-building devices and information dissemination. Technological advances such as the 3D printer will only make arms and weaponry more readily available to these groups. YouTube, Facebook, Twitter, and blogs are utilized by many of these groups to spread propaganda, organize, and gather recruits. These platforms offer cheap and effective means of spreading fear, coercing recruits, and manipulating the narrative around the objectives of militant Islam.

Saudi Arabia, Qatar, and other Persian Gulf countries fund or have funded, both directly and indirectly, many of the Sunni militant groups.

Iran funds the Shiite militant groups. The international community must do more to curtail this funding.

Deobandi, Salafist, and Wahhabi ideologies produce the most radically offensive groups.

As with any text in the field of coercive and surreptitious non-state actors, information on these groups is hard to confirm. This book is not a compendium of field research or exclusive information. Insofar as these groups are constantly transforming, and information regarding their activities and structure is oftentimes an observational estimate, this text is not warranting a strictly authoritative reference. Rather, the intention was to produce an easily digestible pocket guide, of manageable length and complexity to the average reader, to catalog and present readily available information about 44 of the world's most notorious militant Islamic groups. And, although this book documents atrocities against the nationals of the countries where these militant groups operate, it at times highlights the violence inflicted against international citizens. This is intended to remind us that although we may not live in countries ravaged by these groups, the fight against militant Islam is a global one.

The greatest weapon we can possess to counter the efforts of these groups is an informed understanding of their shared tactics and potential for cooperation. It is my hope that this book will illuminate the threat posed by the concerted effort of these extremist groups for worldwide domination, so that a well-informed public can demand an appropriate response from political leaders.

Knowledge, however, is only half of the battle. The ideals of freedom, individualism, participatory government, equality, and inalienable rights must be our banner, both preached and practiced. Narratives of our own that embellish the faults of democracy and capitalism and that overlook the objective superiority of these Western-backed ideals over hard-line Sharia, or autocracy in any form, can create the mental and physical vulnerabilities that Islamic fundamentalists wish to capitalize upon. Despite the amalgamation of militant Islam, our greatest enemy may just be the potential for our own moral equivocation. We must, together, understand militant Islam, resist the spread of its ideology, and confront it nobly.

—BRYAN GRIFFIN

ABDULLAH AZZAM BRIGADES (AAB)

ABDULLAH AZZAM
BRIGADES (AAB)

Main Area(s) of Operation	Lebanon, Arabian Peninsula
Founder or Spiritual Leader	Abdullah Azzam
Known or Suspected Leader	Saleh al Qarawi
Approximate Year Founded	2004
Approximate Size	Hundreds to thousands among multiple branches
Alliances & Cooperations	Al Qaeda, al-Nusra
Enemies/Rivals	Hezbollah
Ideological Sect/Affiliation	Salafist
Flag	

THE ABDULLAH AZZAM BRIGADES (AAB) is a Sunni jihadist group that operates primarily out of Lebanon and the Arabian Peninsula, with some activities in Afghanistan and Pakistan. The group has several branches and factions.

The group is named after Osama bin Laden's mentor, Abdullah Azzam, who was also the cofounder of **Al Qaeda**. Azzam was Palestinian, and led a massive recruitment campaign of mujahideen fighters from across the Middle East to converge in Afghanistan and fight the Soviets in the 1980s. He was also instrumental in the founding of **Hamas**. Azzam was assassinated in Peshawar, Pakistan, in 1989.

Allegedly, the assassination was arranged by the current leader of **Al Qaeda**, Ayman al-Zawahiri, with whom Azzam had frequent disagreements.

The AAB's original objective was to fight Western interests in the Middle East, but activities have expanded to include offensives against Israel. The AAB has called for the overthrow of the Saudi monarchy and a regime change in Lebanon. Additionally, AAB militants have traveled to Syria to fight alongside rebels against Bashar al-Assad's regime.

FOUNDING

The AAB was founded in 2004 to aid **Al Qaeda**'s efforts in targeting Syria, Lebanon, Israel, and the Palestinian territories. Its founder was Saleh al Qarawi, who says he was personally ordered by **Al Qaeda** leader Abu Musab al Zarqawi to form the group.

The various branches of the AAB were formed as operations expanded around the Middle East. One of the branches, called the Ziad al Jarrah Battalion, which is based in Lebanon, was named after the hijacker of United Airlines flight 93 that crashed in a field in Pennsylvania on September 11, 2001. The Arabian Peninsula-based battalion is called the al-'Uyayri Battalion, named after a former leader of **Al Qaeda**.

In February 2014, a group called Saraya Yehya Ayyash released a video of its activities from the Gaza Strip. The video depicted a targeting of the January funeral for former Israeli prime minister Ariel Sharon. Pictures posted to social media sites show the group launching rockets into Israel. Saraya Yehya Ayyash claims it has integrated into the AAB.

Through YouTube, Twitter, and various other social media outlets, the group has become proficient in releasing propaganda and widely disseminated calls for jihad. It releases new propaganda regularly.

LEADERSHIP

Saleh al Qarawi has led the group since founding it. Suleiman Hamad Al-Hablain is a senior member who is wanted internationally for constructing explosive devices. The AAB spokesperson is Sirajeddine Zurayqat, who has released numerous videos and Twitter posts calling for jihadist fighting on behalf of the AAB, particularly proclaiming that Sunnis in Lebanon should focus their efforts on combating **Hezbollah**.

One of the group's high-ranking commanders was Majid Bin-Muhammad al Majid, who took power in June 2012. In 2014, he died from kidney failure in Lebanese custody in Beirut.

VIOLENCE

In 2005, the AAB bombed two U.S. Navy ships, the **Kearsarge** and the **Ashland**, as well as the Egyptian Museum in Cairo. A separate AAB-claimed series of car bombings in the tourist-heavy site of Sharm al Shaykh, Egypt, killed 88 and injured 200. AAB suicide bombings in June 2009 in the Perl Continental Hotel in Peshawar, Pakistan, killed 17 and injured 46. In 2010, the AAB executed a suicide bombing of a Japanese oil tanker. In 2011, it led an armed assault against NATO oil tankers in Afghanistan, killing 15.

In November 2013, the group carried out two suicide bombings on the Iranian embassy in Beirut, Lebanon. The attack killed 25 and injured 150, causing significant damage to the small community that housed the embassy. An AAB spokesman praised the bombers as "heroes" on Twitter following the attack.

A double suicide bombing in 2014 at the Iranian Cultural Center in Beirut killed 129.

A 2005 AAB rocket attack was aimed at American ships in Aqaba, Jordan. The AAB has claimed responsibility for launching rockets into Israel from Gaza in 2009, 2011, and multiple times in 2014, often posting photos of the launches on Twitter. The targets are typically busy population centers in northern Israel.

TIES

The AAB's formation was ordered by the **Al Qaeda** branch in Iraq, and the group has referred to itself as "Al Qaeda in the Levant." In 2013 and 2014, it partnered with **Al Nusra** in Lebanon to launch rocket attacks at **Hezbollah** targets.

AAB's integrated Palestinian sub-group, Saraya Yehya Ayyash, is named after a top **Hamas** explosives expert who was killed in 1996. Equally notable, Abdullah Azzam was a founder of **Hamas**.

FUNDING

AAB financial support likely comes from **Al Qaeda**.

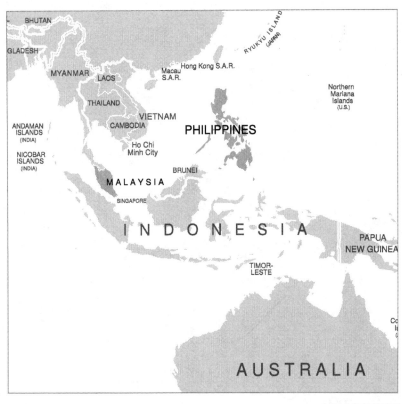

ABU SAYYAF

ABU SAYYAF

Main Area(s) of Operation	Philippines, Malaysia
Founder or Spiritual Leader	Abdurajak Janjalani
Known or Suspected Leader	Khadaffy Janjalani
Approximate Year Founded	1991
Approximate Size	400+
Alliances & Cooperations	Al Qaeda, Jemaah Islamiyah, Moro Islamic Liberation Front, Islamic State
Name Meaning	"Bearer of the Sword"
Flag	

ABU SAYYAF, translated as "Bearer of the Sword," is a militant separatist Islamic group based in the southern Philippines. Its mission is to establish an independent Muslim state. According to the National Counter Terrorism Center, Abu Sayyaf is "the most violent of the Islamic separatist groups" in the region.[1]

It operates predominantly in the southern Philippine islands of Mindanao and the Sulu Archipelago, the region that the group ultimately desires to become the new Muslim state, but they have been known to venture as far as Malaysia to commit kidnappings.

Abu Sayyaf's strength was severely weakened in 2007 following U.S.-Philippine military operations that killed 127 members and captured 38. As recently as 2014, the group committed 72 violent incidents within half a year, and lost another 69 members to combat or capture.

Estimates of its size have fluctuated from the thousands to the hundreds, but the U.S. State Department believes it is growing, thanks to aid from **Jemaah Islamiyah** and the **Moro Islamic Liberation Front**. The most recent estimate is 423 members.

Unlike the **Moro Islamic Liberation Front**, **Abu Sayyaf** has never engaged in peace negotiations with the Philippine government.

FOUNDING
Abu Sayyaf split from the Moro National Liberation Front, a Marxist Philippine separatist group, in 1991. Abdurajak Janjalani, who fought in the international Islam brigade in Afghanistan during the Soviet-Afghan war, founded it. Leadership passed to Khadaffy Janjalani, Abdurajak's younger brother, in 1998 after Abdurajak was killed by Philippine police. Vital to the group's initial growth was a wealthy Saudi businessman living in the Philippines, Mohammad Jamal Khalifa, who provided much of the new group's funding.

LEADERSHIP
Founder Abdurajak Janjalani, as noted, died in 1998. In 2006, leader Khadaffy Janjalani was killed in a skirmish with Philippine troops on Jolo island. His likely successor, Abu Sulaiman, was killed just five months later. Philippine intelligence believes the deaths of Janjalani and Sulaiman presented a significant setback for Abu Sayyaf, as they were the two main points of contact with donors in the Middle East. Since Sulaiman's death, Radullan Sahiron has been appointed to the top post, but scholars believe that Abu Sayyaf now lacks "any semblance of central leadership." Other known leaders of the group include Isnilon Hapilon, Yasir Igasan, and Kahir Mundos.

Abu Sayyaf targets the impoverished and young recruits and is known to welcome foreign jihadists into its ranks.

VIOLENCE
Abu Sayyaf's favored tactics include kidnappings, bombings, assassinations, and guerrilla warfare. Kidnappings vary from a single individ-

ual to groups of 20 or more. In 2000, it kidnapped 21 from a resort in Malaysia. In 2001, it kidnapped three Americans and 17 Filipinos from a resort in Palawan, Philippines, later beheading several of the hostages. That same year, it took American Guillermo Sobero hostage and beheaded him.

In February 2004, Abu Sayyaf members bombed a passenger ferry in Manila Bay, killing 116 people. In 2005, the group detonated bombs in Manila, General Santos, and Davao, targeting civilians. Eight were killed and more than 150 injured.

Abu Sayyaf frequently engages in guerilla warfare with the Philippine military (the Armed Forces of the Philippines, or AFP). It utilizes cover provided by other militant Islamic groups and frequently is aided by armed local community militias. Bombings of Philippine military installments are common.

In 2007, an Abu Sayyaf motorcycle bomb was detonated outside of the Philippine Congress, killing a congressman and three staffers. A 2008 Abu Sayyaf plot to assassinate Philippine president Gloria Arroyo was stopped by Philippine security forces. In 2009, the group kidnapped three American Red Cross workers, holding one captive for half a year.

TIES

The group is known to associate with **Al Qaeda** and work with **Jemaah Islamiyah**. It provides haven for fugitive foreign jihadists and wanted members of local militant groups. Abu Sayyaf networks are believed to be linked with those of the **Moro Islamic Liberation Front**, although the **MILF** denies any connection. Often, Abu Sayyaf members will flee combat with the Armed Forces of the Philippines to take refuge on **MILF-** and MNLF-controlled islands.

Abu Sayyaf has pledged public allegiance to the **Islamic State**, but experts consider the gesture a "publicity stunt." One analyst, Joseph Franco, said in an interview: "Latching on to the **Islamic State** brand is an attempt to prop up its flagging reputation." Abu Sayyaf is "known for their clever use of media and propaganda," Franco said.[2]

FUNDING

Abu Sayyaf relies heavily on kidnapping and extortion to fund its ventures. Kidnapping is performed strategically to result either in the highest possible ransom or leverage over the Armed Forces of the Philippines for the release of captured members.

Kidnappings are facilitated by a kidnapping industry. Victims are taken from remote islands, often tourist destinations, to various villages, where supporters of the group, known as facilitators, run hidden detention facilities.

Abu Sayyaf once was "flush with cash" from ransom payments. Victims range from locals, to tourists, to religious figures. In April 2014, Abu Sayyaf kidnapped two high-profile Germans and held them for ransom, around $5.5 million each.

NOTES

[1] Abu Sayyaf Group (ASG) entry on The National Counterterrorism Center website. <http://www.nctc.gov/site/groups/asg.html>.

[2] Dominguez, Gabriel. "Abu Sayyaf 'Seeking Global Attention' with Hostage Kill Threat." Deutsche Welle. 25 Sept. 2014. <http://www.dw.de/abu-sayyaf-seeking-global-attention-with-hostage-kill-threat/a-17954921>.

ADEN-ABYAN ISLAMIC ARMY (AAIA)

ADEN-ABYAN ISLAMIC ARMY (AAIA)

Main Area(s) of Operation	Yemen
Founder or Spiritual Leader	Abu Hasan al-Abadin al Mihdhar
Known or Suspected Leader	Khalid Abd al-Nabi
Approximate Year Founded	Early 1990s
Approximate Size	Dozens to hundreds (estimate)
Alliances & Cooperations	Al Qaeda
Enemies/Rivals	Houthis (at times)

THE ADEN-ABYAN ISLAMIC ARMY (AAIA) is a militant group in Yemen. Its goal is to "hoist the banner of al-Jihad, and fight secularism in Yemen and the Arab countries."[1]

Abyan is a governorate in Yemen, on the southern coast of the Arabian Peninsula and on the Gulf of Aden. Aden is a city in Abyan. The Gulf of Aden is the mouth to the Red Sea from the Indian Ocean, and it is a bottleneck for the shipping of oil and other precious commodities into and out of the Middle East.

The group's name, referencing the city of Aden and the governorate of Abyan, harks back to the former People's Democratic Republic of Yemen, one of two former states that later became the single country of Yemen. The PDRY was composed of Yemen's southern lands and coastlines, and the Yemeni government at the time was accused by the PDRY of sponsoring terrorism and supporting the Soviet Union.

The AAIA recognizes the advantage of operating at this shipping and transportation hub, and has utilized the geography to organize attacks intended to create economic hardship for Western countries, particularly the United States.

FOUNDING

The founding members of the Aden-Abyan Islamic Army were returning to Yemen from Afghanistan, where many of them had fought in the Soviet-Afghan war. According to the Jamestown Foundation's Terrorism Monitor:

> Yemen, unlike most other Arab countries, proved to be a hospitable environment for the returned fighters. Training camps were established, some with quasi-official support from government officials, and the men were kept well-supplied and content....The unification of the communist south with the tribal north in 1990 created a unique environment that allowed the AAIA to flourish.[2]

In the early 1990s, Abu Hasan al-Abidin al-Mihdhar organized the AAIA under the banner of a hadith that references an end-of-times army that would come from the Aden-Abyan region.

The Yemeni Socialist Party (YSP) had nationalized many lands and farms that belonged to native Muslims, including those owned by prominent AAIA member Tariq al-Fadhli. The Yemeni Socialist Party remains, at present, a democratic group that opposes the unified Yemeni government.

In 1998 the AAIA issued a formal statement of intent to overthrow the Yemeni government.

LEADERSHIP

Al-Mihdhar was executed by the Yemeni government in 1999 after the group kidnapped 16 Western tourists in Yemen. Command passed to Khalid Abd al-Nabi, who was arrested in 2003 but later pardoned by the Yemeni government and released. He continues to make public statements on behalf of the group, but his role is unclear. Al-Nabi bargained with former Yemeni president Ali Abdullah Saleh for the release of various AAIA members, or the commuting of their sentences. President Saleh pardoned AAIA members when useful to influence the balance of power among insurgency and terrorist groups that were fighting amongst themselves to control large parts of the country.

Al-Nabi was arrested again in 2008 after he and other AAIA members engaged in an armed skirmish with Yemeni security forces.

VIOLENCE

AAIA members were implicated in a 1992 plot to bomb the Gold Mohur hotel in Aden, where it was believed U.S. soldiers were staying. The plot was credited to **Al Qaeda** by many sources, and is considered the first **Al Qaeda** attack on U.S. interests.

In 1998, the AAIA kidnapped 16 Western tourists in Yemen.

In 2000, the AAIA was linked to an **Al Qaeda** suicide boat bombing. Militants filled an inflatable motorboat with explosives and ran it into the side of the U.S.S. *Cole*, killing 17 and injuring 40.

In 2001, the AAIA claimed responsibility for a church bombing in Aden and rocket attacks at a hotel in Yemen. In the same year, it set off bombs near Aden International Airport and the SABA news agency building, and three AAIA members perpetrated serial bombings in the southernmost port of Aden. In 2002, the AAIA was involved in an attack on a French oil tanker in the Gulf of Aden. In 2003, the group plotted an attack on a U.S. embassy in Sana'a, but it was foiled.

TIES

The AAIA operates in southern Yemen under the newly formed Ansar al-Sharia banner, an umbrella organization for jihadist groups in the Arabian Peninsula and Islamic Maghreb. Ansar al-Sharia is considered a subsidiary of **Al Qaeda in the Arabian Peninsula (AQAP)**. The **Houthis**, with their armed military wing called Ansar Allah, operate out of north Yemen. The groups are considered at odds but share a common enemy in the secular Yemeni government.

A 2015 article in the *Yemen Times* acknowledged the growing presence of both groups and a number of similarities:

The militants of Ansar Al-Sharia view themselves as better than other militants. Their belief in their own superiority is reminiscent of the Houthis theory of Devine [sic] Selection.

The groups of Ansar Al-Shariah and Ansar Allah are opposites in the sense that the former represents Sunni fundamentalism and the other Shiite extremism. However, their way of thinking is similar as both groups tend to use violence to achieve their aims.

While the Houthis' Ansar Allah group expands their military presence in north Yemen, the Ansar Al-Shariah group intensifies their fighting against the Yemeni army in south Yemen.[3]

The AAIA has previously denied links to **Al Qaeda**, but experts have called them "close affiliates." **Al Qaeda** in Yemen, the branch with which the AAIA is believed to have cooperated in terrorist activities, merged into **Al Qaeda in the Arabian Peninsula** in 2009. In 2010, **AQAP** founded a new Aden-Abyan Islamic Army, referencing the same hadith, and essentially usurped the original AAIA's leadership. Experts suggest the AAIA was disbanded and that its members now belong to **AQAP**.

FUNDING

Initial funding for the AAIA was provided in part by Osama bin Laden, as the group was formed to combat the socialist southern Yemeni government and other secular political groups. While northern Yemen was in conflict with the YSP in the south, some members of the AAIA were paid by the north Yemeni government. Prominent member Tariq al-Fadhli had a salaried position as a colonel in the Yemeni army.

The AAIA has received funding and support from **Al Qaeda**. It also self-finances through ransom payments from kidnappings.

NOTES

[1] Aden-Abyan Islamic Army section on Terrorism Research and Analysis Consortium website. <http://www.trackingterrorism.org/group/aden-abyan-islamic-army>.

[2] Johnsen, Gregory D. "The Resiliency of Yemen's Aden-Abyan Islamic Army." *Terrorism Monitor*. The Jamestown Foundation. 13 July 2006. <http://

www.jamestown.org/programs/tm/single/?tx_ttnews%5Btt_news%5D=838&tx_
ttnews%5BbackPid%5D=181&no_cache=1#.VPU0YvnF98E>.

[3] Sallam, Mohamed Bin. "Yemen Caught Between Ansar Allah and Ansar Al-Sha-riah." *Yemen Times.* 5 Apr. 2012. <http://www.yementimes.com/en/1561/report/678/ Yemen-caught-between-Ansar-Allah-and-Ansar-Al-Shariah.htm>.

AL-AQSA MARTYRS BRIGADE (AAMB)

AL-AQSA MARTYRS BRIGADE (AAMB)

Main Area(s) of Operation	Israel/Palestine
Known or Suspected Leader	Fatah leadership (alleged)
Approximate Year Founded	2000
Alliances & Cooperations	Hamas, Palestinian Islamic Jihad
Ideological Sect/Affiliation	Palestinian nationalism, socialism

AL-AQSA MARTYRS BRIGADE (AAMB) is a Fatah offshoot based in Palestine, intent on removing any Israeli presence from the West Bank and Gaza Strip. The group emerged around 2000 and was one of the driving forces of the Second Intifada. Initially, the group targeted only Israeli military personnel and outposts, but eventually AAMB joined up with **Hamas** and the **Palestinian Islamic Jihad** to commit acts of terrorism aimed at Israeli citizens.

The brigade is a collection of independent groups that share the common mission of extremist Palestinian nationalism. The decentralized nature of the group has made it increasingly difficult for the U.S. to identify its leaders and operational commanders.

The group's name is derived from a reference to Israeli political leader (and later prime minister) Ariel Sharon's visit to the Islamic holy site of the al-Aqsa mosque—which is located on the same site as the Jewish Temple on the Mount. The group believes Sharon's walk on this site was an offense to Islam, and it has served as the motivating narrative behind their violent crusade.

Although AAMB claims to be a secular movement, the Council on Foreign Relations notes that its suicide bombings and attacks closely resemble those of militant Islamic groups **Palestinian Islamic Jihad** and **Hamas**. Furthermore, the group's logo and name have Koranic elements.

AAMB has often teamed with **Hamas** in skirmishes. Since the 2006 political victory by **Hamas** in the Gaza Strip, cells of AAMB in the Gaza Strip and cells of AAMB in the West Bank have been less coordinated on attacks.

FOUNDING

AAMB was founded during the second major Palestinian uprising, or intifada, in September 2000.

LEADERSHIP

AAMB is composed of numerous autonomous cells, each one a different militia. Because of the independence of those cells, recognizing a distinct leader of the group has been difficult for U.S. intelligence. Some sources believe the group's members to be mostly veterans of older militant groups. Many of the commanders of the various groups that have been able to be identified have been killed by the Israel Defense Forces. Cells are divided geographically, with leaders at the head of each regional operation. Leaders likely change often due to the effectiveness of Israeli operations. Groups also form and fold with varying regional interests, so new leaders emerge frequently. As AAMB was a Fatah offshoot, cells were loyal to Palestinian Authority president Yasser Arafat until his death in 2004. At present, the lone wolf leaders may coordinate on attacks, but it is unclear as to whether a central leadership exists.

VIOLENCE

AAMB shifted its targets from Israeli military units in the West Bank to Israeli citizens in 2002. The group has been responsible for suicide bombings that have killed hundreds of citizens. The largest bombings have occurred in Jerusalem and Tel Aviv. Other bombings have been carried out at various Israeli security checkpoints. The group has also claimed responsibility for a number of situations that amounted to tense stand-offs but, ultimately, ended with AAMB's backing down. In 2006, AAMB kidnapped a college student in Israel, mistaking him for an Israeli citizen. The group tried to use him as leverage to get Palestinian prisoners released, but let him go after realizing his nationality was not Israeli. Likewise, in 2006, an AAMB group stormed the European Union mission in Gaza and demanded apologies from Danish and Norwegian publishers that printed cartoon sketches of Muhammad, only to leave 30 minutes later. AAMB formed the first female unit of Fatah fighters and suicide bombers, and the group claimed responsibility for the first female-led suicide bombing in Jerusalem in 2002, which claimed 40 lives.

The group has been known to carry out sporadic and regular anti-Israeli rocket attacks. In 2007, a disarmament agreement entered into by Fatah leader Mahmoud Abbas included AAMB and a pardon of over 200 AAMB members by Israel in exchange for the group's promise to end the violence. In 2009, Israel's successful Operation Cast Lead forced Hamas into a cease-fire, and AAMB mostly complied. However, after the 2014 launch of the Israeli Operation Protective Edge, aimed at reducing missile fire into Israel from Palestinian territories, AAMB publicly announced its return and promised "open war against the Zionist enemy." It is not clear if Abbas authorized the reemergence of AAMB.

TIES

The official leader of the Fatah, the movement for the liberation of Palestine, of which AAMB claims to be the acting military wing , is Mahmoud Abbas, the head of the Palestinian Liberation Organization (PLO). While direct orders have not been found to have been communicated between Abbas and AAMB, it is believed that orders were probably delivered to the group by Yasser Arafat. Arafat was chairman of the PLO until his death in 2004.

Although Fatah leadership initially denied that AAMB was an official part of the movement, Palestinian prime minister Ahmed Qurei said in 2004, "...the AAMB are part of Fatah. We are committed to them and Fatah bears full responsibility for the group."

FUNDING
Payments from Fatah to AAMB have been discovered, to the tune of $50,000 a month.

AL-NUSRA FRONT (JABHAT AL-NUSRA)

AL-NUSRA FRONT
(JABHAT AL-NUSRA)

Main Area(s) of Operation	Syria, Lebanon
Founder or Spiritual Leader	Abu Muhammad al-Julani
Known or Suspected Leader	Salqin Idlib
Approximate Year Founded	2011
Approximate Size	7,000+
Alliances & Cooperations	Al Qaeda, Islamic State
Enemies/Rivals	Hezbollah
Ideological Sect/Affiliation	Salafism
Name Meaning	"Support Front for the People of Al-Sham"
Flag	

THE AL-NUSRA FRONT EMERGED from the civil war in Syria, with several organized factions fighting the Syrian government, led by Bashar al-Assad. Unlike other Syrian rebel groups, including those aided by the U.S. government, al-Nusra's mission is both political and ideological. Al-Nusra, or Jabhat al-Nusra, translates to "Victory Front," and the group's goal is to establish an Islamic caliphate in Syria.

Other Syrian rebel groups fight for political liberation from the al-Assad regime. Groups like the Free Syrian Army fight for democracy in the country. Al-Nusra has made it clear that it fights for the implementation of Sharia under an Islamic state. Because of al-Nusra's commitment to militant Islam and use of violent tactics against civilians, moderate opposition efforts of other rebel groups and international support of democracy in the region have been hindered.

According to a statement by the U.S. State Department, al-Nusra "has sought to portray itself as part of the legitimate Syrian opposition while it is, in fact, an attempt by **Al Qaeda** in Iraq to hijack the struggles of the Syrian people for its own malign purposes."

In 2013, al-Nusra pledged formal allegiance to **Al Qaeda**, days after **Al Qaeda** leader Ayman al-Zawahiri publicly called for a rally to jihad and for supporters to do "everything possible" to establish an Islamic state in Syria.

In a 2012 video released online, al-Nusra leaders claimed:

> We are Syrian mujahideen, back from various jihad fronts to restore God's rule on Earth and avenge the Syrians' violated honor and spilled blood....Jabhat al-Nusra has taken upon itself to be the Muslim nation's weapon in this land.[1]

In 2012 the group had an estimated 300 to 400 members, and in just two years that number rose to over 7,000.

Al-Nusra gets many of its recruits from across the Syrian border as well. Many have joined from across the Middle East, Chechnya, and Europe. Six Americans have been arrested in attempts to join al-Nusra's ranks.

FOUNDING

In 2011, **Al Qaeda** leader Abu Bakr al-Baghdadi sent Abu Muhammad al-Julani to Syria to organize a jihadist movement. Using **Al Qaeda** networks and donors, al-Nusra quickly amassed sizable stockpiles of arms and recruits. Initially, many rebel groups admired its quick growth, although favor among other rebel groups has fallen since al-Nusra claimed responsibility for a series of March 2011 bombings, making it the first Syrian group to claim responsibility for attacks that targeted civilians.

LEADERSHIP

Al-Nusra is exceedingly efficient at using propaganda, including handouts, to gain favor among Syrian civilians and other rebel groups. It has taken over bakeries in the Syrian city of Aleppo, distributing flour and baked goods to the needy. As a result, al-Nusra has set up a Sharia court there to administer Islamic law.

According to a BBC profile: "Al-Nusra's propaganda often appear designed to appeal to ordinary Muslims...It emphasizes purported efforts to avoid civilian casualties...[S]tatements and videos are usually issued by its media group, al-Manara al-Baida, and are regularly posted to jihadist, social media and video-sharing websites. There is even a Facebook page dedicated to the group."[2]

Abu Muhammad al-Julani retains a key leadership role in al-Nusra. In addition, Abdul Mohsen Abdullah Ibrahim al-Sharikh and Hamid Hamad Hamid al-Ali are two members of **Al Qaeda** who traveled from Iraq to Syria to become senior al-Nusra leaders. Another individual, Abu Yousef al-Turki, was a senior al-Nusra member and sniper recruit trainer, but was killed by a U.S. airstrike.

VIOLENCE

A string of 2011 suicide bombings was claimed by al-Nusra in a video released in 2012. That same year, two more suicide bombings targeting government forces killed 26 in the capital city of Damascus and dozens in Aleppo.

In early 2013, an al-Nusra leader was killed by a civilian from the small village of Albu Saray. Al-Nusra surrounded the village and took every male hostage. Many were executed and numerous homes were destroyed in retaliation.

In December 2013, al-Nusra kidnapped 13 nuns from a Christian town, releasing them unharmed in March 2014.

Al-Nusra has captured Syrian army encampments and arms depots, as well as **Hezbollah** bases and territories controlled by moderate Syrian rebel forces.

TIES

Al-Nusra's ties to other militant groups in the region are complex and constantly changing. It consistently reaffirms allegiance to **Al Qaeda**, and **Al Qaeda** continues to provide the group with financial support, personnel, and weaponry.

In 2013, **Al Qaeda**'s leader in Iraq, Abu Bakr al-Baghdadi, announced the merger of his group with the **Islamic State**. Al-Nusra leader Muhammad al-Julani rejected the merger and publicly renewed his group's allegiance to **Al Qaeda** commander Ayman al-Zawahiri. However, a number of al-Nusra fighters have defected to join the **Islamic State**. Battles between al-Nusra and **Islamic State** armed factions have killed over 3,000 militants. In the summer of 2014, the **Islamic State** successfully captured al-Nusra bases in Deir al-Zor, Syria, and many of the oil fields that al-Nusra relied upon for continued funding.

Despite the hostilities between the **Islamic State** and al-Nusra, evidence exists of cooperation between the two groups when advantageous for both. Al-Nusra and the **Islamic State** released a joint video from Lebanon depicting Lebanese soldiers held hostage. Al-Nusra has proclaimed that it will set up a Sunni Islamic state in Syria with support from other Islamist groups.

Al-Nusra, a Sunni Islamist group, has conducted a number of attacks targeting Shiite groups in Lebanon. Additionally, al-Nusra and **Hezbollah** engage readily in conflict, as **Hezbollah** actively supports the Bashar al-Assad regime, which al-Nusra fights in Syria.

According to experts, al-Nusra gained favor and support from other rebel groups that were demoralized by the U.S.'s decision not to intervene in 2013. In November 2014, al-Nusra led a successful large-scale attack on moderate rebel groups, including the Syrian Revolutionary Front and Harkat Hazm (which has ties to the Free Syrian Army), claiming the groups were spies for the United States.

FUNDING

Evidence suggests that a majority of al-Nusra's resources are imported into Syria. The group has also overtaken Syrian arms stockpiles. Previous to **Islamic State**-induced tensions between al-Nusra and **Al Qaeda**, **Al Qaeda** claimed to provide al-Nusra with half of its operational budget. Al-Nusra also controls Syrian oil fields, wheat stores, factories, and gas fields, and pilfers local towns and villages. It is estimated to operate in 11 of the 13 Syrian provinces, and controls over a dozen towns, in which it carries out government welfare services. The group is known for targeting impoverished towns and gaining local favor with handouts.

Senior al-Nusra commander Ghaith Abdul-Ahad told a crowd of people in a town shortly after its capture:

> Go and ask the people in the streets whether there a liberated town or city anywhere in Syria that is ruled as efficiently as this one. There is electricity, water, and bread and security. Inshallah, this will be the nucleus of a new Syrian Islamic Caliphate![3]

In regards to the region's oil fields and wheat stores, he says, "All this wealth is for the Muslims."

Al-Nusra also conducts kidnappings to collect ransom money. In August 2014, together with the **Islamic State**, it kidnapped a unit of Lebanese soldiers to pressure **Hezbollah** to take action. Fortunately, Al-Nusra did release American writer Theo Curtis and 45 UN peacekeepers that were in the group's captivity.

NOTES

[1] "Profile: Syria's Al-Nusra Front." BBC. 10 Apr. 2013. <http://www.bbc.co.uk/news/world-middle-east-18048033>.

[2] Ibid.

[3] Ahad, Abdul. "Syria's Al-Nusra Front – Ruthless, Organised and Taking Control." *The Guardian*. 10 July 2013. <http://www.theguardian.com/world/2013/jul/10/syria-al-nusra-front-jihadi>.

AL QAEDA

AL QAEDA

Main Area(s) of Operation	Global, mainly concentrated in the Middle East and northern Africa
Founder or Spiritual Leader	Osama bin Laden
Known or Suspected Leader	Ayman al-Zawahiri
Approximate Year Founded	1988
Approximate Size	20,000–30,000
Alliances & Cooperations	Taliban, Boko Haram, Ansar Dine, al-Shabaab, al-Nusra, Egyptian Islamic Jihad, Libyan Islamic Fighting Group, Lashkar-e-Taiba, Jaish-e-Muhammad, Armed Islamic Group of Algeria, Aby Sayyaf, Jemaah Islamiyah (among many others)
Enemies/Rivals	Islamic State (at times)
Ideological Sect/Affiliation	Salafism
Name Meaning	"The Base"
Flag	

THE NAME AL QAEDA TRANSLATES as "The Base." It is an international Salafi jihadist group of militant Islamists that seeks to replace Muslim countries' secular governments with fundamental Islamic regimes, and obliterate Western influences from the world.

On September 11, 2001, 19 Al Qaeda operatives carried out the most devastating terrorist attack to ever occur on American soil. Four commercial airplanes were hijacked. Two were flown into the World

Trade Center buildings in New York City, causing their collapse. One was flown into the U.S. Pentagon building, severely damaging an entire wing. The fourth plane, surely destined for another iconic American target, was instead flown to an empty field in Pennsylvania, thanks to the heroic efforts of its passengers. In New York, amidst the chaos, thousands of brave men and women in the police and fire departments jumped into action to help. Hundreds lost their lives while trying to save others. In all, the attack claimed 2,977 victims.

According to an assessment by the Council on Foreign Relations in 2012, Al Qaeda is the top terrorist threat facing the United States. In 2001, as a response to the 9/11 terror attacks, the United States launched a major campaign to defeat Al Qaeda in Iraq and the **Taliban** in Afghanistan. Despite American victories and the removal of Saddam Hussein's Al Qaeda-complicit regime, many Al Qaeda members successfully escaped decimation by fleeing to the FATA region of Pakistan for shelter, where the group has been able to recover its operational strength and size.

Al Qaeda leads the global jihad movement. It has franchised groups acting across the globe, including Al Qaeda in Iraq, Al Qaeda in the Islamic Maghreb, and Al Qaeda in the Arabian Peninsula. According to some, including the Obama administration, "core" Al Qaeda has suffered decimation and a depleted leadership, thanks to continued targeted U.S. strikes. Yet the expanding power of Al Qaeda through its subsidiaries is underestimated by this assessment. The Council on Foreign Relation argues:

A number of [Al Qaeda] affiliated groups have gained prominence in recent years, complicating the task of containing the organization.[1]

Al Qaeda propaganda is strong, and its ideology has quickly spread from the Middle East to Southeast Asia, Africa, and even the United Kingdom and the United States. Al Qaeda popularized suicide bombings, and successfully helped transform Islamic Sunni jihad from a local struggle against regimes to an all-out war on the Western world. Al Qaeda's successful propaganda has drawn dozens of Americans to join their ranks, mostly younger men and women, many of whom are stopped before they can reach the group.

Al Qaeda capitalized on the U.S. efforts in Afghanistan and Iraq and authored the anti-Western narrative of fundamental Islam with the U.S. as its antagonist with some degree of success. However, in Iraq, citizens and tribal leaders have worked with U.S. forces to defeat the terror group that has shown no mercy to Iraqi citizens.

Still, Al Qaeda continues to be resilient. According to a 2014 report by terrorism experts Peter Bergen and Jennifer Rowland, the group now "control[s] more territory in the Arab world…than at any time in its history."[6]

FOUNDING

Al Qaeda's origins reach back to the end of the Soviet-Afghan war. Its most iconic founding member, Osama bin Laden, was a driving force behind its initial organization, recruitment, and messaging.

Osama bin Laden was born in 1957 to a billionaire Saudi Arabian construction magnate, Mohammed bin Awad bin Laden and his 10th wife. Osama bin Laden inherited an estimated $25 to $30 million from his father. Using this money and much more that was provided to him by his brothers and sisters, he bankrolled significant portions of the mujahideen efforts in Afghanistan against the Soviet Union, including providing arms and construction equipment to dig trenches for warfare.

According to *The Economist*:

Keenly, he followed the media coverage of the atrocities he inspired, playing the world's press like a violin when he chose. He built the brand and turned it into a global franchise; his face advertised it, even as he disappeared….His mind and approach were those of a businessman.[2]

Osama bin Laden's religious mentor and teacher was Abdullah Azzam, a Palestinian theoretician who fervently touted Islamic jihad. His right-hand man, often the operational commander he used to direct the activity of Al Qaeda, was Ayman al-Zawahiri. As a team, the three capitalized on the victories over the Soviets in Afghanistan and built Al Qaeda.

When Saddam Hussein invaded Kuwait in 1991, bin Laden saw the opportunity to capitalize on the events and put his Al Qaeda militia to the test. He petitioned Saudi Arabia to endorse his group to battle Saddam's regime, but Saudi Arabia instead opted for American backing. This choice prompted bin Laden's first fatwa, in 1996, which declared war against America.

The group was soon exiled from Saudi Arabia, but found shelter under the **Taliban** regime that controlled Afghanistan. It amassed many recruits from madrassas in neighboring Pakistan. In 1998, bin Laden declared his second fatwa, calling for global jihad and violent resistance to America, Jews, and any infidels who did not follow Salafist Islam.

Al Qaeda justifies terrorism using an Islamic principle known as rukhsa, or a "relaxation of religious law." It rationalizes violence and terrorism on the basis of the size of the West and the threat it poses. Al Qaeda's propaganda wing, the al-Sahab media organization, releases regular grievances against the West (particularly the United States), to solicit favor among receptive (usually young and impressionable) supporters. Al Qaeda propaganda effectively twists religious doctrine to support its goals, and capitalizes on the frustrations and hardships of poor or disenfranchised citizens of Muslim countries. According to the American Foreign Policy Council's World Almanac of Islam, Al Qaeda propaganda is so effective that even "Westerners are not immune to the Al Qaeda vision, as demonstrated by mainstream Western acceptance that Al Qaeda's war is entirely fueled by grievances against the West— even when Bin Laden himself asserted that the animosity between the West and the Muslim world is inherent."[3]

Al Qaeda's September 11 attack and the subsequent American response forced the group into the FATA region of Pakistan, and largely into a covert existence. However, it has capitalized on the largely lawless region to rebuild its base and, more significantly, its brand. It has franchised into three formidable groups: Al Qaeda in Iraq, Al Qaeda in the Islamic Maghreb, and Al Qaeda in the Arabian Peninsula. Each has become a sizable organization and committed atrocities under the banner of Al Qaeda. It uses the Internet to disseminate its propaganda and encourage jihad worldwide.

LEADERSHIP

On May 2, 2011, U.S. Navy SEAL team 6 killed Osama bin Laden in his compound in Abbottabad, Pakistan. After his death, bin Laden's right hand and longtime associate, Ayman al-Zawahiri, took command of Al Qaeda, and still commands the group. Other high-level commanders include Pakistan and Afghanistan Al Qaeda commander Khalid al-Habib, overseas operations leader Adnan el Shukrijumah, Mustafa Abu al-Yazid, Saif al-Adel, Mustafa Hamid, Matiur Rehman, and Abu Khalil al-Madani. The top operational command of Al Qaeda is a leadership council that makes big-picture organizational decisions. Many top Al Qaeda leaders, including notorious Al Qaeda in Iraq founder Abu Musab al-Zarqawi, have been killed by U.S. military strikes. Other top leaders are imprisoned at Guantanamo Bay, Cuba.

VIOLENCE

Al Qaeda's violent history is extensive. It began in the early 1990s, when Osama bin Laden was living in and recruiting from Sudan, expanding the Al Qaeda network into Africa. Among the many groups he connected with in the region were those that played a role in the 1993 World Trade Center bombing that killed six and injured 1,500. Attacks persisted throughout the '90s, many aimed at the United States. In 1993, a Somalia-based Al Qaeda cell reportedly shot down a U.S. Black Hawk helicopter, and an assassination attempt was made on U.S. president Bill Clinton in 1996.

In August 1998, serial suicide bombings at U.S. embassies in Dar es Salaam in Tanzania, and Nairobi in Kenya, killed 258 and injured 5,000. In October 2000, Al Qaeda suicide bombers ran a boat of explosives into the side of the U.S.S. *Cole*, killing 17 and injuring 40.

On September 11, 2001, as noted above, Al Qaeda committed the unthinkable.

While fighting in Iraq and Afghanistan, Al Qaeda and its affiliates have committed hundreds of terrorist attacks and successfully claimed the lives of thousands of innocent people. While the group focuses on Western targets, the majority of its victims are other Muslims. Its major attacks include:

— A 2002 bombing of a synagogue in Djerba, Tunisia, that killed 10 and injured 22.

— A 2003 suicide car bombing of residential compounds in Riyadh, Saudi Arabia, that killed 17 and injured 122.

— Bombings of the London Underground subway system in 2005 that killed 56, considered the worst terrorist attack in British history.

Additionally, numerous acts of terror and violence have been committed by Al Qaeda's three large franchises and network of supporting militant groups, including:

— A 2007 serial suicide bombing of five Kurdish villages, killing 300 Iraqis and injuring hundreds more, committed by Al Qaeda in Iraq.

— A 2012 Al Qaeda in the Islamic Maghreb-backed attack on the U.S. consulate in Benghazi, Libya, killing Ambassador Chris Stevens and three others.

— A January 2015 massacre at French satirical magazine Charlie Hebdo's headquarters that claimed 12 lives, by members of Al Qaeda in the Arabian Peninsula.

TIES

The **Taliban**'s rule of Afghanistan from 1996 to 2001 provided a haven nation in which Al Qaeda was able to thrive and grow into the international jihadist organization it is today. The **Taliban**'s shelter was instrumental to Al Qaeda's growth and recruitment. When the Taliban was removed from power in 2001, Al Qaeda's operations were moved to the FATA region of Pakistan, which made for a more dangerous and lawless base of operations.

Al Qaeda in the Arabian Peninsula (AQAP)

AQAP was formed from the amalgamation of Al Qaeda cells in Saudi Arabia and Yemen. AQAP's leader, Nasser al-Wuhayshi, was appointed by al-Zawahiri to be Al Qaeda's overall second-in-command, behind al-Zawahiri himself. The group funds itself through robbery and kidnapping and is estimated to have a thousand active members. In Yemen, it has conquered significant territory and has continued to present a violent threat to the stability of the Yemeni government.

Al Qaeda in the Islamic Maghreb (AQIM)

AQIM was formed from Al Qaeda cells in northern Africa, absorbing the militant Group for Call and Combat. AQIM sponsors various militant efforts at overthrowing Muslim African countries through violent means. AQIM leader Abdelmalek Droukdel is estimated to command around 1,000 active operatives. The group operates out of Mali, Niger, Mauritania, Algeria, and Libya. It has cooperated with and supported **Boko Haram**, **Ansar Dine**, and **al-Shabaab**.

Al Qaeda in Iraq (AQI)

AQI returned to prominence in Iraq after the American troop withdrawal and, with close cooperation with **Al-Nusra**, soon rebranded itself as the **Islamic State** in Iraq and Syria (ISIS). Internal disputes over leadership cased al-Zawahiri to disavow the group. The two distinct groups now compete for dominance over a shared ideology in the global jihad effort.

Other groups that Al Qaeda supports include the **Egyptian Islamic Jihad**, the **Libyan Islamic Fighting Group**, **Lashkar-e-Taiba**, **Jaish-e-Muhammad**, the **Armed Islamic Group of Algeria**, **Abu Sayyaf**, and **Jemaah Islamiyah**. Intelligence also exists that shows Al Qaeda's cooperation with **Hezbollah** on operational logistics and recruit training, despite the Sunni-Shia difference between the groups.

FUNDING

Initial support for Al Qaeda was provided by Osama bin Laden, and reportedly by Saudi Arabia, Kuwait, and the UAE. Al Qaeda benefits from money funneled through Islamic charities and private donors. It also capitalizes on criminal activities for fundraising, including kidnapping.

While Al Qaeda has suffered substantial setbacks, it has rebranded and reformulated, finding a new level of effectiveness. Much of Al Qaeda's financing has been transformed into open-source terror sponsorship inspired by Al Qaeda's ideology.

In [the years after 9/11], Al Qaeda transformed from what was once a hierarchical organization with a large operating budget into an ideological movement. Whereas Al Qaeda once trained its own operatives and deployed them to carry out attacks, it is just as likely to inspire individuals or small groups to carry out attacks, often with no operational support from the larger organization.[4]

NOTES

[1] Bajoria, Jayshree, and Greg Bruno. Al-Qaeda section on Council on Foreign Relations website. 6 June 2012. <http://www.cfr.org/terrorist-organizations-and-networks/al-qaeda-k-al-qaida-al-qaida/p9126>.

[2] "Osama Bin Laden." The Economist. 5 May 2011. <http://www.economist.com/node/18648254>.

[3] Al Qaeda section in World Almanac of Islam. The American Foreign Policy Council. 13 Oct. 2014. <http://almanac.afpc.org/al-qaeda>.

[4] Jayshree and Bruno, Al-Qaeda section on Council on Foreign Relations website.

AL-SHABAAB

AL-SHABAAB

Main Area(s) of Operation	Somalia
Founder or Spiritual Leader	Hassan Dahir Aweys
Known or Suspected Leader	Ahmad Umar
Approximate Year Founded	2003–2006
Approximate Size	7,000–9,000
Alliances & Cooperations	Al Qaeda, Boko Haram
Ideological Sect/Affiliation	Salafism, Wahhabism
Name Meaning	"The Youth"
Flag	

AL-SHABAAB IS A MILITANT Wahhabi group based in the East African nation of Somalia. Its objective is to overturn the Somali government and replace it with an Islamic state.

Al-Shabaab translates as "The Youth." The group has committed terror attacks in Somalia, Kenya, and Ethiopia, and reportedly draws numerous international recruits. It also boasts of ties to **Al Qaeda**. Washington, D.C., officials have expressed concern over potential Al-Shabaab attacks on the U.S.

Al-Shabaab has an estimated 7,000 to 9,000 members. It controls most of southern and central Somalia.

FOUNDING

Somalia is an extremely impoverished country that has seen numerous regime changes. In 2013, the U.S. formally recognized the first legitimate government in Somalia in over 20 years. The Siad Barre military regime ruled Somalia from 1969 to 1991. In 1991, armed groups overthrew the government, and a massive civil war erupted among Somali insurgencies. For the next 10 years, various militant groups controlled the country autonomously, and armed groups formed and grew without significant resistance.

One such armed group was Al-Ittihad Al Islami (AIAI), which translates as "Unity of Islam." AIAI was funded by Osama bin Laden and **Al Qaeda**, and was composed of extremists determined to set up an emirate in Somalia. Eventually, the Ethiopian army and Somali allies exiled most of the members, who left the country to fight in the Afghan-Soviet war.

Factionalization in AIAI in 2003 led to a splinter group of young members who sought a more fundamental Islamic rule for Somalia. The splinter group agreed to become the armed branch of an organized collection of Islamic Sharia courts that called themselves the Islamic Courts Union. The militant youths organized under the banner of Al-Shabaab.

By 2006, Al-Shabaab and the Islamic Courts Union controlled considerable portions of Somalia, including the capital city of Mogadishu. The new national Somali government looked to neighboring Ethiopia for assistance. Reportedly, Ethiopia has also received numerous terror attack threats from members of the Islamic Courts Union. In December 2006, the Ethiopian Army invaded, exiling the Islamic Courts Union and causing Al-Shabaab to retreat to the south of the country.

From 2006 to 2008, Al-Shabaab recruited with the help of **Al Qaeda**.

A transnational government later formed in Somalia, backed by member nations of the African Union, including Uganda, Kenya, Burundi, Djibouti, and Sierra Leone, operating as the African Mission in Somalia (AMISOM). AMISON's interests and security forces have increasingly become a target for Al-Shabaab.

LEADERSHIP

Al-Shabaab's ideological leader is former Siad Barre colonel Hassan Dahir Aweys. After the Siad Barre regime fell, Aweys became commander of AIAI's military wing and, later, leader of the Islamic Courts Union. Aden Hashi Ayro, selected by Aweys to be operational commander of Al-Shabaab in 2006, was killed in 2008 by a U.S. missile strike. The command passed to Ahmed Abdi Godane, cofounder of Al-Shabaab. Internal factionalization produced Godane loyalists, who killed two senior Al-Shabaab members in 2013, speaking to Godane's harsh and vengeful leadership tactics. Later in 2013, Aweys turned himself in to Somali authorities to escape retribution from disagreements with Godane, and Al-Shabaab's second-in-command, Mukhtar Robow, went into hiding in south Somalia for the same reason.

In September 2014, the U.S. announced it had killed Godane via airstrike. Shortly after, the group released on online statement naming Ahmed Umar the new leader of Al-Shabaab. Local sources indicated that Umar joined Al-Shabaab in 2006, likely as a close confidant of the late Godane.

Al-Shabaab's recruitment methods include kidnapping young men and forcing them to fight on the group's behalf. It has a Twitter account and a video production branch that has created propaganda such as a 2009 rap video, in English, that boasts of sending enemies to hell. Somalis living in America are frequently recruited to join the group, according to the FBI. The first two confirmed American suicide bombers, Shirwa Ahmed and Farah Mohamad of Minnesota, were recruited and trained by Al-Shabaab. Omar Hammami of Alabama was a leader of Al-Shabaab until he was killed in 2013.

VIOLENCE

Al-Shabaab-controlled areas of Somalia are under strict Sharia rule. Amputations and stoning are liberally distributed punishments. The group is known to behead Christians, attack humanitarian workers, and defile graves of non-Muslims and moderate Muslims.

In 2010, Al-Shabaab executed a series of suicide bombings aimed at World Cup viewers in Kampala, Uganda, killing 74. This was its first recorded international terror attack. In 2011, Al-Shabaab members kidnapped and attacked numerous Kenyans living in border towns.

In 2013, Al-Shabaab claimed responsibility for an attack on the Westgate Shopping Center in Nairobi, Kenya, where it took hostages and killed numerous foreigners. In all, at least 67 were killed in a four-day siege of the mall.

In April of 2015, five Al-Shabaab gunmen stormed Garissa University College, near Nairobi, and indiscriminately shot at students in halls and classrooms. Many students were reported to have been found with their throats cut. The university was likely targeted because it was known for having many Christian students and offering a Western-style education. In all, 147 were killed in the daylong siege.

TIES

Al-Shabaab and its parent organization, AIAI, have received funding and recruitment support from **Al Qaeda** and, formerly, Osama bin Laden. In 2010, an Al-Shabaab leader released a statement in which he promised to "connect the horn of Africa jihad to the one led by **Al Qaeda** and its leader Sheikh Osama bin Laden." In February 2012, Al-Shabaab formally declared allegiance to **Al Qaeda**.

Al-Shabaab reportedly also cooperates with **Boko Haram**.

FUNDING

Al-Shabaab partly self-finances, through Somali piracy, kidnapping, extortion, and illegal trade. It has an elaborate racketeering operation in which it controls a sizable portion of the sugar and charcoal trade with Kenya.

Al-Shabaab also profits from running charities and welfare programs, and uses these entities to gain favor and support from local populations. When Western countries offered food aid in 2011 to distribute to Somali citizens suffering from famine, Al-Shabaab refused to accept it.

Allegedly, Gulf states including Saudi Arabia, Yemen, Syria, Iran, Eritrea, and Qatar also have provided funding to Al-Shabaab.

ANSAR DINE

ANSAR DINE

Main Area(s) of Operation	Mali
Founder or Spiritual Leader	Iyad Ag Ghaly
Known or Suspected Leader	Iyad Ag Ghaly
Approximate Year Founded	2012
Approximate Size	Hundreds to thousands
Alliances & Cooperations	Al Qaeda (AQIM)
Name Meaning	"Defenders of the Faith"
Flag	

ANSAR DINE ("DEFENDERS OF THE FAITH") is one of five major militant Islamic groups operating in the African country of Mali. The others are Jama'at Tawhid Wal Jiad fi Garbi Afriqqiya ("Movement for United and Jihad in West Africa"), **Al Qaeda in the Islamic Maghreb**, the Signed-in-Blood Battalion, and the Islamic Movement for Azawad.

Many of the groups claim they formed as a reaction to French colonialism, which ended in Mali in the 1960s. Ansar Dine's objective is to bring Mali under Sharia rule. It takes the most hard-line Islamic approach among the various Malian rebel groups.

Ansar Dine took control of a substantial portion of northern Mali after a series of violent and hostile campaigns for control over various Malian towns. The Ansar Dine-controlled region is roughly equivalent to the size of France.

The group has an estimated several hundred to several thousand members.

FOUNDING

The group is composed of ethnic Tuaregs, who have held a longstanding rivalry with the Malian central government. Its founder reportedly led numerous Tuareg rebel groups until he split off and formed Ansar Dine in 2012.

LEADERSHIP

Ansar Dine is led by Iyad Ag Ghaly, who in the 1990s was commander of a Malian military group and received Salafist religious education from Pakistani missionaries. One of Ghaly's cousins is a commander in **Al Qaeda in the Islamic Maghreb**. Ghaly founded Ansar Dine after failing to gain control of the Islamic Movement for Azawad.

Ansar Dine recruits members from across northern Africa, and has built a substantial online presence and propaganda machine.

VIOLENCE

Since its founding in 2012, Ansar Dine has captured the Malian cities of Agulhok, Tessalit, Kidal, Gao, and Timbuktu. During the hostile takeover of Agulhok, it executed 82 Malian soldiers and kidnapped another 30. Citizens in captured cities are forced to obey Ansar Dine laws, or face torture and execution. As the group continues to amass land under its control, it freely destroys U.N. World Heritage sites, and has displaced an estimated 420,000 people.

TIES

AQIM, or **Al Qaeda in the Islamic Maghreb**, operates in North African countries, including Mali. According to the U.S. State Department, Ansar Dine cooperates closely with **AQIM**. U.S. general Carter F. Ham, former commander of Africa Command, said in July 2012:

> The relationship between **AQIM** and Ansar Dine is one that is—frankly, difficult for us really to understand....The harshness that **AQIM** and Ansar Dine have applied to the people of northern

Mali I think is indicative of this friction between the populace and these extremist organizations.[1]

The confusion results from Ansar Dine's frequent shifts of allegiance between the four other major Islamic militant groups in the region.

In a public announcement in 2014, Ansar Dine and the National Movement for the Liberation of Azawad proclaimed northern Mali to be an independent country known as The Islamic Republic of Azawad. Within months, the two groups battled each other for control of the region; they have since publicly disassociated.

FUNDING

AQIM has supported Ansar Dine since **AQIM's** founding in 2011. Additionally, Ansar Dine is believed to be financially backed by Qatar and Saudi Arabia, where founder Ghaly previously lived.

Moroccan Islamic Combatant Group The Moroccan Islamic Combatant Group (GICM) is an international militant group composed of Moroccan diaspora communities throughout Europe. Its main branches are in Morocco and Britain, but it has cells in Belgium, Italy, the Netherlands, Egypt, Denmark, France, Spain, Turkey, and Scandinavia.

The goals of the GICM are to establish an Islamic caliphate in Morocco and to support **Al Qaeda** in its pursuit of global jihad. The GICM subscribes to Salafi ideology.

NOTES

[1] Ansar Al Din ("Defenders of the Faith") section on GlobalSecurity.org. <http://www.globalsecurity.org/military/world/para/ansar-al-din.htm>.

ARMED ISLAMIC GROUP OF ALGERIA (GIA)

ARMED ISLAMIC GROUP
OF ALGERIA (GIA)

Main Area(s) of Operation	Algeria, France
Founder or Spiritual Leader	Mansour Meliani
Known or Suspected Leader	Numerous
Approximate Year Founded	1992–1993
Approximate Size	Several hundred
Alliances & Cooperations	Al Qaeda
Ideological Sect/Affiliation	Takfiri

KNOWN SIMPLY AS the Armed Islamic Group (GIA), this Algerian-based militant group sought to overthrow the Algerian government and replace it with a fundamentalist Islamic state. The GIA's violent history displayed a proclivity for attacks targeted at civilians, designed to kill as many as possible in an indiscriminate fashion.

There is currently debate as to whether al-Jama'ah al-Islamiyah al-Musallaha, a violent and similarly destructive group that operates within Algeria, is a separate group or an alias for offshoots of GIA.

The GIA, now splintered, was once considered one of Algeria's most radical and violent extremist groups.

GIA violence was so horrific that it received negative pushback from foreign extremist Islamic groups. As a result, beginning in 1997, several members of the GIA split to form independent groups. Those include:

— The Salafist Group for Preaching and Combat (GSPC), which later merged into Al Qaeda in the Islamic Maghreb

— The Islamic League for Preaching and Combat

— The Islamic Front for Armed Jihad (FIDA)

— The Defenders of Salafist Preaching (HDS)

— The Salafist Combatant Group (GSC)

— The Salafist Group for Jihad (GSD)

FOUNDING

The GIA is said to have been formed in reaction to the Algerian government's canceling of a 1992 election that was expected to produce large victories for the Islamic Salvation Front (FIS) political party. Following this event, Algeria experienced one of the most violent civil wars in recorded world history. The GIA played an active part in this violence with regular rural executions.

The group's founder and first leader, Mansour Meliani, was soon after arrested. Abdelhak Layada then revived the group under the teachings of Omar El-Eulmi.

The GIA's activities during the civil war focused on the murder of journalists and women. GIA leaders stated, "Those who fight against us by the pen will die by the sword."[8] Women who did not dress in appropriate Muslim attire, who held professional jobs, or who had short marriages were killed under the principle of takfiri.

According to the Council on Foreign Relations, the GIA recruited up to an estimated 500 members a week by 1994.

The last terror attack publicly claimed by the GIA occurred in 2001. After that, the GIA split into many smaller terror groups, one of which later transformed into **Al Qaeda in the Islamic Maghreb**. A 2004 crackdown by the Algerian government led to the arrest of 400 GIA members. The group's members now operate under many different banners.

LEADERSHIP

The GIA's leaders have changed frequently due to killings and arrests. One of the last reported leaders, Boulenouar Oukil, was arrested in

2005. GIA members now follow the leadership of their various splinter groups.

VIOLENCE

GIA violence is particularly horrific and devastating. Estimates place GIA-related deaths at approximately 70,000 from 1993 to 1998, in a total of 174 attacks.

In 1994, GIA slaughtered seven Italian sailors, kidnapped ambassadors from Yemen and Oman, killed five in the French embassy in Algiers, and hijacked an Air France flight. It threatened to set off a bomb in the plane as it flew over Paris. The French military retook the plane when it landed in nearby Marseilles, after three passengers had been killed. The GIA hijackers were also killed in the recapture of the aircraft, so the group killed French Catholic priests in Algeria in retaliation.

As France became a more prominent target in GIA's objectives, more attacks were perpetrated across the Mediterranean Sea on French soil with the use of improvised explosive devices (IEDs). In 1995, the group bombed a train station in Paris, killing four and injuring 84. In 1996, the GIA systematically attacked rural villages around Algiers and executed over 120 civilians by cutting their throats. It also assassinated the French archbishop of Oran at his home in Algeria in August of the same year.

GIA bombings in 1997 killed over 50, and similar rural executions were conducted in Sidi Youssef, Algeria. In 1999, GIA killed 27 civilians in Bechar, Algeria. In 2002, GIA killed 60 civilians in Chlef province and bombed a market outside of Algiers, killing an additional 35. A 2004 attack in Meda province killed 16, and a 2005 attack in Blida province killed 14.

TIES

Al Qaeda leader Ayman al-Zawahiri made public justifications of GIA's violent activities when criticism of the group was at its peak. Ten members of the GIA were identified as also belonging to **Al Qaeda** when they were captured in Italy in 2004. Two of the GIA's splinter groups are the Defenders of Salafist Preaching (HDS) and the Salafist Group for Preaching and Combat, which later transformed into **Al Qaeda in the Islamic Maghreb**.

FUNDING

Osama bin Laden provided early financial support for GIA bombings in France, particularly those in 1995. The GIA also maintained a financial network composed of North African expatriates living in Europe, including many residents of France. The group ran extortion and smuggling rings throughout Europe and collected charitable donations in mosques.

BOKO HARAM

BOKO HARAM

Main Area(s) of Operation	Nigeria and surrounding countries
Founder or Spiritual Leader	Mohammed Yusuf
Known or Suspected Leader	Abubakar Shekau
Approximate Year Founded	2002
Approximate Size	10,000+
Alliances & Cooperations	Al Qaeda, al-Shabaab
Ideological Sect/Affiliation	Wahhabism, Salafism
Name Meaning	"Western Education Is Forbidden"
Flag	

BOKO HARAM IS THE WORLD'S DEADLIEST extremist group. From 2013 to 2014, the group's violence increased over 300% and claimed nearly 7,000 lives—surpassing the Islamic State in its body count. Together with the Islamic State, the two groups are responsible for approximately 50 percent of deaths by terror worldwide.

The name Boko Haram roughly translates to "Western Education Is Forbidden." The group's name, though it speaks largely for itself, also refers to the forbidden nature of engaging in any Western activity, from participating in democracy to receiving a secular education. Boko Haram's full name is Jama'atu Ahlis Sunna Lidda'awati wal-Jihad, or "the People Committed to the Propagation of the Prophet's Teachings and Jihad." Through jihad, the group wants to combat the influence of

Western traditions and education that may detract from fundamental adherence to Islam.

Boko Haram is best known today for their public abductions, totaling in the thousands of individuals to date, with the largest being the kidnapping of 276 schoolgirls from Chibok in April 2014. Their violent campaigns have also uprooted more than 300,000 people from their homes and businesses. In 2010, the United States officially declared Boko Haram a terrorist organization.

Before their world-headline-grabbing status, the group was conceived and grew in a bloodied and turbulent setting. Boko Haram continues to recruit poor Nigerian youth, college students, and unemployed college graduates. The group uses handouts and welfare programs to gain followers and recruits. As it expanded, many in the region began calling it "The Nigerian Taliban," which added to its recognition and notoriety.

Boko Haram is based in the West African country of Nigeria. Its members believe that the current Nigerian government, though largely Muslim, is led by a corrupt group of false followers of Islamic ideology, and the group has declared war on that government. Nigeria is composed of many different groups of people. Nigerians speak various languages, belong to various ethnic tribes, and practice different religions. Since it became independent in 1958, Nigeria has had 14 heads of state, but only five have been elected. About half of the country is Christian, and the other half Muslim. Boko Haram has used violence, terrorism, kidnapping, and torture to capitalize on Nigerian ethnic civil conflicts to achieve its end of ruling the country under strict Islamic Sharia.

Most Boko Haram recruits originally came from the Kanuri tribe, based in the northeast of the country. The Kanuri tribe predates the modern Nigerian border, so its influence extends into the countries of Niger, Chad, and Cameroon. It is believed that these relationships facilitate Boko Haram's ability to buy and import weapons and illegal goods. Most of Boko Haram's terrorist activities have taken place in the northern and northeastern parts of Nigeria.

FOUNDING

The organization's founder and spiritual leader was a Muslim cleric named Mohammed Yusuf. Yusuf was a Salafist who followed the teachings of a 13th-century religious scholar named Ibn Taymiyya, who taught that communities suffer when leaders do not follow a "true Muslim faith." In interviews, Yusuf argued that Muslims should reject the Western lifestyle, particularly Western education. Yusuf lived and operated in the northeastern Nigerian city of Maiduguri, which is riddled with poverty and has a population of about 1 million people. Yusuf had four wives and a dozen children. He spoke clear English, was well educated, and drove a Mercedes-Benz.

Despite his lavish lifestyle among the impoverished and hungry, Yusuf believed the greatest threat to his fellow citizens was education. In an interview, he stated that education "spoils the belief in one God" and explained how he rejected such concepts as rain forming by evaporation and the idea of a spherical Earth. He was killed in 2009 by Nigerian security forces while trying to escape arrest.

LEADERSHIP

In 2002 Mohammed Yusuf started a religious complex in Maiduguri, which included a mosque and an Islamic school. He recruited students from poor Muslim families across the country. The school undoubtedly had an agenda: to recruit and train mujahideen to fight for a desired Islamic state. Yusuf, as founder, maintained a leadership role in the group. After Yusuf's death in 2009, three new leaders emerged: Abubakar Shekau, Kabiru Sokoto, and Abu Muhammed. Boko Haram's acting commander is Abubakar Shekau. Shekau uses online videos to post threats, calls for jihad, and anti-American rhetoric. More than once he has been presumed dead, only to appear again in an online video proving he is still alive. Some experts consider Shekau to be a more dangerous leader than Yusuf was, because Shekau is reckless, aggressive, and opportunistic. Worse still, Shekau has had multiple attempts on his life by Nigerian security forces—in one clash he was shot, and he's out for revenge. For Shekau it may be for the glory of God, but the resentment he harbors is also quite personal.

VIOLENCE

In 2009, authorities in the Nigerian state of Bauchi prohibited the group from preaching and recruiting in public. In July, a crackdown on motorcycle helmet infractions prompted Boko Haram's first violent pushback. (Motorcycles are the signature style of transportation for many of the group's members and a calling card. Many in the group saw this crackdown as a targeted attack on their members by the authorities.) Seventeen members of Boko Haram were killed when the confrontation escalated. Two weeks later, Boko Haram launched an attack on the police station in Bauchi. Additionally, Boko Haram members in the cities of Maiduguri, Lamisulu, Yobe, and Gamboru attacked other municipal police stations, schools, and churches, killing at least 50 civilians in four days. Eventually the Nigerian army was deployed—but over 800 people died before the violence subsided. In late July 2009, Yusuf was executed and many members of the organization were captured or killed.

Boko Haram remained largely in exile for the second half of 2009 after the remaining members fled the country. During this time, they reportedly trained and continued to recruit. There are reports of the group's receiving training in rebel camps in Mali, and of high-profile Boko Haram leaders living in northern Cameroon.

Boko Haram returned to Maiduguri in 2010 and began a campaign of hit-and-run attacks and assassinations of police and local political leaders. Group members frequently used motorcycles to attack police and take their weapons. Another favorite tactic still used is initiating major attacks on civilians during Western holidays. On Christmas Eve 2010, Boko Haram planted six bombs near churches and open-air markets, and detonated them in the presence of civilians. On New Year's Eve of the same year, they detonated another explosive in a fish market, killing 10. The group favors armed assaults and bombings. In 2010, they killed 127 people with explosives and 35 with armed assaults. In 2011, those figures jumped to 587 and 89, respectively. Though most attacks have been on the Nigerian Christian population, many have also been on prominent local Muslims. The attacks have spread from the group's base in the northeastern region of Nigeria to the west and south, and have been reported in dozens of new cities and the nation's capital, Abuja. In 2012, 800 people were killed during the course of 215 Boko Haram attacks. In

2013, over 1,200 more were killed, and in 2014, the death toll rose to over 6,600. Attacks by Boko Haram are consistently becoming more violent and claiming more lives.

Their notoriety led Nigerian president Goodluck Johnathan to declare a state of emergency in late 2014. Two days after Johnathan's declaration, Boko Haram gave all southern Nigerians living in the northern part of the country an ultimatum: "Leave or die." For those remaining, Boko Haram has made life treacherous. Since 2011, the group has carried out attacks on nearly a weekly basis.

Because democracy is viewed by Boko Haram as a Western institution to be opposed, many of Boko Haram's assassinations and acts of terror have coincided with elections. Following Johnathan's 2010 presidential election defeat of Muhammadu Buhari (a Muslim born in northern Nigeria), Boko Haram committed several bombings that took the lives of prominent political and religious figures, such as Abba Anas Ibn Umar Garbai, the brother of the second most prominent Muslim religious figure in the country. In 2014, Boko Haram sought to spread its influence and intimidation into Cameroon with group abductions that included the wife of a deputy prime minister. It is estimated that its terror activities have displaced at least 30,000 people.

On August 26, 2011, a Boko Haram suicide car bomber blew up the United Nations building in Abuja. The bomb killed 18 and injured 100 more. On January 20, 2012, Boko Haram attacked a police station in the city of Kano, killing 190 people through a combined assault with car bombs, suicide bombers, and rocketed missiles. In April 2014, Boko Haram kidnapped 276 schoolgirls from the city of Chibok. The group stated the goal of the kidnappings was to gain international media attention and profit from ransom money. Fifty girls have escaped safely; the rest remain captured. The kidnapping of the schoolgirls garnered international attention and drew Western attention in a "hashtag" campaign, #bringbackourgirls. In April 2015, the Nigerian government successfully rescued over 300 females from Boko Haram. More rescues throughout 2015 proved successful, with around 180 rescued in August. Despite these successes, the captured schoolgirls still remain with Boko Haram.

In January 2015, Boko Haram committed one of its deadliest attacks to date. Members entered the Nigerian town of Baga and 16 of the surrounding villages. They arrived in armored trucks and indiscriminately sprayed bullets from assault rifles at everyone in sight. When some of the attacked took shelter in their homes, members of Boko Haram barricaded them inside and burned the buildings. Over 3,700 homes and businesses were burned or destroyed. An estimated 2,000 people were killed in the attack. In July 2015, Boko Haram outfitted a 13-year-old girl with a suicide vest. She detonated near a major mosque in the city of Kano, killing only herself. More than 50 were killed in the city of Sabon Gari when Boko Haram detonated a bomb in a busy market in August 2015. In November 2015, another bomb detonated in a busy vegetable market in the city of Yola killed 30 and sent over 50 more to the hospital.

A Boko Haram fighter appearing in a video posted in 2015 coldly states, "Our job is to shoot, slaughter, and kill."[1]

Nigeria's national, state, and local governments are feeling increasingly powerless against the growing threat. Borno state governor Kashim Shettima worries that "Boko Haram are better armed and are better motivated than our own troops. Given the present state of affairs...it is absolutely impossible for us to defeat Boko Haram."

Boko Haram now controls land in northeastern and eastern Nigeria, including in the states of Borno, Adamawe, and Yobe. After capturing the city of Gwoza in Borno, Boko Haram leader Shekau released a video claiming the town was now part of "an Islamic caliphate."

An estimated 20,000 have been killed by Boko Haram, in total, since its 2009 resurgence.

TIES

In 2009 after Boko Haram founder Yusuf was executed, temporary leader Sani Umar published the following statement:

> Boko Haram is an Islamic Revolution which impact [sic] is not limited to northern Nigeria, in fact, we are spread across all the 36 states in Nigeria, and Boko Haram is just a version of the Al Qaeda which we align with and respect. We support Osama bin

Laden, we shall carry out his command in Nigeria until the country is totally Islamized which is according to the wish of Allah.[2]

During Boko Haram's brief 2009 to 2010 exile, it likely formed allegiances with **al-Shabaab**, another Salafi group based in Somalia. Though an alliance between the two groups has not been firmly established, suicide bombings and video releases by both groups have notably similar forms.

Analysts have acknowledged ideological similarities between Boko Haram and **Al Qaeda**.

FUNDING

Boko Haram seems to fund most of its operations by robbing local banks and stealing weapons from local police. A spokesperson for the Central Bank of Nigeria attributed at least 30 bank robberies to the group in 2011 alone. Additionally, a number of powerful independent and government actors have been arrested on suspicion of financially supporting Boko Haram, including state officials in Borno and a member of the Nigerian Senate. It is not clear whether these supporters are motivated by a common ideology or have other, more complex reasons. Experts have referred to the funding network as elusive and diverse. Boko Haram has released videos threatening to sell abducted women into black markets, involving both local and foreign buyers. **Al Qaeda** and other wealthy Middle Eastern militant groups are thought to be part of the elaborate fundraising apparatus of Boko Haram.

NOTES

[1] Jacinto, Leela. "The Boko Haram Terror Chief Who Came Back from the Dead." France 24. 25 Sept. 2014. <http://www.france24.com/en/20120111-terror-chief-boko-haram-imam-shekau-youtube-nigeria-goodluck-jonathan-al-qaeda-oil>.

[2] Cook, David. "The Rise of Boko Haram in Nigeria." Combating Terrorism Center at West Point. 26 Sept. 2011. <https://www.ctc.usma.edu/posts/the-rise-of-boko-haram-in-nigeria>.

CAUCASUS EMIRATES (CE)

CAUCASUS EMIRATES (CE)

Main Area(s) of Operation	Russia
Founder or Spiritual Leader	Doku Umarov
Known or Suspected Leader	Magomed Muleymanov
Approximate Year Founded	2007
Approximate Size	Hundreds to thousands
Alliances & Cooperations	Islamic State, Al Qaeda,
Ideological Sect/Affiliation	Salafism
Name Meaning	"Islamic Empire of the Caucasus Region"
Flag	

THE CAUCASUS EMIRATES (CE) is an umbrella organization of Islamic jihadist groups that seek to establish an independent Islamic emirate, ruled under Sharia, to aid in a global jihad.

The Caucasus region consists of the region around the Caucasus Mountains on the border of Europe and Asia. It includes parts of Russia in the north, and the countries of Armenia, Azerbaijan, and Georgia and parts of Iran and Turkey in the south. It is one of the most ethnically and linguistically diverse regions in the world.

The groups that form the Caucasus Emirates are largely independent and self-sufficient. They include the following known terror groups:

— Yarmuk Jamaat
— Dagestani Shari'ah

— Ingush Jamaat
— Riyad us-Saliheyn Martyrs Brigade

The CE frequently targets Western interests as part of its mission to facilitate global jihad. In 2013, it released a video statement calling for Islamic militants to "derail" the winter Olympic games in Sochi. The group's leader said, "We have an obligation to use all means to prevent this."[1] Another video from the group called for fighters in Syria to return to Russia to help attack the games. The CE's motive was both to harm Westerners and discredit the Russian government by causing the internationally attended games to be disrupted and unsafe. In addition, the CE is suspected of having connections with the Tsarnaev brothers, perpetrators of the 2013 Boston Marathon bombing.

FOUNDING

The Caucasus Emirates was founded by Doku Umarov, following his resignation as president of the self-proclaimed secessionist government of Chechnya, the Republic of Ichkeria, in 2007.

The CE grows its membership by operating youth training camps in the Caucasus region, and with support from **Al Qaeda** and the **Taliban**.

LEADERSHIP

The CE maintains six regional substructures, or provinces, all of which are led by emirs who originally reported to Umarov. These provinces include Chechnya, Ingushetia and north Ossetia, Nogay Steppe, Cherkess and southern Krasnodar Krai, Dagestan, and Kabardino-Balkaria and Karachay. The Russian government has an active and dedicated security force tasked with eliminating CE factions and regional leaders, which means the local emirs constantly change.

In March 2014, it was reported that Umarov was poisoned by Russian security forces. He was succeeded by Ali Abu Mohammed al-Dagestani. Al-Dagestani was killed by Russian security forces in August 2015, bringing the CE emir turnover rate to more than three in just one and a half years. A new emir has yet to be publicly announced.

VIOLENCE

In 2005, the CE attacked the city of Nalchik, killing 100 while attacking Russian security forces, apparently unfazed by the collateral damage. In 2006 the group had another deadly skirmish with Russian forces, and in 2008 it committed seven more attacks. In 2009, the CE assassinated an Orthodox priest in Moscow. It also planted bombs in high-traffic subway infrastructure, one on a rail line between Moscow and St. Petersburg, which killed 35 and injured 95. Two CE female suicide bombers killed 40 and injured 100 by detonating explosives in Moscow subway stations at rush hour. Other attacks include a 2010 bombing of the Chechen Parliament building, a 2011 bombing of the Domodedovo International Airport that killed 37 and injured 180, and a bus bombing near Sochi that killed six.

The 2013 Boston Marathon bombers are allegedly linked with the Caucasus Emirates. That attack closely resembled CE-led attacks in Chechnya, and it is believed that the brothers suspected of carrying out the attack spent time as children in the CE-populous Dagestan region, where the group's influence would have been probable. The CE has publicly denied any involvement in the attack.

From January 1999 to December 2011, the CE was linked to 30 terror attacks. In the three years following, the number of CE terror attacks escalated to an estimated 500 or more, primarily bombings and armed assaults. Casualties from CE acts of violence are estimated at 1,500 in the group's seven-year existence.

TIES

According to the *Moscow Times*, the CE is "deeply embedded in the global jihad revolutionary movement which the **Islamic State** and **Al Qaeda** are fighting to lead." Numerous CE members and leaders have left the Caucasus for Iraq and Syria to join the **Islamic State** and **Al Qaeda**.

One former CE leader, Abu Umar al-Shishani, joined the **Islamic State** in 2013 and has risen through the ranks to become military emir of the **Islamic State**'s northern front. Al-Shishani is just one of many from the CE who have become leaders within the **Islamic State**.

FUNDING

The CE receives financial support from **Al Qaeda** and allegedly from high-level officials in the Chechen government. As CE members increasingly find newer and higher posts within the Islamic State, it is likely that they are sending money back to CE for operational use.

NOTES

[1] Caucasus Emirate (CE) section on Terrorism Research and Analysis Consortium website. <http://www.trackingterrorism.org/group/caucasus-emirate-ce>.

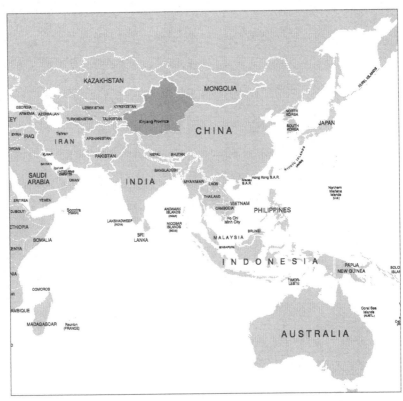

EAST TURKESTAN ISLAMIC MOVEMENT (ETIM)

EAST TURKESTAN ISLAMIC MOVEMENT (ETIM)

Main Area(s) of Operation	Xinjiang province of China
Founder or Spiritual Leader	Hasan Mahsum, Abudukadir Yapuquan
Approximate Year Founded	1997
Approximate Size	Unknown; at least 40 cells
Alliances & Cooperations	Islamic Movement of Uzbekistan, Al Qaeda, Taliban
Ideological Sect/Affiliation	Uyghur nationalism

THE EAST TURKESTAN ISLAMIC MOVEMENT (ETIM), also known as the Turkestan Islamic Party, is a militant Islamic separatist group based in the Xinjiang province in northwest China. The ETIM is composed of Uighur people from the Turkic ethnic majority of Xinjiang.

Xinjiang province is large and has a low population density. It borders eight countries, including Afghanistan and Pakistan. Thus, information about the extent of ETIM activities and the size of its network is sparse. According to anthropology professor Dru Gladney, who actively studies the Xinjiang region, "There is no reliable independently verified information on this organization, [sic] there's widespread suspicions among experts that this so called ETIM is an umbrella term for several small groups or individuals acting alone."[1]

China has banned ETIM activities within its borders, so many ETIM training camps and operational bases are in Pakistan and Afghanistan, near the Chinese border. The U.S. previously held 22

ETIM members at Guantanamo Bay, given into U.S. custody by Pakistani forces. However, most of them have since been released.

The State Department indicates that the strength of the ETIM is "unknown" but regards it as "one of the more extreme separatist groups."[2] It is believed that over 40 ETIM cells exist around and within Xinjiang province.

The goal of the ETIM is to establish an independent state in East Turkestan that would include parts of China, Turkey, Kazakhstan, Kyrgyzstan, Uzbekistan, Pakistan, and Afghanistan.

FOUNDING

East Turkestan was a territory independent of China, but under its protection, until the Qing Dynasty incorporated it as the Xinjiang province (officially recognized in 1884). The region was home to both Russians and Chinese, and the ethnic tensions played into a series of Sino-Soviet power plays. Eventually, the Russians ceded the territory to China, but conflict among the various ethnic groups in the region remains.

The East Turkestan Islamic Movement began in 1993 to separate the region from China under the banner of an independent Islamic state. In 1997, Hasan Mahsum and Abudukadir Yapuquan reinvented the movement, moving operations to the Afghan capital of Kabul and training under the **Taliban**.

Mahsum was a student of Xinjiang-based Islamic scholar and fundamentalist Abdul Hakeem. He followed Hakeem around Xinjiang for years, frequently teaching at underground religious schools. In 1990 and 1993, he was detained for participating in rebellions. While in prison, Mahsum radicalized and made numerous contacts with Uighur separatists and other extremists. He organized armed resistances against Chinese security forces with varied success, and in the 1990s brought a number of militants together to travel to Afghanistan to prepare for jihad. Mahsum then founded ETIM, remaining abroad to direct operations in Xinjiang to keep from being caught by Chinese security forces. He led a group of fighters to resist American efforts in Afghanistan in 2001, fighting alongside the **Taliban**, until he was killed by Pakistani security forces in 2003.

After Mahsum's death, Abdul Haq became leader of the ETIM. Haq had quit school at age 9 to follow Islamic clerics and study Islam. In the late 1990s, he traveled to Afghanistan and Pakistan and met Mahsum. Haq was quickly appointed to the overseeing advisory body of the ETIM, and led militant ETIM training operations in Afghanistan.

The ETIM was weakened during U.S. efforts in Afghanistan and Iraq, but after the U.S. withdrew troops in the region, attacks credited to the group have become more violent and numerous.

LEADERSHIP

Haq led the group until he was killed in Pakistan in 2010. The Chinese government has named several individuals now suspected of holding leadership roles, but the group's splintered structure makes pinpointing leadership difficult. One individual to surface as recently as 2014 and speak on behalf of the group in online videos is Abdullah Mansour.

VIOLENCE

The ETIM was responsible for over 200 attacks between 1990 and 2001. According to the Council on Foreign Relations, these include "bombing buses, markets, and government institutions—as well as assassinating local officials, Muslim leaders, and civilians—in attacks that [during that time period] killed 162 people."[3]

In the late 1990s, the ETIM detonated two bombs at the Chinese embassy in Turkey. In 2002, it was prevented from attacking the U.S. embassy in China, and in 2008 it received international attention when it threatened to attack the Beijing Olympics.

In 2008, the ETIM claimed responsibility for explosions in the Chinese cities of Shanghai and Kunming. In 2011, the group killed 16 with bombs and knives, and a 2013 Tiananmen Square car bombing killed five and injured 40.

Recently, ETIM members have created videos that have been widely disseminated on the Internet, including on social media sites, calling for Uighur people living in Xinjiang to participate in jihad.

TIES

Experts believe the ETIM works closely with the **Islamic Movement of Uzbekistan**, another militant separatist group operating around the Turkestan region. The Chinese government has indicated that the ETIM has ties to **Al Qaeda**, the **Taliban**, and, when he was alive, Osama bin Laden, who was involved in the group's formation in **Taliban** training camps after it left Xinjiang for Afghanistan in the 1990s. The U.S. government was reluctant to list the organization as a terror group, partly because of the political situation surrounding the Uighur people's grievances with the Chinese government; however, the Bush administration took action against the group in 2002 by freezing its assets and labeling it a terrorist organization.

FUNDING

The Chinese government has released findings that show financial ties between **Al Qaeda**, the **Taliban**, and the ETIM. These reports detail **Al Qaeda**-led training initiatives of ETIM members, who are then sent back into Xinjiang to set up terrorist cells.

The U.S. government has also issued reports of ties between the ETIM and **Al Qaeda**. ETIM operatives are known to have fought alongside **Al Qaeda** against the United States in Afghanistan.

NOTES

[1] "What Is the East Turkestan Islamic Movement?" *Voice of America*. 3 Aug. 2011. <http://www.voanews.com/content/what-is-the-east-turkestan-islamic-movement-126763973/167829.html>.

[2] Xu, Beina, Holly Fletcher, and Jayshree Bajoria. The East Turkestan Islamic Movement (ETIM). Backgrounder section on Council on Foreign Relations website. 4 Sept. 2014. <http://www.cfr.org/china/east-turkestan-islamic-movement-etim/p9179>.

[3] Ibid.

EGYPTIAN ISLAMIC JIHAD (EJJ)

EGYPTIAN ISLAMIC JIHAD (EJJ)

Main Area(s) of Operation	Egypt
Founder or Spiritual Leader	Ayman al-Zawahiri, Omar Abdel Rahman
Known or Suspected Leader	Ayman al-Zawahiri
Approximate Year Founded	1979
Approximate Size	300+
Alliances & Cooperations	Al Qaeda

THE EGYPTIAN ISLAMIC JIHAD is a militant Islamic group that seeks to replace the Egyptian government with a fundamentalist Islamic state, as well as attack U.S. and Israeli interests abroad. The group was led by Ayman al-Zawahiri, Osama bin Laden's second-in-command, from 1991 to 2001, when it was integrated into **Al Qaeda**. Despite the merger, the EIJ is believed to maintain limited independent operations, with most remaining active members operating in Afghanistan, Pakistan, Lebanon, Yemen, and the United Kingdom.

EIJ had an estimated 300 members in 2001.

FOUNDING

EIJ was founded in 1979 when members of two other Egyptian militant groups united under a common manifesto called *Al-Faridah al-Gha'ibah*, translated as "The Neglected Duty." The manifesto calls for violent jihad in the struggle against the impious, and places an affirmative duty on all Muslims to act in accordance. Ayman al-Zawa-hiri helped facilitate the merger and the founding of EIJ.

LEADERSHIP
EIJ's spiritual leader is Omar Abdel Rahman, whose teaching provided guidance for the group's early manifesto and struggle against the Egyptian state. Since the group's founding, al-Zawahiri has been a senior member or leader, and he continues to hold authority as the leader of **Al Qaeda**.

VIOLENCE
From 1979 to 2001, EIJ focused primarily on its efforts in Egypt against the secular government. Since 2001, it has shifted its priorities to facilitating attacks against the United States and Israel. According to the U.S. State Department, "EIJ is thought to be involved with most of the terrorist attacks on the United States in the last two decades, and its operatives played a key role in both attacks on the World Trade Center."[1]

The Australian government estimates that EIJ has abandoned nationalist goals for a global jihad focus since its last major attack within Egyptian borders in 1993.

While attempting to manipulate the Egyptian state, EIJ's most notorious attack was its assassination of Egyptian president Anwar al-Sadat in 1981. In 1993, the group also attempted to assassinate Egyptian prime minister Atef Sedky and Egyptian interior minister Hassan al-Alfi.

In 1995, the EIJ bombed the Egyptian embassy in Islamabad, Pakistan, by driving a truck filled with explosives into the side of the compound. The attack killed 15. The same year, the group attempted to assassinate Egyptian president Hosni Mubarak in Addis Ababa, Ethiopia. In 1998, EIJ targeted the U.S. embassy in Algeria, but that plan was foiled. However, a successful simultaneous bombing of the U.S. embassies in Nairobi and Tanzania killed 223 and injured over 4,000. This attack was executed with the help of the **Al Qaeda** network and Osama bin Laden's resources.

TIES

The EIJ's successful assassination of Egyptian president Anwar al-Sadat was in conjunction with a **Muslim Brotherhood** offshoot group and the **Palestinian Islamic Jihad**.

EIJ largely merged with **Al Qaeda** in 2001, under the direction of its longtime leader, al-Zawahiri. Al-Zawahiri also succeeded Osama bin Laden to lead **Al Qaeda** at large.

Many members of EIJ were members of the **Muslim Brotherhood** who left that group when it publicly denounced violence. For its assassination of President Sadat in 1981, EIJ coordinated with the Egyptian-based Jamaat al-Islamiya terror group.

FUNDING

Initial funding sources are unknown, but one was likely Osama bin Laden, as al-Zawahiri developed his relationship with the **Al Qaeda** leader throughout the '80s and '90s. EIJ gained access to **Al Qaeda** funding networks after the merger in 2001.

NOTES

[1] Fletcher, Holly. Egyptian Islamic Jihad. Backgrounder section on Council on Foreign Relations website. 30 May 2008. <http://www.cfr.org/egypt/egyptian-islamic-jihad/p16376>.

GREAT EASTERN ISLAMIC RAIDERS' FRONT (IBDA-C)

GREAT EASTERN ISLAMIC RAIDERS' FRONT (IBDA-C)

Main Area(s) of Operation	Turkey
Founder or Spiritual Leader	Necip Fazil Kisakurek (ideological role model), Salih Izzet Erdis
Known or Suspected Leader	Salih Izzet Erdis
Approximate Year Founded	1970s
Approximate Size	Dozens to hundreds (estimate)
Alliances & Cooperations	Al Qaeda
Ideological Sect/Affiliation	Salafist, communism
Flag	

THE GREAT EASTERN ISLAMIC RAIDERS' FRONT (IBDA-C) is a Turkey-based militant Islamic group that follows a communist, Wahhabi-like ideology, though it is composed of Sunni Salafists. Its mission is to establish a fundamentalist Islamic nation in Turkey based on Sharia. The Turkish caliphate would then be a base of operations from which a global war of jihad could be launched.

FOUNDING
The IBDA-C was loosely formed in the 1970s under the ideology of Islamic historian and poet Necip Fazil Kisakurek, author of over 130 published books. His works detail a unique conceptualization of the

path to Islamic salvation, which IBDA-C claims it strives to implement as its guiding purpose under "Islamic truth." In Kisakurek's "Ideal Islamic Society," the evil secular Turkish government has been replaced with one that restores "pure," fundamental Islamic values. According to the Intelligence and Terrorism Information Center, the IBDA-C school of thought developed by Kisakurek is "ideologically opposed to virtually every other Islamic movement....However, this radical ideological opposition has not kept it from cooperating with other organizations trying to destabilize the system of Turkey."[1]

Founding members of the IBDA-C had defected from the Islamic Salvation Party, a Turkish political party to which former Turkish prime minister Nejmettin Erbakan belonged. Erbakan was the nation's first Islamist prime minister, who was forced to resign in 1997 after he violated the Turkish constitution's provision separating church and state.

The group's official founding came in 1985 by Salih Izzet Erdis.

LEADERSHIP

Erdis remains the leader and is known by IBDA-C members as "the Commander." He was arrested in 1998 and tried in 1999 on charges of "attempting to overthrow the constitutional order by use of arms." He received a death sentence, but in 2002 his sentence was converted to life imprisonment, and in 2015 he was released after he filed for a retrial.

The IBDA-C has a propaganda wing that publishes books and pamphlets, and organizes conferences. Erdis headlined one such conference after his recent release from prison. The IBDA-C also controls a number of bookstores, and from these locations operates training seminars. Its model is to inspire independent violent action on behalf of the group's ideological purposes.

VIOLENCE

The IBDA-C targets civilians and advertises its attacks in publications to encourage public assistance. In 1993, the group firebombed a hotel in Sivas, Turkey, killing 37. It was tied to a 1994 assassination attempt on a prominent Jewish businessman in Turkey, and an attack on the Greek Orthodox Church in Istanbul.

In 2003, the IBDA-C claimed responsibility with **Al Qaeda** for four bombings in Istanbul, with targets such as the British consulate and the Turkish headquarters of banking company HSBC. Fifty-two people were killed in the blasts and hundreds injured.

TIES

The IBDA-C, despite ideological differences, has been linked to various Turkish terrorism groups, the Jerusalem Brigades (a part of the **Iranian Revolutionary Guard Corps**), and **Al Qaeda**.

FUNDING

IBDA-C attacks are "open sourced." The group invites the public to join and encourages donations of resources. It is also believed to receive funding from Al Qaeda.

NOTES

[1] Fighel, Yoni. "The Great East Islamic Raiders Front (IBDA-C)" report, Intelligence and Terrorism Information Center at the Center for Special Studies (C.S.S.). <http://www.terrorism-info.org.il/Data/articles/Art_506/dec_03b_1580673991.pdf>.

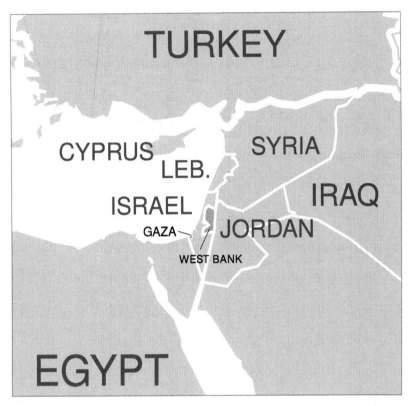

HAMAS

HAMAS

Main Area(s) of Operation	Palestine (Gaza Strip)
Founder or Spiritual Leader	Ahmed Yassin
Known or Suspected Leader	Khaled Meshaal
Approximate Year Founded	1987
Approximate Size	1,000+
Alliances & Cooperations	Muslim Brotherhood, Palestinian Islamic Jihad
Name Meaning	"Zeal"; also an acronym for "Harkat al-Muqawama al-Islamiya" or "Islamic Resistance Movement"
Flag	

HAMAS IS THE LARGEST MILITANT GROUP in Palestine, elected to political leadership in the Gaza Strip in 2006. It is the first militant Islamic extremist group in the world to gain autonomous power democratically.

"Hamas" is related to the Arabic word for "zeal," but is also an acronym for Harkat al-Muqawama al-Islamiya, which translates as "Islamic Resistance Movement."

The Palestinian National Authority (PNA) is the governing entity of the Palestinian territories, which include the Gaza Strip and the West Bank. At present, Hamas controls the PNA in the Gaza Strip, and Fatah controls the PNA in the West Bank. Fatah, formerly the Palestinian National Liberation Movement, is the largest political party among the coalition of Palestinian political entities known as the Palestinian

Liberation Organization (PLO). The president of the PNA is Mahmoud Abbas, of Fatah.

The charter of Hamas expressly states the group's objective as the destruction of the state of Israel, to be followed by the establishment of an Islamic state on the same land.

FOUNDING

Hamas was founded in 1987 following the First Intifada against Israel.

Instrumental in its founding was Ahmed Yassin, a member of the **Muslim Brotherhood** who traveled to Palestine from Egypt in the 1960s. In 1973, Yassin formed al-Mujamma' al-Islami as a political arm of the Muslim Brotherhood and to coordinate its efforts in Palestine. After the Hamas charter, which called for violent tactics and the destruction of Israel, was written in 1988, the **Muslim Brotherhood** distanced itself from Hamas. Yassin was killed by Israeli security forces in 2004.

The first Hamas-organized suicide bombing took place in 1993 in the Gaza Strip. Five months later, PLO leader Yasser Arafat signed the Oslo Accords, a treaty with Israel that granted the PNA authority to rule the Palestinian territories. Hamas condemned the accords because they required the PLO to recognize Israel as a nation.

During the Second Intifada, Hamas substantially increased its suicide bombings and violent attacks. It directly and indirectly targets both Israeli *and* Palestinian civilians. According to the Council on Foreign Relations, "In both [the First and the Second Intifadas], Palestinian fatalities far exceeded Israeli ones."[2]

Hamas's original group structure had two parts: a militant branch called the Izzedine al-Qassam Brigades, and a branch that ran social welfare programs for Palestinians. The militant branch was founded by Salah Shehadeh, who was killed in 2002 in an airstrike. Hamas became involved in Palestinian politics in 2005. Its 2006 election victory is credited to its welfare offerings and to its split with the rival Palestinian political party Fatah. After Hamas won political authority, most social welfare services stopped coming from Hamas, and the need has been filled by the UN and humanitarian organizations.

LEADERSHIP

According to the U.S. State Department, Hamas's highest-ranking decision makers operate from hideouts in neighboring countries. The chief decision maker is Khaled Meshaal, in Doha, Qatar. Ismail Haniyeh, considered by some sources to be "Gaza's de facto prime minister," retains some leadership in the group even though Mahmoud Abbas dismissed him from formal PNA leadership in 2007. Salah al-Arouri commands Hamas's West Bank operations from an undisclosed location abroad. The Izzedine al-Qassam Brigades are commanded by Marwan Issa and Mohammed Deif.

Hamas recruits are typically young idealists. In many cases, suicide bombers are paid for their training, and the families of the bombers are paid after the suicide bomber's death. According to a Council on Foreign Relations profile published by the *Washington Post*:

> Shortly before the "sacred explosion," as Hamas calls it, the bomber records a video testament. To draw inspiration, he repeatedly watches his video and those made by his predecessors and then sets off for his would-be martyrdom after performing a ritual ablution and donning clean clothes. Hamas clerics assure the bombers their deaths will be painless and that dozens of virgins await them in paradise. The average bombing costs about $150.[2]

VIOLENCE

From 1993 until 2005, through the First and Second Intifadas, Hamas resorted to suicide bombings and armed attacks on the Israeli population, launched from both Gaza and the West Bank. Since 1993, it has committed over 350 attacks that have killed more than 500 people.

In 1994, Hamas claimed responsibility for a suicide bombing in the central bus station of Hadera, Israel, and in the Israeli town of Afula. Together, the attacks killed eight. In February 1996, a Hamas suicide bombing in Jerusalem killed 26, and another in March killed 19. In 1997, Hamas suicide bombings in Jerusalem claimed another 14 lives and injured 150. In June 2001, a bombing at a nightclub in Tel Aviv killed 140. In August, another Hamas suicide bomber targeted a busy restaurant in Jerusalem, killing 15 and injuring 90. A 2003 bombing on an Israeli bus killed 20, six children included, and injured 100.

After its legislative victory in 2006, Hamas changed its approach and began acting as a sovereignty in warfare. A 2006 suicide bombing in Tel Aviv, which killed nine, was claimed by the **Palestinian Islamic Jihad**. In its new role, Hamas didn't claim responsibility, but did defend the attacks as "self-defense."

When Hamas gained power in Gaza, it used the PNA's infrastructure and arms and weaponry networks to begin a continuous missile barrage against Israel from the Gaza Strip. It fires rockets indiscriminately at Israeli civilians and cities, to cause maximum casualties. According to estimates by the Israel Defense Forces, rocket attacks from Gaza into Israel number as follows:

— 2001: 510
— 2002: 661
— 2003: 848
— 2004: 1,528
— 2005: 488
— 2006: 1,123
— 2007: 2,427
— 2008: 3,278
— 2009: 774
— 2010: 231
— 2011: 627
— 2012: 2,248
— 2013: 41
— 2014: 450

These numbers equate to roughly three missile or rocket attacks a day, for a total of 15,200-plus rockets, missiles, and mortars since 2001. The launched explosives used by Hamas include the 9KG Qassam model, the 45KG GRAD model, the 60KG M-75 model, and the M-302 144K model. The M series of launched explosives have a range that allows them to reach most of Israel from Gaza, including the most populous cities: Haifa, Be'er Sheva, Tel Aviv, and Jerusalem.

Hamas uses civilian centers, buildings, schools, hospitals, and homes in Gaza to store, launch, and coordinate missile attacks. In June 2014, the United Nations Relief and Works Agency condemned Hamas when it was discovered that 20 rockets were hidden in a school in Gaza.

To gain international support and to control its public image, Hamas encourages Israeli attacks on Palestinian civilians; Hamas operatives intimidate reporters so they don't disclose these deplorable tactics. A report by New Delhi television reporter Sreenivasan Jain exposed Hamas's firing rockets at a residential neighborhood in Gaza in August 2014 to draw Israeli fire. According to an article in the *Algemeiner*, "It's the most graphic evidence yet of Hamas deliberately acting in, and from civilian areas—in the hopes of drawing Israeli fire that will cause civilian casualties and increase international criticism of Israel."[9] A French reporter, Radjaa Abu Dagga, also wrote of similar tactics he witnessed during his time in a hospital used as an operations base.

In late 2014, the Israel Defense Forces procured a Hamas recruit manual, titled *Urban Warfare*, which gives instructions on how Hamas operatives could use Gaza civilians to military advantage. The manual encourages Hamas militants to attack places with civilians nearby, because they create for Israelis "Problems with opening fire, Problems in controlling the civilian population during operations and afterward; [and capitalize on the Israeli] Assurance of supplying medical care to civilians who need it."[9] Another portion of the manual encourages damaging civilian property to increase international rebuke of Israel.

Hamas denies use of these tactics and accuses the IDF and Israel of intentionally attacking Palestinian civilians. According to Israel, a series of warning tactics are used before offensive measures are taken on a Hamas target in Gaza, including phoning and texting residents, dropping leaflets warning civilians of impending attacks, and firing harmless warning missiles called "roof-knocking" bombs.

TIES

After the 2006 Hamas electoral victory in the Gaza Strip, Fatah and Hamas became violent rivals, and in 2007, clashes occurred between them. The two groups initiated peace agreements in 2011, and an April 2014 reconciliation deal rebuilt the Palestinian national unity government. Fatah has renounced violent tactics, but Hamas continues to defend their use.

Hamas originated from the **Muslim Brotherhood**, but remains at odds with the group since the split following the publishing of the 1988 Hamas charter.

Hamas and the **Palestinian Islamic Jihad** cooperate on attacks. From 2001 to 2003, the two groups together executed dozens of suicide bombings in Israeli cafes, shops, and restaurants, and on public transportation—eventually prompting Israel to construct a wall around portions of the Gaza Strip where attackers frequently entered Israel with explosives.

FUNDING

Hamas's initial funding sources included Palestinian expatriates and Gulf State donors, and money funneled through Western Islamic charities.

Hamas, designated a terrorist group by the U.S., the EU, and Israel, gets no financial assistance from the West, and is subject to border and maritime blockades. As a workaround, Hamas constructed more than a thousand tunnels from the Gaza Strip to Egypt, through which it smuggles food, weapons, gas, medicine, building materials, and money. It taxes illicit tunnel trade for a profit. Since 2013, Israel and Egypt have made a concerted effort to close and destroy the tunnel network.

Hamas historically maintained financial ties with Iran (and, thus, the **Iranian Revolutionary Guard Corps**), which by some account was its "primary benefactor," with financial aid estimated at $20 million to $30 million per year. However, since 2001, Iran's support for the Syrian Bashar al-Assad regime has been creating tensions between Iran and Hamas.

NOTES

[1] Hamas. Backgrounder section on Council on Foreign Relations website. 1 Aug. 2014. <http://www.cfr.org/israel/hamas/p8968 >.

[2] Ibid.

[3] Phillips, Moshe, and Benyamin Korn. "Conclusive Proof That Hamas Uses Palestinians as Human Shields." The Algemeiner. 7 Aug. 2014. <http://www.algemeiner.com/2014/08/07/conclusive-proof-that-hamas-uses-palestinians-as-human-shields/#>.

HAQQANI NETWORK

HAQQANI NETWORK

Main Area(s) of Operation	Afghanistan, Pakistan, Arabian Peninsula
Founder or Spiritual Leader	Jalaluddin Haqqani
Known or Suspected Leader	Sirajuddin Haqqani, Badruddin Haqqani, Nasiruddin Haqqani
Approximate Year Founded	1980s
Approximate Size	10,000
Alliances & Cooperations	Taliban, Al Qaeda, Islamic Movement of Uzbekistan, Harkat-ul-Mujahideen al-Islami, Tehrik-e-Taliban Pakistan, Lashkar-e-Taiba
Ideological Sect/Affiliation	Deobandi

THE HAQQANI NETWORK is a militant group based in Afghanistan that seeks to attack U.S-led coalition forces in the region. Its namesake is a family of business owners who funnel proceeds from legal business ventures in Afghanistan, Pakistan, and Gulf states into terrorist activities. Haqqani attacks are often elaborate and intricately planned and executed, thanks to the resources provided through the network. The network has killed or injured over 1,300 U.S. troops.

Of the 52 designated terrorist groups on the U.S. Foreign Terrorist Organizations list in 2012, the Haqqani Network was regarded by *The Economist* as the one involved in the most "direct, regular and violent attacks on Americans." U.S. command in Afghanistan has called the group its "most formidable enemy."[1]

The Haqqani Network has an estimated 10,000 fighters, in addition to extensive training and recruitment centers in Miranshah, Pakistan.

FOUNDING

Jalaluddin Haqqani was an Afghan Jadran tribesman who came to prominence during the Afghan-Soviet war in the 1980s. He formed a militia of fighters during his time in the Hezb-e-Islami militant group that he led in battle against the Soviets. Through this campaign, he developed regional recognition. After the beginning of the Soviet Union's withdrawal, his forces were the first to seize a major Afghan city–Khost—which his fighters conquered in 1991. Working thereafter with the **Taliban**, he was eventually appointed interior minister and then commander of the **Taliban**'s armed forces.

At the war's conclusion, Jalaluddin Haqqani traveled the Middle East building relationships, gathering investors, and creating a network of support for continued mujahideen efforts. With the help of his sons (he had six), he organized and maintained an offensive against U.S. interests that entered Afghanistan in 2001. After the U.S. campaign began in the Middle East in 2001, Jalaluddin "turned against the West with a vengeance," dedicating his bases and resources to be used against troops and for the purposes of Western-oriented terror attacks.[2]

Currently, the Haqqani network recruits from Afghanistan, Pakistan, Uzbekistan, Chechnya, and Turkey.

LEADERSHIP

In 2015, it was confirmed that Jalaluddin had died from illness in Afghanistan. Various unconfirmed reports exist of exactly when he died, with some contending it was up to six years prior. Control of the network evidently passed from Jalaluddin Haqqani to three of his sons, Sirajuddin, Badruddin, and Nasiruddin, and his brother, Ibrahim. Sirajuddin, the most radical and violent member of the family, is considered to have ultimate authority. He has been described as "a brutal criminal murderer" and "very much into the global extremism of Al Qaeda."[3]

VIOLENCE

The Haqqani Network organizes and executes complex suicide bombings against American interests in Afghanistan. Its primary targets include U.S. troops and high-level personnel.

In 2008, a Haqqani car bomb was detonated at the Kabul Serena Hotel, and Haqqani militants thereafter open-fired on the hotel residents, killing six and injuring six more. In 2010, a suicide car bomb killed 18 in a NATO convoy, including five U.S. soldiers, and injured 52. In 2011, 77 U.S. soldiers were injured in a truck bomb attack outside of the Combat Outpost Sayed Abad in Wardak, Afghanistan. Later in the same month, a Haqqani-armed attack on the U.S. embassy in Kabul claimed 11 lives and injured 23.

TIES

The Haqqani Network, a business-minded enterprise, appreciates the significance of creating and maintaining alliances with like-minded terror groups.

It is supported by the Pakistani ISI to maintain influence over Indian interests In Afghanistan. The group is believed to be based out of the FATA region of Pakistan and is allowed to operate its businesses and maintain its headquarters freely.

The Haqqani Network is allied with the **Taliban**, which protects and supports its activities in Afghanistan. It is also believed to be aligned with **Al Qaeda**. Jalaluddin Haqqani had a relationship with Osama bin Laden throughout the 1980s.

The **Islamic Movement of Uzbekistan** provides fighters to aid Haqqani Network efforts. Ties between the Haqqani Network and **Harkat-ul-Mujahideen** and **Tehrik-i-Taliban Pakistan** also exist, and are believed to exist with **Lashkar-e-Taiba**.

FUNDING

After gaining recognition as a mujahideen fighter in the Afghan-Soviet war in the 1980s, Jalaluddin Haqqani traveled the Middle East raising funds and building a network of financial investors. Jalaluddin turned his initial investments into an extensive enterprise of legal businesses, including car dealerships, construction companies, import and export operations, and commercial and residential real estate holdings. These investments have paid off handsomely and have financed Haqqani-orchestrated attacks.

The Haqqani Network also profits from illegal business activities, including illicit minerals, timber, jewels, and metal smuggling. It has utilized extortion and kidnapping as a supplemental source of funding. The **Taliban** and **Al Qaeda** provide weapons, explosives, training, and recruits to the Haqqani Network as needed.

NOTES

[1] "The Haqqani Network: Blacklisted." *The Economist*. 15 Sept. 2015. <http://www.economist.com/node/21562974>.

[2] "Afghan Militant Leader Jalaluddin Haqqani 'Has Died'" BBC. 31 July 2015. <http://www.bbc.com/news/world-asia-33740337>.

[3] Fantz, Ashley. "The Haqqani Network, a Family and a Terror Group." CNN. 7 Sept. 2012. <http://www.cnn.com/2012/09/07/world/who-is-haqqani/>.

HARKAT-UL-JIHAD AL-ISLAMI (HUJI)

HARKAT-UL-JIHAD AL-ISLAMI (HUJI)

Main Area(s) of Operation	Pakistan, India, Bangladesh
Founder or Spiritual Leader	Qari Saifullah Akhtar
Known or Suspected Leader	Qari Saifullah Akhtar, Muhammad Ilyas Kashmiri, Shahid Bilal, Mohammad Tariq Qasmi
Approximate Year Founded	1984
Approximate Size	500–700
Alliances & Cooperations	Jaish-e-Muhammed, Harkat-ul-Mujahideen al-Islami, Lashkar-e-Taiba, Taliban, Al Qaeda
Ideological Sect/Affiliation	Deobandi Islam
Name Meaning	"Islamic Jihad Movement"

HARKAT-UL-JIHAD AL-ISLAMI (HUJI) is a militant Islamic group with factions operating in Pakistan, Bangladesh (there, HuJI-B), and India since the early 1990s. HuJI formed in Pakistan in conjunction with other large jihadist groups, including **Lashkar-e-Taiba, Jaish-e-Muhammed, and Harkat-ul-Mujahideen al-Islami**. These groups have their own distinct internal agendas but share origins, motivations, objectives, and recruitment techniques. Many of these groups began as paramilitary organizations to counter Soviet objectives in Afghanistan and the region. Additionally, all of these groups at some point received favorable treatment from the state of Pakistan and the Pakistani Inter-Services Intelligence agency.

HuJI is a Deobandi radical Islamist group that seeks to establish an Islamic caliphate through jihad. It is self-described as "the second line of defense for every Muslim." One branch of HuJI operates in Pakistan, with the objective of separating Jammu and Kashmir from India and annexing it to Pakistan. HuJI-B seeks to establish Islamic rule in Bangladesh. Both branches are known to associate with the **Taliban**. The group once had a slogan that translated as "We will all become **Taliban** and we will turn Bangladesh into Afghanistan."

HuJI-B has an estimated 500 to 750 members. There are reports of a HuJI-B presence and activities in over 20 nations, including the U.S. and the U.K.

FOUNDING

In 1980, Jaimat Ansarul Afghaneen (JAA), or Party of the Friends of the Afghan People, formed with the purpose of fighting in the Soviet-Afghan war. After the war, the group renamed itself HuJI and reoriented its mission to aid Muslims in Jammu and Kashmir in the fight to separate from India and rejoin Pakistan.

In 1989, the group merged with Harkat-ul-Mujahideen (HUM) to strengthen terrorist operations in Jammu and Kashmir, and adopted the name Harkat-al-Ansar (HUA). When the U.S. sought to name Harkat-al-Ansar as a terrorist organization in 1997 and ban all of its operations in the country, a portion of the group broke off and reverted to the name Harkat-ul-Mujahideen in Pakistan, while the Bangladesh affiliate adopted the name HuJI-B.

LEADERSHIP

Qari Saifullah Akhtar, under the guidance of Harkat-ul-Mujahideen leader Maulana Fazalur Rehman Khalil, became leader of HuJI after it broke off from HUA. Before the September 11 attacks and American involvement in the Middle East, Akhtar oversaw the unchecked swelling of HuJI's membership, and facilitated many of its members' eventually joining Al Qaeda.

The U.S. involvement in Afghanistan caused Akhtar and other early leaders to relocate to Pakistan. Akhtar worked to bring together Osama bin Laden and Mullah Omar (commander of the **Taliban**) as partners-in-jihad. Akhtar served as a trusted advisor to Omar and worked to build and reinforce terror networks and ties between HuJI, **Al Qaeda**, and the **Taliban**.

While Akhtar was busy bringing various jihadist leaders together in the region, others assumed operational leadership roles in HuJI and HuJI-B. Bashir Ahmed Mir, born in Jammu and Kashmir, was trained in Pakistan and initially assigned to recruitment. He was appointed HuJI commander in 2004. In 2008, he was killed by police in the Doda district of Jammu and Kashmir. The operations of Pakistani HuJI efforts are now believed to be led by Shahid Bilal or Mohammed Amjad, but reports vary on whether one or the other is alive and in command. Akhtar was arrested in Pakistan in 2008, released a month later, arrested again in 2010, and again released only four months after his arrest. Some believe the second arrest, made by the Pakistani ISI, was more a protective measure after Akhtar was injured by a 2010 drone strike. Regardless, Akhtar for a second time was released by the ISI for "lack of evidence."

HuJI-B commander Ilyas Kashmiri was killed by a U.S. drone in 2011. He was believed to be instrumental in a 2010 bombing in Pune, India. He has been succeeded by Shah Sahib.

VIOLENCE

HuJI and HuJI-B have been responsible for numerous multi-casualty terrorist attacks. They particularly utilize female suicide bombers, detonate explosives in highly populated civilian areas, and engage in politics through assassinations. Many attacks by HuJI in Pakistan are aimed at Indian police forces in Jammu and Kashmir. There have been over 20 HuJI attacks from 1998 to 2008. HuJI-B attempted to assassinate the prime minister of Bangladesh in 2005, and the British high commissioner in 2004. Assassination attempts are typically made with thrown grenades. In 2005 the group assassinated former Bangladesh finance minister and UN executive secretary Shah AMS Kibria. HuJI bombed the Andhra Pradesh police force's counterterrorism unit in 2005, the Sankat Mochan temple in 2007, and a Marriott hotel in

Islamabad in 2008, and have claimed responsibility for serial blasts of four Indian cities in 2008 and serials bombings in Delhi in 2008 and 2011. In 2012, HuJI members bombed three courthouses in cities in India. HuJI has targeted American interests on many occasions; most notably in a 1995 attack on a meeting of American counterterrorism diplomats (killing four) and in an attack in 2006 on the U.S. consulate in Karachi, Pakistan (killing four).

TIES
When HuJI-B shifted operations from Pakistan to Bangladesh, it originally assimilated into an existing jihad movement under the leadership of Fazlur Rahman, a radical Islamist who signed a declaration in 1998 committing to a holy war under Osama bin Laden's fatwa titled "World Islamic Front for Jihad Against the Jews and Crusaders." HuJi-B later grew into its own group.

HuJI is believed to have support from the Taliban and **Al Qaeda**, as well as the Pakistani ISI through ISI-sponsored training camps in Pakistan. The anti-India attacks are believed to be coordinated and facilitated by ISI in conjunction with efforts by **Lashkar-e-Taiba** and **Jaish-e-Muhammed**.

FUNDING
HuJI is allegedly funded by supporters within the Pakistani ISI. It is also believed to get other financial assistance from Pakistan, Saudi Arabia, and Afghanistan. HuJI-B gets funding through NGOs operating in Bangladesh, and profitable terror activities.

HARKAT-UL-MUJAHIDEEN AL-ISLAMI (HUM)

HARKAT-UL-MUJAHIDEEN
AL-ISLAMI (HUM)

Main Area(s) of Operation	Pakistan, Jammu and Kashmir
Known or Suspected Leader	Farooq Kashmiri Khalil
Approximate Year Founded	1985
Approximate Size	Several thousand
Alliances & Cooperations	Harkat-ul-Jihad al-Islami, Taliban, Al Qaeda, Sipah-e-Sahaba Pakistan, Lashkar-e-Jhangvi, Jaish-e-Muhammed
Ideological Sect/Affiliation	Wahhabi, Deobandi
Name Meaning	"Islamic Mujahideen Movement"
Flag	

HARKAT-UL-MUJAHIDEEN AL-ISLAMI (HUM) is a Sunni organization that shares similarities with Wahhabi and Deobandi schools of thought. HuM maintains a strict interpretation of Islam that regards democracy as a negative Western influence. The Pakistani-based group aims to "liberate" the Jammu and Kashmir regions of India, and advance an Islamic caliphate and anti-Western campaign through jihad. HuM also helps operate terrorist training camps in Afghanistan. The group's longtime leader, Fazlur Rehman Khalil, had multiple ties to Osama bin Laden while bin Laden was alive, and served as his consultant when bin Laden authored his first fatwa in 1998.

HuM reportedly operates publicly in Pakistan. According to the *Long War Journal*, "HuM operates freely…with the permission of the Pakistani establishment, including the military and powerful Inter-services Intelligence Directorate. [Fazlur Rehman] Khalil, HuM's leader, lives openly in Pakistan's capital of Islamabad."[1]

HuM has several hundred armed members living in Pakistan, Afghanistan, and India.

FOUNDING

HuM began as part of **Harkat-ul-Jihad al-Islami**, a group formed in the 1980s to combat the Soviets in the Afghan-Soviet war. The group broke away in 1985 due to ideological differences. After the war in 1989, the group initiated efforts to wage jihad within Jammu and Kashmir, which is still its objective.

The group has changed its name multiple times to cover its public operations, most notably in 1993, when it switched to Harkat-ul-Ansar, and in 2003, when it became Jaimat-ul-Ansar. Pakistan banned both groups, and the group has reverted to the HuM name.

LEADERSHIP

Fazlur Rehman Khalil led HuM from 1989 to 2000, was a consultant to Osama bin Laden, and was a signatory of his 1998 fatwa calling for attacks on the West. Khalil studied at a radical madrassa in Karachi among founders of the Deobandi movement. After 2011, Khalil led fighters into Afghanistan to fight U.S. troops, and assisted **Taliban** troop coordination efforts. He has since stepped down from his leadership post, and Farooq Kashmiri Khalil, his son, has taken control.

In a 2003 interview with *60 Minutes*, Fazlur Khalil referenced a personal initiative to see HuM obtain nuclear capabilities. "God has ordered us to build nuclear weapons," he stated.

Masood Azhur and Sheikh Omar were both prominent HuM members who splintered from the group to create **Jaish-e-Muhammed** in 1999. Both also had ties to Osama bin Laden while he was alive.

VIOLENCE

In December 1999, HuM hijacked Indian flight IC 814 en route from Nepal to Delhi and rerouted the flight to Afghanistan. It then used the hostages to barter for the release of jailed HuM leaders Masood Azhur and Sheikh Omar.

HuM assisted in the kidnapping of five Westerners in 1995, all of whom were executed by the group within the year. HuM attacks on Indian civilians resulted in at least 15 deaths in 2005. In 2007 and 2008, HuM skirmishes with Indian police forces led to the deaths of several Indian police and military members. Leaders of Indian political parties supposedly received death threats from HuM in 2009.

TIES

HuM maintains ties with the **Taliban** and **Al Qaeda**. It also coordinates with the Pakistani-based militant group **Sipah-e-Sahaba Pakistan**. Reportedly, HuM provided safe houses for members of **Lashkar-e-Jhangvi** after their assassination attempt on Pakistani prime minister Nawaz Sharif in 1999.

Many members of HuM left the organization to create **Jaish-e-Muhammed** in 1999, following former HuM member Masood Azhar's departure from the organization when he was released from prison. The split occurred despite HuM's having initiated the plot that led to the successful trade of hostages for his release.

FUNDING

HuM utilizes magazine ads and pamphlets to solicit donations from members of the regional public. It had bank accounts and multiple investments until 2001, when the Pakistani government froze its assets.

The Pakistani ISI allegedly funded the group initially. HuM also receives financial support from wealthy independent backers living in Saudi Arabia and its Gulf neighbors, maintaining an extensive cooperative relationship with them to continue to fund its terrorist activities.

NOTES

[1] Roggio, Bill. "Harakat-ul-Mujahideen 'Operates Terrorist Training Camps in Eastern Afghanistan'." *The Long War Journal*. 8 Aug. 2014. <http://www.longwarjournal.org/archives/2014/08/harakat-ul-mujahidee.php>.

HEZBOLLAH

HEZBOLLAH

Main Area(s) of Operation	Lebanon
Founder or Spiritual Leader	Lebanese Amal Movement party of Lebanon
Known or Suspected Leader	Hassan Nasrallah
Approximate Year Founded	1985
Approximate Size	Several thousand
Alliances & Cooperations	Iranian Revolutionary Guard, Hamas
Name Meaning	"Party of Allah"

HEZBOLLAH, TRANSLATED AS "the Party of Allah," has three objectives: to implement Sharia in Lebanon; to expel "foreign" entities from Lebanon; and to destroy the nation of Israel and reclaim the capital city of Jerusalem.

According to the Terrorism Research and Analysis Consortium:

> Hezbollah feels committed, ideologically and in practice, to strive for an ongoing conflict with Israel with all means possible on all fronts. In light of this, Hezbollah constantly stresses its basic approach to Israel and its goal to destroy it.[1]

Hezbollah is a Shiite organization, and has extensive ties with Khomeini's Islamic Republic that formed after the 1979 revolution in Iran. Hezbollah is also supported by Syria.

Hezbollah has three parts: a political wing, a social provisions wing, and a military wing.

Hezbollah operates from Lebanon but has international influence. It has recently been successful in its political endeavors, winning 10 out of 128 seats in the Lebanese Parliament in the 2009 election. It also controls the Lebanese Agriculture and Administrative Reform departments.

Hezbollah frames its violent activities as justified means by which to retake Lebanese lands wrongly claimed by Israel. In May 2000, Israel withdrew from most of the lands that Hezbollah asserted to be occupied, and since that time Israel and the U.S. have provided funding and support to the Lebanese Armed Forces to counteract Hezbollah's influence. However, according to the United States Congressional Research Service, "even if disputed areas were secured, the group would seek to maintain a role...in providing for Lebanon's national defense and would resist any Lebanese or international efforts to disarm it."[2]

According to Hezbollah's statement of purpose, the group seeks to use Islam as a "guardian for human rights." The same statement insists that, though the group is intent on establishing Islam among people, it does not seek to do so "by force or violence." From just its involvement in the Syrian civil war, Hezbollah's contributed death toll over a four-year period (2011–2015) tops 1,200.

A 2010 report from the White House included the following:

> [Hezbollah is] the most technically capable terrorist group in the world....[It has] thousands of supporters, several thousand members, and a few hundred terrorist operatives.[3]

FOUNDING

In 1982, Israel invaded Lebanon in what would come to be called the First Lebanese War. Israel's reason for the invasion was to secure regional peace and stability. In June 1982, gunmen from the organization of Abu Nidal, a faction of the Palestinian Liberation Organization, attempted an assassination of the Israeli ambassador to the United Kingdom. The PLO and Syrian forces both had expansive operational camps and influence over the southern Lebanese region, and were using that area to launch attacks against Israel. Detractors claim that Abu Nidal was at odds with the PLO, and Israel's invasion was unjustified. After the region was stabilized, Israel removed forces from Lebanon and returned most land holdings.

As a response to the 1982 invasion, a reactionary political party known as the Lebanese Amal Movement was formed. Shortly after, a group of Shiite leaders who wanted a more militant response to Israel broke away from the group to establish an independent militant alternative, called the Islamic Amal. The Islamic Amal began to receive support from the **Iranian Revolutionary Guards Corps**, and grew and organized into a larger and more influential operation. The Islamic Amal initiated a number of attacks on Israel and the Southern Lebanese Army, including a bombing of the U.S. embassy and U.S. Marine barracks in 1983 that killed 258 Americans and 58 French servicemen.

In a publicly released statement in 1985, Hezbollah announced its formation. The statement identified the United States as one of Islam's primary enemies and called for the "obliteration" of Israel.

LEADERSHIP

Hezbollah's command structure is complex. It is hierarchical, with the top commander being the general secretary. The general secretary is selected by a seven-member consultative body called the Shura Council, which sits in the middle of the command hierarchy. The Shura Council oversees five sub-councils: the political assembly, the jihad assembly, the parliamentary assembly, the executive assembly, and the judicial assembly.

Abbas al-Musawi, a cofounder of the group, was the second secretary general until he was killed in 1992 by Israeli security forces. Al-Musawi was replaced by Hassan Nasrallah, who is still secretary general. Nasrallah was a member of a group called al-Dawa al-Islamiyah, which is considered to be an ideological influence of Hezbollah's and which followed the teachings of Islamic cleric Mohammed Baqir al-Sadr.

Hassan Nasrallah was born in 1960 in Beirut, Lebanon. Nasrallah claimed his family was never involved in political activity, but he became involved in various political groups as he progressed in his studies and grew up in Lebanon. Eventually, he married and had children. His 18-year-old son, Hadi, was killed fighting in Israel. Since his death, Hadi has been martyred, and Nasrallah heralds his son's death as a symbol of the struggle he leads, which shores up his appeal among Hezbollah members and supporters.

Nasrallah contends that Hezbollah is more than a group with a mission, but a political doctrine and an ideology. Among the tactics Nasrallah sanctions to accomplish his group's goals, death is highly regarded. "Death is nothing but a gateway....Some people pass through this gateway with difficulty and agony, and some do it with ease and willingness," he says.[4] Nasrallah is adamantly anti-Israel. Hezbollah's motto includes "death to Israel," but Nasrallah has gone much further in his statements:

— If [the Jews] all gather in Israel, it will save us the trouble of going after them worldwide.[5]

— I am against any reconciliation with Israel. I do not even recognize the presence of a state called "Israel."[6]

— The Jews invented the legend of the Nazi atrocities.[7]

According to Nasrallah, victory for Hezbollah is achieved as long as they can still fight:

As long as there is a missile that is fired from Lebanon and targets the Zionists, as long as there is one fighter who fires his rifle, and as long as there is someone who plants a bomb against the Israelis, then that means resistance is still there.[8]

Hezbollah's second-in-command is Naim Qassem.

On the international front, one of Hezbollah's top attack coordinators, Imad Fauez Mugniyah, was killed in a car bombing in Syria in 2008.

VIOLENCE

Hezbollah operates primarily out of southern Lebanon, a Shiite-dominated region, with a presence also in Beirut and the Bekaa Valley in the east. Hezbollah commits both terrorist activities for publicity for their cause, and concerted attacks against Israeli forces. Hezbollah has engaged in extended guerilla activities against the Lebanese Army and Israeli security forces throughout Lebanon.

A civil war raged in Lebanon in 1989, and Hezbollah was a significant actor. In a 1989 peace agreement brokered by Saudi Arabia, Hezbollah formally joined Lebanese politics.

In February 2005, a bombing near the St. Georges Hotel in Beirut successfully assassinated Lebanese prime minister Rafic Hariri and killed 21 others. Hezbollah denied involvement and pointed to Israel for culpability, but a UN tribunal indicted four of Hezbollah's members for the attack.

In the summer of 2006, Hezbollah launched thousands of rockets into Israel and killed eight soldiers in a border attack.

In 2008, the Lebanese government took measures to reduce Hezbollah's influence, including shutting down the group's telecommunications networks and removing an airport security chief believed to be tied to the group. Hezbollah responded by taking over much of the capital city of Beirut in a violent effort that killed 81 and nearly catalyzed a civil war. In an agreement to end the conflict, the Lebanese government gave Hezbollah veto power over any cabinet decisions in what was termed the Doha agreement.

In 2011, Hezbollah helped overthrow the administration of Saad Hariri, who was the Sunni-backed president of Lebanon. It subsequently helped install a new prime minister, and then forced him from office in 2013, during an overall collapse of the government, after a dispute with Lebanese security forces.

Hezbollah's international presence includes forces in South America, Asia, Africa, and Europe. In 1985, it hijacked TWA flight 847 from Cairo to London. Hostages were held for days and flown to multiple continents, and American Navy diver Robert Stethem was killed. In 1992, Hezbollah used a car bomb to attack the Israeli embassy in Argentina. In 1996, the group allegedly detonated an explosive in the Khobar Towers in Saudi Arabia. In 2012, a Hezbollah car bombing of Israeli tourists in Bulgaria killed six.

TIES

Hezbollah's primary supporter is the **Iranian Revolutionary Guard Corps**. According to a 2010 report from the White House:

> Iran, through its longstanding relationship with Lebanese Hezbollah, maintains a capability to strike Israel directly and threaten Israeli and U.S. interests worldwide....On 4 November [2009] Israel interdicted the merchant vessel FRANCOP, which had 36 containers, 60 tons, of weapons for Hezbollah to include 122mm katyushas [Soviet-style short-range rockets], 107mm rockets, 106mm antitank shells, hand grenades, light-weapon ammunition. The [**Iranian Revolutionary Guard Corps**] operates training camps in Lebanon, training as many as 3,000 or more LH fighters.[9]

Hezbollah has received operational support from Syria, and in return has sent fighters to support the Bashar al-Assad regime in the Syrian civil conflict. In 2013, Hezbollah secretary general Nasrallah publicly pledged support to al-Assad, stating, "I promise you victory." Hezbollah troop support to al-Assad's forces is estimated to be in the several thousands.

Hezbollah supplies a number of Palestinian terrorist organizations, including **Hamas**, with arms and weaponry.

FUNDING

Hezbollah receives funding and support from Iran and **the Iranian Revolutionary Guard Corps** and Syria. Iran provides Hezbollah with training, weapons, and explosives, and offers the group "political, diplomatic, and organizational aid," plus an estimated $200 million a year. Syria provides "diplomatic, political, and logistical support" and reportedly provided Scud missiles in 2010.[10]

Hezbollah uses its foreign aid to, in turn, supply Palestinian terrorist organizations with weapons and aid. Likewise, it trains Iraqi Shiite insurgents on how to construct improvised explosive devices (IEDs) and arm trucks and vehicles.

NOTES

[1] Hezbollah section on Terrorism Research and Analysis Consortium website. <http://www.trackingterrorism.org/group/hezbollah>.

[2] Addis, Casey L., and Christopher M. Blanchard. "Hezbollah: Background and Issues for Congreess." Congressional Research Service, posted on FAS Project on Government Secrecy wesbite. 3 Jan. 2011. <http://fas.org/sgp/crs/mideast/R41446.pdf>.

[3] Ibid.

[4] Schwartz, Stephen, ed. *Hassan Nasrallah: In His Own Words.* New York, New York: Pamphleteer, LLC, 2006.

[5] Ibid.

[6] Ibid.

[7] Ibid.

[8] Ibid.

[9] Addis and Blanchard, "Hezbollah: Background and Issues for Congress."

[10] Masters, Jonathan, and Zachary Laub. Hezbollah (a.k.a. Hizbollah, Hizbu'llah). Backgrounder section on Council on Foreign Relations website. 3 Jan. 2014. <http://www.cfr.org/lebanon/hezbollah-k-hizbollah-hizbullah/p9155>.

HIZBUL MUJAHIDEEN (HM)

HIZBUL MUJAHIDEEN (HM)

Main Area(s) of Operation	Jammu and Kashmir
Founder or Spiritual Leader	Abdul Mujeed Dar
Known or Suspected Leader	Syed Salahuddin
Approximate Year Founded	1989
Approximate Size	1,500
Name Meaning	"Party of Holy Warriors"

WITH A STRONG INTERNATIONAL recruiting campaign, Hizbul Mujahideen (HM), or the "Party of Warriors," is one of the largest militant Islamic groups in Jammu and Kashmir. The group has an estimated 1,500 members. Unlike many other separatist Islamic groups operating in Jammu and Kashmir, HM is ardently pro-Pakistan. HM's mission is to support the full integration of Jammu and Kashmir into Pakistan. The group also calls for the implementation of fundamental Islamic practice throughout Kashmir.

Its members are largely ethnic Kashmiris from the Indian-administered regions of Kashmir.

FOUNDING
Hizbul Mujahideen was founded in 1989 by Abdul Majeed Dar, as the militant wing of another Islamic group, Jamaat-e-Islami (Jel). Jamaat-e-Islami was reportedly set up by the Pakistani Inter-Services Intelligence (ISI) agency to counter the separatist group Jammu and Kashmir Liberation Front (JKLF), which sought independence for the region from Pakistan.

In 1990, HM organized its leadership into two primary positions, a patron and an emir. Mohammed Yusuf Shah, also known as Syed Salahuddin, was appointed patron, and Hilal Admed Mir was appointed emir. Founder Dar retained a prominent position until he was exiled in 2002; he was assassinated a year later in his home.

The group split from **Jamaat-e-Islami** when differences arose. In 1997, JeI publicly distanced itself from HM. Salahuddin took leadership of the breakaway group that was to become HM, and Mir remained in control of the JeI-affiliated faction until he was killed in 1993. HM's history is one of deep internal factions. The two most prominent factions were loyal to either Salahuddin or Dar. Even after Dar's death, there is conflict within the group, and the factions often carry out attacks independently, at times passing blame to one another.

According to Salahuddin, HM is allowed to operate numerous recruitment camps across Pakistan without consequence from the Pakistani government. In a 2011 interview with the *Times of India*, he stated:

> Our mujahideen can come and go at their own will. There is no question that the army can stop us. And we have hundreds of training camps in the state where we recruit and train the mujahideen.[1]

LEADERSHIP

Hizbul Mujahideen is headquartered in Kashmir, with Salahuddin now the group's emir. Its patron is Ghulam Nabi Nusheri, and its operational commander is Ghazi Nasiruddin. Its spokesperson is Saleem Hashmi.

Syed Salahuddin was born in Kashmir and attended university in the region, achieving a master's degree at the University of Kashmir. At university, he became radicalized under the influence of **Jamaat-e-Islami**. Now he is also the head of the United Jihad Council, formed in 1990 to coordinate the efforts of the various Pakistani groups fighting in the Jammu and Kashmir region. In his public statements on behalf of the Council, he has encouraged and welcomed the support of Al Qaeda, the Taliban, and any group willing to help further the cause of the militant separatists in Jammu and Kashmir. Speaking in an interview, Salahuddin insisted the solution to the Jammu and Kashmir conflict between India and Pakistan is one that can be resolved only through militancy—and that peaceful negotiations are not considered possible by his group.

The group has five divisions based on operations in districts of Pakistani Kashmir. Those include a central division in Srinagar, a northern division in Kupwara-Bandipora-Baramulla, a southern division in Anantnag and Pulwama, the Chenab division in Doda and the Gool division in Udhampur (a single unit), and the Pir Panjal division in Rajouri and Poonch. HM also operates a news agency, the Kashmir Press, and a women's cell called Banat-ul-Islam.

VIOLENCE

HM targets Indian security forces, police units, and politicians. It claimed responsibility for a 2013 attack on the Indian Central Reserve Police Force camp in Bemina, which killed five. HM also targets civilians. In 2012, it attacked three Indian liquor shops in a government-run hotel, killing one and injuring four.

From 1989 to 2008, HM was responsible for an estimated 75 attacks.

TIES

When the Indian subcontinent was apportioned by Great Britain in the 1940s, a condition of Indian and Pakistani statehood was that minor outlying territories chose incorporation into one of the two nations. The Jammu and Kashmir province went through a number of internal referendums and reviews by the United Nations, and was caught between larger military activities of Pakistan and India, both with an interest in maintaining the region. Though it was eventually recognized as a political entity of India, Pakistan has held the claim in contention. HM, founded as a militant wing of **Jamaat-e-Islami**, was reportedly supported by the Pakistani ISI to assist in reclaiming the Jammu and Kashmir region for Pakistan. Syed Salahuddin, as the head of the United Jihad Council, has publicly stated he welcomes the support of any militant group to his cause, specifically the **Taliban** or **Al Qaeda**. However, Salahuddin has also increasingly pushed for the Islamization of the region, and has stated that his group is willing to fight against Pakistan, as well as India, if these objectives are not supported.

FUNDING
Initial funding for HM likely came from the Pakistani ISI. It allegedly receives financial support from two American groups, Kashmir American Council and the World Kashmir Freedom Movement.

NOTES
[1] "Pak Supports Militants in Kashmir: Hizbul Mujahideen Chief." *The Times of India*. 27 May 2011. <http://timesofindia.indiatimes.com/world/pakistan/Pak-supports-militants-in-Kashmir-Hizbul-Mujahideen-chief/articleshow/8594878.cms>.

HIZB UT-TAHRIR (HT)

HIZB UT-TAHRIR (HT)

Main Area(s) of Operation	global
Founder or Spiritual Leader	Taqi al-Din Nabhani
Known or Suspected Leader	Naveed Butt (spokesperson)
Approximate Year Founded	1953
Approximate Size	Hundreds of thousands worldwide (not all engaged in terror activities)
Ideological Sect/Affiliation	Salafism
Name Meaning	"Party of Liberation"

HIZB UT-TAHRIR (HT) DESCRIBES ITSELF as a global initiative and political organization. The name translates to "Party of Liberation." According to their website, the group is committed to "[resuming] the Islamic way of life and [conveying] the Islamic da'wah to the world." Unique among many of the other militant Islamic groups operating in Pakistan, Hizb ut-Tahrir acts covertly. It also has a different target audience than the general South Asian civilian population. Hizb ut-Tahrir recruits senior military officers, civil bureaucrats, doctors, engineers, accountants, and other professionals.

Hizb ut-Tahrir is one of the largest groups listed in this encyclopedia, because it has undertaken a successful global digital outreach. The Hizb ut-Tahrir website (http://www.hizbuttahrir.org/) has a lengthy and complex mission statement, suggested reading, "political analyses" of various regions worldwide, and even a visitor poll. The poll question that closed on March 3, 2015, was "[Do you agree that] the

Syrian Civil War is part of the American Project against Islam?" Of the respondents, 85.7% agreed.

According to HT members who have spoken out after defecting from the organization, the group's goal is to establish a caliphate in a Muslim-ruled country that can be used as a base of operations to unify all Muslim countries in the world by conquest. The final aim is to conquer the Western world through a grand-scale war. According to the *Terrorism Monitor*, groups such as **Al Qaeda** aim to control countries through Islamic revolution, with some form of Muslim-only participatory government, but HT has stated it seeks to achieve its objectives through sheer force and authoritarianism. From the Hizb ut-Tahrir website:

> Hizb ut-Tahrir must be a political party that undertakes within the Ummah[1] this task and works towards seizing the reins of power through her; thus Hizb ut-Tahrir is not a spiritual bloc, nor is it a moralistic or a scientific bloc, but rather a political bloc that works towards the management of the Ummah's affairs as a whole according to Islam.[*]

HT's aim for its initial Islamic nation is Pakistan, because the country has a predominantly Muslim population with a history of military-led regime changes, has an overall low literacy rate, and is armed with nuclear weapons capabilities.

FOUNDING

HT was founded in 1953 in Jerusalem by Taqi al-Din Nabhani, who was an Islamic cleric and a former member of the **Muslim Brotherhood**. Reportedly, the group was founded as a reaction to the establishment of the Jewish state of Israel. HT has spread across both Arab and non-Arab countries around the Middle East and South Asia. HT is active all over the world, with one of its largest bases in Western Europe. Branches of the group are known to exist in Uzbekistan, Tajikistan, Kyrgyzstan, and Kazakhstan. One of the largest branches of the

---

[*] The "ummah" is the global body of Muslims as a whole.

group was founded in Pakistan in 1999 to better recruit members. The group's Pakistani base was founded by seven individuals: Imtiaz Malik, Taimur Butt, Imran Yousafzai, Shahzad Shaikh, Muhammed Irfan, Naveed Butt, and Maajid Nawaz. Imtiaz Malik was born in Britain; Naveed Butt graduated the University of Illinois and worked for Motorola before leaving the company to become the Pakistan-based spokesman of HT.

The group, like **Al Qaeda**, holds a Salafist ideology.

LEADERSHIP

Naveed Butt, one of the seven founding members of the Pakistani HT organization, is the group's spokesman. He has broadcast videotaped messages to the Pakistani military, asking them to rebel against the Pakistani state and join the HT cause. There have been three Pakistani coup attempts since HT's founding, and 13 members of the Pakistani Special Services Group did defect to join HT. One defector, a Pakistani brigadier named Ali Khan, helped to continuously recruit fellow officers in the Pakistani military until he was arrested in 2012.

The group has counterparts in countries across South Asia. In Dhaka, the capital city of Bangladesh, it has been banned from operating, but more than 10,000 members are known to still be active. In Bangladesh, the group has divided into small groups to carry out police skirmishes and reach more civilians with their message, while operating more covertly to prevent an effective state response.

According to data on HT's recruiting methods, members are selected from Islamic followers at large, despite different ideologies within the religion. The group claims to be a political party, but is rarely involved in national politics, mostly in an effort to prevent acknowledging the legitimacy of existing governments.

VIOLENCE

HT is a secretive and clandestine group, and has never overtly claimed responsibility for a violent attack. In fact, HT publicly rejects violence as a methodology to achieve their goal. It was, however, blamed for a 1999 bombing in Tashkent, the capital of Uzbekistan. There are also reports of its funding and aiding other terrorist outfits in Central Asia. Many countries have banned the group from operating publicly, and hundreds of individuals claiming membership in HT have been arrested. Russia is particularly suspicious of the group's involvement in supplying separatist fighters with militant support on behalf of the efforts to break Chechnya from Russia, and has listed the group as a terrorist organization. Many other countries allow the group to operate openly. HT is a *legally* recognized group in the United States and Britain.

Membership in HT is estimated at hundreds of thousands worldwide.

TIES

HT considers America to be an "American raj," or an open and hostile enemy to Muslims. It also rejects the legitimacy of the Pakistani government, although it reportedly has sympathizers in the Pakistani ISI.

HT has not had extensive contact with other militant organizations in the region, but in many regards supports the Jamaat al-Islami efforts against the U.S. and the Pakistani government. It does not believe in participating in a democratic process, so it stays out of the Pakistani political affairs that Jamaat al-Islami engages in.

Other militant groups in the region condemn HT for refusing to publicly support violence. However, HT recently issued a call in the *Times of London* for a "bloodless, military coup" in Pakistan that would allow them to control it by "military means" if needed. The group is also very active in Britain. According to an ex-member of HT, "Britain remains vital to [HT], for it gives the group access to the global media and provides a fertile recruiting ground at mosques and universities." The British HT's website explicitly calls for the dismantling of the state of Israel.

FUNDING

HT's membership is numerous and spread across the globe. Thus, sources of funding for the group vary. On many occasions, HT leaders have been known to hold positions in Islamic charity groups and publicly funded programs. In England, an entity called the Islamic Shakhsiyah Foundation was given as much as £113,000 a year in public grants before it was cut off due to ties to HT. The foundation's proprietor and some of its trustees were high-ranking figures in HT. The foundation used the money to run a nursery and two primary schools. The schools' website openly stated a goal of creating an "Islamic personality" in children through a curriculum that teaches that "there must be one ruler of the khilafah [caliphate]" and "in the glorious history of Islam...the Sharia was the norm."[1] According to an interview by *The Telegraph*, a former teacher said the schools were a "great way of creating Hizb ut-Tahrir propaganda."[2]

NOTES

[1] Gilligan, Andrew. "Council Suspends Funding to Schools Linked to Hizb Ut-Tahrir." *The Telegraph*. 31 Oct. 2009.

[2] Ibid.

HOUTHIS

HOUTHIS

Main Area(s) of Operation	Yemen
Founder or Spiritual Leader	Hussein Badr al-Din al-Houthi
Known or Suspected Leader	Abdul Malik al-Houthi
Approximate Year Founded	1994
Approximate Size	100,000
Alliances & Cooperations	Iranian National Guard
Enemies/Rivals	Al Qaeda (AQAP), Aden-Abyan Islamic Army (at times)
Ideological Sect/Affiliation	Zaidism
Name Meaning	"Supporters of God" from alternate name, Ansar Allah
Flag	الله أكبر الموت لأمريكا الموت لإسرائيل اللعنة على اليهود النصر للإسلام

THE HOUTHIS ARE A MILITANT rebel group based in the country of Yemen. They are Shiites who ascribe to Zaidism, a branch of Islam with which one-third of the Yemeni population identifies. Zaidis ruled a large portion of northern Yemen for over 1,000 years until the consolidated Yemeni government came to power in 1962 after a civil war.

Over 10 million Yemenis are estimated to be food-insecure. Poverty levels are high, and many demographic groups, including the Zaidis, believe themselves to be unrepresented in the Yemeni government. Internal conflict eventually reached a breaking point in 2011, when protests and demonstrations led to the ousting of President Ali Abdullah Saleh.

During the instability of the 2011 protests and regime change, the Houthis took the opportunity to expand their control and influence on the nation. They have participated in tribal warfare and violent confrontations with the government. By many accounts, the expansion of their power in Yemen has caused a resurgence of **Al Qaeda**'s operations in the country. Numerous reports exist that Iran and the **Iranian Revolutionary Guard** support the Houthis' activities.

The Houthis' justification for insurgency cites government corruption, oppression, and lack of access to national politics. Additionally, the Houthis contend that the Yemeni government has numerous Wahhabi influences and has cooperated with Saudi Arabia to found a variety of state-sponsored education initiatives to supplant Shiite ideology with Salafi Sunni Islam. Houthis often state the objective of autonomy for the Zaidi population from the Yemeni government.

The Houthis deny the objective of instituting a Zaidi imamate, but former spiritual leaders, including Badr al Din al Houthi, have called for such an outcome.

Part of the Houthi motto translates as "Death to Israel, Death to America." The full motto reads: "God is Great; Death to America; Death to Israel; Damnation to the Jews; Victory to Islam."[1]

The Houthis are active primarily in the Sa'ada and Amran provinces of Yemen.

FOUNDING

The Houthis, also known as Ansar Allah (translated as "Partisans of God") derived their name from the leader of the group's first uprising, in 2004. Hussein Badr al-Din al-Houthi was a Zaidi religious scholar. He founded a group in the 1990s called the Believing Youth, from which the Houthis later evolved. Following the attacks of September 11, 2001, the Yemeni government agreed to aid U.S. efforts in the Middle East, which caused Hussein Houthi to spearhead numerous anti-U.S. and anti-government demonstrations.

Hussein Houthi was killed by Yemeni security forces in 2004, but his family led five more rebellions from the time of his death to 2010. The Houthis engaged in peace talks in 2010, but actively participated in the 2011 rebellions and demonstrations that ousted the Yemeni president, and quickly took advantage of the opportunity to gain more power.

LEADERSHIP

Hussein Badr al-Din al-Houthi lived for a time in Iran, and allegedly participated in writing a book that favorably featured Iranian ayatollah Ruhollah Khomeini. He was a member of the Yemeni Parliament from 1993 to 1997, at which point he focused entirely on fostering the Believing Youth.

After Hussein al-Houthi's death in 2004, leadership of the group passed to his father, Badr al-Din al-Houthi, and Abdullah Ayed al Ruzami. Badr al-Houthi was against democratic rule and led the group through many of the armed clashes with the Yemeni government between 2004 and 2010. Eventually, both Badr al-Houthi and al Ruzami were killed. In 2006, leadership passed to Abdul Malik al-Houthi, another member of the al-Houthi family. Abdul al-Houthi's deputy is Youssef al-Midani, who may now lead the group following reports of Abdul al-Houthi's possible death or severe injury in 2010.

A senior leader of the Houthis, Yahya al-Houthi, was a member of the Yemeni Parliament who fled the country for Germany and then Libya. He has been tried by the Yemeni government for spying and participating in a plot to assassinate an American ambassador. The Houthi spokesman is Mohammed Abdul Salem, which may be a nom de guerre for a group of individuals.

VIOLENCE

The Houthis have continued to forcibly expand their influence and control in Yemen. In the mid- to late 2000s, the Houthis took over schools, hospitals, mosques, and military buildings in northern Yemen. They have engaged in violent clashes with Yemeni government forces, despite multiple attempts at peace negotiations.

Since September 2014, the Houthis have had a violent presence in the Yemeni capital city of Sanaa, when the rebels' tactics transitioned from sit-ins and nearby encampments to bombing buildings, causing hundreds to flee their homes. When the Houthis mounted a full-on invasion in late 2014, many Yemeni soldiers surrendered, yet concerned civilians took up arms to take their place. The fighting has persisted and is growing increasingly more violent.

In early 2015, the Houthis made significant advances on Yemeni government interests. On January 17, they kidnapped the chief of staff to the Yemeni president. A few days later, the group overran Sanaa, seizing control of the presidential palace and most of the national government buildings, and killing nine. Protestors who marched against the insurgent occupation of the capital in late January were beaten and detained by Houthi militants.

On February 6, 2015, the Houthis officially gained control of the Yemeni government and forced President Abd Rabbuh Mansur Hadi to flee his palace in Sanaa. The Houthis pronounced their own government under Mohammed Ali al-Houthi, cousin of Abdul al-Houthi. President Hadi fled to Aden, which he declared to be a provisional capital. Fighting has continued between the two groups as each vies to assert the control of their government. A coalition of regional powers led by Saudi Arabia has entered the fight, siding with Hadi against the insurgents and laying heavy fire to Houthi positions within the former capital city.

TIES

The Houthis are supported by **Iran and the Iranian Revolutionary Guard**. Hussein al-Houthi spent part of his life in Iran and had ties to the Iranian ayatollah. According to the *New York Times*, "Yemeni authorities have seized ships carrying Iranian weapons that they say were being sent to the Houthis."[2]

The Houthis are regularly involved in conflict with the Yemeni-based **Al Qaeda in the Arabian Peninsula (AQAP)**. Since they have seized control of Sanaa, **AQAP** has regularly perpetrated attacks in the city, including an October bombing at a Houthi rally that killed 40. Houthi conflict with the Yemeni government is cited as an opportunity for the expansion of **AQAP** power and control.

FUNDING

Houthi funding reportedly comes from Iran and other Shiite interests, as well as from government and civilian institutions seized by Houthi forces in Yemen.

NOTES

[1] "Houthis' Rise in Yemen Risks Empowering Al-Qaeda." *Time*. 22 Jan. 2015. <http://time.com/3677676/houthis-yemen-al-qaeda/>.

[2] "Who Are the Houthis of Yemen?" *The New York Times*. 20 Jan. 2015. <http://www.nytimes.com/2015/01/21/world/middleeast/who-are-the-houthis-of-yemen.html?_r=0>.

INDIAN MUJAHIDEEN (IM)

INDIAN MUJAHIDEEN (IM)

Main Area(s) of Operation	India
Founder or Spiritual Leader	50 students from the Students Islamic Movement of India
Known or Suspected Leader	Abdul Subhan Usman Qureshi
Approximate Year Founded	2007
Approximate Size	Hundreds
Alliances & Cooperations	Lashkar-e-Taiba, Harkat-ul-Jihad al-Islami, Jaish-e-Muhammed
Name Meaning	"Holy Warriors of India"

THE INDIAN MUJAHIDEEN, also known as the Islamic Security Force, is a covert group that operates in India and is allegedly supported by the Pakistani ISI. It targets Indian civilians, foreigners of all nationalities, and non-Muslims. The group uses coded emails to communicate and meets in Saudi Arabia under the auspices of religious pilgrimages to plan and collaborate with Pakistani supporters. Its mission is to carry out terror attacks to facilitate the creation of an Islamic caliphate in South Asia.

FOUNDING

The IM was founded in 2007 by 50 members of the Students Islamic Movement of India (SIMI), who trained in a jihadist camp in southern India. The Institute for Defense Studies and Analysis reports:

> According to Indian intelligence, the IM is not a well-knit organization with a hierarchical structure like other more established

groups like **Lashkar-e-Taiba**. Rather, it is a loose network of Islamic organizations which includes the Students Islamic Movement of India (SIMI), certain individuals from the state of Uttar Pradesh with alleged links with the **Harkat-ul-Jihad al-Islami**, and the terror cartel of Aftab Ansari.[1]

LEADERSHIP

The IM claims responsibility for bombings using email manifestos signed by Abdul Subhan Usman Qureshi, its assumed leader. Qureshi grew up in Mumbai, India, in a wealthy household. He obtained a degree in industrial electronics and worked for two large software companies before leaving to pursue activism with SIMI. SIMI became radical throughout the 1990s. In 2001, Qureshi organized a SIMI-led student conference that hosted 25,000 participants. He is believed to have masterminded many of the IM's large-scale serial bombings across India.

Other former software professionals have leadership roles in the IM, designing propaganda, hacking security entities, and planning bombings.

VIOLENCE

The IM has committed dozens of terror attacks since 2005 that have claimed hundreds of lives.

Its signature method of attack is to detonate explosives in crowded civilian areas. A serial bombing by the group in 2008 in the Indian city of Jaipur killed 80 and injured 200. A July 2008 attack that included 21 bomb detonations in Ahmedabad killed 45. Later that same year, the group detonated explosives at a World War I monument, a crowded tourist market, and a children's park, killing 24 and injuring at least 63. In 2010, it bombed a German bakery in the city of Pune, a known tourist destination, killing 17 and injuring 60. The group placed a bomb outside of a high court in Delhi in 2011 that killed 12 and injured 65. In 2013, the group detonated explosives at a bus stop, a fruit market, and a theater that killed 15 and injured 50.

TIES

The IM cooperated with **Harkat-ul-Jihad al-Islami** to carry out bombings in 2011. It aided **Lashkar-e-Taiba** in its deadly 2008 bombings in Mumbai that killed 163.

According to the U.S. State Department, the IM has ties to **Jaish-e-Muhammed,** "significant links to Pakistan," and Indian intelligence believes the group's efforts are supported by the Pakistani ISI.[2]

FUNDING

Financing for IM activities is believed to come from West Asia, facilitated by the Indian terror cartel Aftab Ansari. Aid from **Lashkar-e-Taiba, Harkat-ul-Jihad al-Islami**, and the Pakistani ISI is also likely.

NOTES

[1] Goswami, Namrata. "Who Is the Indian Mujahideen?" Institute for Defence Studies and Analyses. 3 Feb. 2009. <http://www.idsa.in/backgrounder/IndianMujahideen>.

[2] "Terrorist Designations of the Indian Mujahideen" media note from the Office of the Spokesperson, U.S. Department of State. 15 Sept. 2011. <http://www.state.gov/r/pa/prs/ps/2011/09/172442.htm>.

IRANIAN REVOLUTIONARY GUARD CORPS (IRGC)

IRANIAN REVOLUTIONARY GUARD CORPS (IRGC)

Main Area(s) of Operation	Iran
Founder or Spiritual Leader	Ruhollah Khomeini
Known or Suspected Leader	Mohammad Ali Jafari
Approximate Year Founded	1979
Approximate Size	150,000
Alliances & Cooperations	Hezbollah, Taliban, Houthis
Enemies/Rivals	Islamic State
Flag	

THE IRANIAN REVOLUTIONARY GUARD CORPS is the only group in this encyclopedia that is part of a recognized sovereign nation's government.

The Iranian national power structure is complex. Iran has a supreme leader, who is the highest religious and political leader in the country. The position of supreme leader is the most powerful in Iranian politics. This position is currently held by Ali Khamenei. He is indirectly elected by voters: Voters elect a Council of Experts, who then appoint the supreme leader. There have been two only in Iran's history:

Ruhollah Khomeini, the founding ayatollah at the beginning of the Iranian Islamic Republic (in 1979), and Ali Khamenei.

The supreme leader shares executive power with the president, including the ability to decide many high-level appointments. He appoints half of the members of the Guardian Council, which is a 12-person body that determines who is eligible to run for national office and what laws may be brought before the Iranian Parliament. He also is commander of the armed forces and makes important foreign policy decisions. The Iranian president and members of Parliament are elected.

Of the Iranian population of around 80 million people, only 50 million are eligible to vote. The supreme leader's ultimate influence over the Guardian Council essentially equates to his ultimate say on the list of potential presidential candidates.

The Iranian Revolutionary Guard Corps (known as the Pasdaran) serves the supreme leader, and is an entity separate and distinct from the Iranian army (known as the Artesh). The Revolutionary Guard members serve as the "ideological guardians" of the Iranian theocracy. They have been known to support terrorist organizations and activities at home and abroad.

The IRGC is estimated to have 150,000 members, and it controls Iran's ballistic missile arsenal. Experts believe the IRGC to have influence or control over Iran's nuclear program, though the extent to which is unclear. As commander of the armed forces, Ayatollah Khamenei would have control over any nuclear arsenal, and the IRGC operates for and on his behalf. Many of Iran's contentious nuclear facilities are built as part of IRGC bases. Also, scientists in the nuclear program are also members of the IRGC, including the former head of the Atomic Energy Organization, Fereydoun Abbasi. With its mix of military and public works roles, the IRGC has set itself up to work closely with nuclear programs while simultaneously maintaining the perfect cover to do so.

FOUNDING

The IRGC was founded shortly after the 1979 Iranian revolution that set up an Islamic theocracy in the country. It was designed to defend the new government against both external and internal threats to stability.

The idea for the Revolutionary Guard was conceived by then-supreme leader Ayatollah Ruhollah Khomeini. Having been the successful leader of an insurgent force himself, Khomeini wanted to prevent the same fate from befalling his new Islamic republic. The first commander of the IRGC was Akbar Torkan, a civilian.

In the 1980s, the IRGC was called regularly to respond to Iraqi assaults on the Iranian border during the Iran-Iraq war. This led to the formalization of the structure of the IRGC, with commanders and a structured hierarchy of roles.

As the IRGC expanded, so did its role. A paramilitary branch of the IRGC with 10,000 to 15,000 members soon began conducting international foreign policy missions on behalf of the IRGC, and was named the Quds Force. According to military analysts, the Quds Force in the 1980s was tasked with "exporting the ideas of the revolution throughout the Middle East."

The IRGC also has a branch, the Ashura Brigades, dedicated to countering civil unrest. Another group of 90,000 is directed by the IRGC under the name Basij Resistance Force, an Islamic volunteer militia. After the sham reelection of Iranian president Mahmoud Ahmadinejad in 2009, the Ashura Brigades and Basij Resistance Force members beat and killed opposition supporters across the country. Participants of political rallies for moderate presidential candidates in 2013 have likewise been arrested and intimidated.

LEADERSHIP

The IRGC has naval, air, and ground forces. It reports to the supreme leader, and the president has very little control over it.

The IRGC plays an increasingly economic and political role in Iran. Former members have been appointed to high-level government jobs by Khamenei. Ahmadinejad was a former IRGC member.

The current commander of the IRGC is Mohammad Ali Jafari, formerly the head of the Basij militia. The Quds Force is commanded by Hossein Hamadani, who effectively operates as second-in-command in determining foreign policy, under the supreme leader.

The IRGC continues to expand its role and influence in Iran. According to Ali Alfoneh, expert on the IRGC and fellow at the American

Enterprise Institute, "For the past thirty years, the Islamic Republic has been based on a fundamental alliance with the clergy and the Revolutionary Guards. Where the clerics have been ruling the country, and the Revolutionary Guards have guarded the Islamic Republic...the Revolutionary Guards are now both ruling and guarding."[1]

VIOLENCE

Since its formation, the Quds Force has supported terrorist activities and armed militant groups in Lebanon, Palestine, Iraq, and Afghanistan. The Quds provided explosives and projectiles to anti-American forces in Iraq during U.S. efforts in 2007.

The U.S. Treasury Department has designated the group a terrorist organization for aiding the **Taliban**. The U.S. and European Union also believe the Quds Force has supported the Bashar al-Assad regime in the Syrian conflict and plotted to assassinate the United States ambassador to Saudi Arabia.

TIES

The IRGC operates training camps and arms supply centers for **Hezbollah**. The IRGC and country of Iran writ large played a substantial role in the establishment of **Hezbollah** following the 1982 conflict between Lebanon and Israel.

In May 2014, IRGC commander Hossein Hamedani admitted to an Iranian news agency that the IRGC is actively fighting in the Syrian conflict: "Today, we fight in Syria for interests such as the Islamic Revolution." He also claimed that 130,000 members of the Basij are being trained by the group to fight on behalf of Iranian interests in Syria, and that Iran will create a "second **Hezbollah**."[2]

Hezbollah and the Quds Force have engaged in a combined effort to train and assist the militant **Houthis** to take control of the government of Yemen. On January 20, 2015, the **Houthis** seized the palace of Yemen's president, and they continue to gain control of government buildings and weapons stockpiles.

The IRGC, like the Shiite nation of Iran, is at odds with the **Islamic State**. Reports in 2014 indicate that the IRGC is fighting **Islamic State** forces in Iraq.

FUNDING

The IRGC, in addition to being a major political player in Iran, has significant assets and economic influence. It controls an estimated $12 billion in construction and engineering assets, and has control over university laboratories, weapons manufacturing facilities, and nuclear technology companies.

Some observers believe the economic sanctions imposed on Iran actually benefit the IRGC. This is because the IRGC operates where foreign businesses won't or are not allowed to; thus it is awarded multiple large government contracts for infrastructural work with little to no competition.

The IRGC also controls a number of charity organizations throughout Iran and frequently awards contracts on behalf of the government. The IRGC is believed to own a majority stake in the Telecommunications Company of Iran.

The IRGC runs the Tidewater port operating company, which manages the busy Bandar Abbas port in addition to six others. Bandar Abbas sees 90 percent of Iran's shipping traffic, and is frequently the port by which the IRGC exports arms and supplies to terrorist organizations internationally.

NOTES

[1] Bruno, Greg, Jayshree Bajoria, and Jonathan Masters. Iran's Revolutionary Guards. Backgrounder section on Council on Foreign Relations website. 14 June 2013. <http://www.cfr.org/iran/irans-revolutionary-guards/p14324>.

[2] "Iranian Commander Lets Slip That Revolutionary Guard Is Fighting in Syria." *Time.* 7 May 2014. <http://time.com/90807/iran-syria-revolutionary-guard/>.

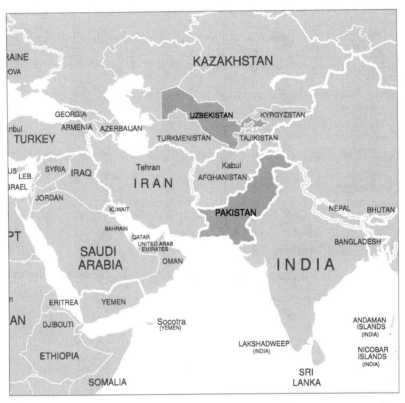

ISLAMIC JIHAD UNION (IJU)

ISLAMIC JIHAD UNION (IJU)

Main Area(s) of Operation	Pakistan, Uzbekistan
Founder or Spiritual Leader	Najmiddin Jalolov, Suhayl Buranov
Known or Suspected Leader	Unknown
Approximate Year Founded	2000
Approximate Size	Hundreds
Alliances & Cooperations	Taliban, Haqqani Network, Al Qaeda, Islamic Movement of Uzbekistan

THE ISLAMIC JIHAD UNION is a splinter group of the **Islamic Movement of Uzbekistan**. Its objective is to overthrow the Uzbekistan government and replace it with an Islamic caliphate. Dissatisfied with their parent organization's focus on fomenting revolution within Uzbekistan, the IJU also calls for an anti-Western global jihad.

To avoid Uzbek authorities, the IJU operates out of Pakistan's FATA region.

Estimates of the group's size are in the hundreds, including two American members, who are prominently featured in IJU propaganda videos.

The IJU is a Sunni outfit.

FOUNDING

The group was founded in 2000 by Najmiddin Jalolov and Suhayl Buranov. The two intended to unite various ethnic groups through a larger common regional heritage, and looked to the broader Caucasus for members. The two were also committed to militant separatist activity against the ruling Uzbek government. The IJU committed its first major terrorist attack in 2004. Afterward, it released a statement saying:

> These martyrdom operations that the group is executing will not stop, God willing. It is for the purpose of repelling the injustice of the apostate government and supporting the jihad of our Muslim brothers in Iraq, Palestine, Afghanistan, and the Hijaz, and in other Muslim countries ruled by infidels and apostates.[1]

From then on, Jalolov would give specific orders to IJU operatives to attack hotels where Westerners were known to stay. Buranov assumed the position of communications director of the group. As the IJU developed, it appeared to shift from being a separatist movement to having broader militant Islamic goals.

LEADERSHIP
Jalolov and Buranov reportedly led the group after they founded it. Concerted efforts by Uzbek, U.S., and European governments have led to many arrests of IJU leaders and members. Jalolov was killed in a 2009 U.S. drone strike. The group is reportedly regrouping while hiding in the Pakistani FATA region.

VIOLENCE
In 2004, the IJU committed a series of suicide bombings. The first targeted a crowded bazaar and local government offices in Tashkent, the capital of Uzbekistan. In the blasts, 47 were killed. A few months later, the IJU simultaneously bombed the U.S. and Israeli embassies in Uzbekistan and the Uzbek prosecutor general's office, killing two and injuring many.

The Sauerland cell of the IJU, composed of four members, attempted to bomb U.S. army facilities in Germany in 2007. In 2008, the IJU attacked a NATO compound and killed several soldiers.

A 2013 IJU-released video shows the IJU attacking an American military base in Paktika, Afghanistan, and IJU members sniping Afghan soldiers.

TIES

From its base in Pakistan along the Afghan border, the group works with the **Taliban** and the **Haqqani network**. The IJU is also known to cooperate with **Al Qaeda** on attacks against U.S. forces in Afghanistan and the region. After a 2007 foiled attempt at attacking U.S. interests in Germany, the IJU launched a media campaign to garner support for its terrorist activities. **Al Qaeda**'s media networks helped disseminate the IJU propaganda.

Despite being an offshoot of the IMU, the IJU is known to have tensions that frequently devolve into conflict with its parent organization, mostly in Pakistan.

FUNDING

Funding for the IJU potentially comes from criminal activity and private donors, and likely Al Qaeda. According to the U.S. Department of the Treasury, the IJU has been affiliated with Al Qaeda since its founding, and like Al Qaeda, the group has been continually increasing the scope of its activity from Uzbekistan to the broader Caucasus and into Europe.

NOTES

[1] Sorcher, Sara. "What Is the Islamic Jihad Union?" *National Journal*. 19 Apr. 2013. <http://news.yahoo.com/islamic-jihad-union-183001458--politics.html >.

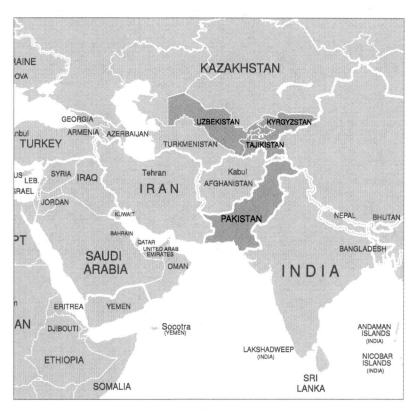

ISLAMIC MOVEMENT OF UZBEKISTAN (IMU)

ISLAMIC MOVEMENT OF UZBEKISTAN (IMU)

Main Area(s) of Operation	Pakistan, Uzbekistan, Tajikistan, Kyrgyzstan
Founder or Spiritual Leader	Tahir Yudashev, Juma Namangani
Known or Suspected Leader	Usmon Odil
Approximate Year Founded	1998
Approximate Size	1,000+
Alliances & Cooperations	Islamic Jihad Union, Taliban, Al Qaeda, Tehrik-e-Taliban Pakistan
Flag	

THE ISLAMIC MOVEMENT of Uzbekistan was formed to overthrow the secular government of Uzbekistan and incorporate the country, along with various other Muslim regions formerly controlled by the Soviet Union, into an Islamic caliphate under Sharia.

FOUNDING
The IMU was founded in 1998 by Tahir Yudashev and Juma Namangani, a former Soviet paratrooper. Before founding the group, Namangani participated in the 1992 to 1997 Tajikistan civil war, building a network of alliances and support that would aid the IMU's mission.

The IMU originally operated out of bases in neighboring Tajikistan. After a series of Uzbek-oriented attacks, Uzbek security forces used airstrikes to attack the group, forcing them to relocate to Afghanistan. However, it still operates a base in Tajikistan that is reportedly protected by sympathetic Tajik politicians.

From its headquarters in Mazar-e-Sharif and Kunduz, Afghanistan, it has trained approximately 2,000 fighters, and continues to launch attacks and violent campaigns around the region.

U.S. efforts in Afghanistan under Operation Enduring Freedom severely crippled the IMU in 2001.

LEADERSHIP

The group's military activities were originally led by Juma Namangani, and its ideological leader was originally Tahir Yudashev (both founders, as noted). When Namangani was killed by a U.S. airstrike in Afghanistan in 2001, Yudashev took control of the group. Shortly after, he pledged allegiance to Taliban leader Mullah Omar.

When the U.S. was successful in Afghanistan, the IMU was forced to relocate once again, this time to the FATA region of Pakistan. While there, it regrouped, and Yudashev engaged in creating various forms of propaganda to support jihad movements across the globe. His intention was to extend the reach of the IMU's mission. Yudashev was killed by a U.S. drone strike in 2009. His successor was Usmon Odil, who was killed in an April 2012 U.S. drone strike in Pakistan. In August of 2012, Odil's deputy Usmon Ghazi was tapped to lead the group.

VIOLENCE

IMU attacks include bombings and assaults on civilians and soldiers in Tajikistan, Kyrgyzstan, Uzbekistan, Pakistan, and Afghanistan.

A February 1999 IMU attack involved the detonation of five car bombs in Uzbekistan's capital city, Tashkent, aimed at assassinating Uzbek president Islam Karimov. The attack missed the president but killed 16 and injured 130.

In 2002 the group bombed a marketplace in Bishkek, Kyrgyzstan, killing six and injuring 40. In 2009, an IMU suicide bombing in Pakistan killed a solider and seven civilians. In 2010, the IMU attacked an Afghan police headquarters, killing a policeman. In September 2010, it ambushed Tajik troops, killing 25 and injuring 20 more.

It attacked the Peshawar airport in Pakistan in 2012 and the airport in Karachi in June 2014.

IMU kidnappings include four Japanese geologists and the head of the Kyrgyz Ministry of Interior Troops in 1999, and four American hikers in 2000.

TIES

While operating out of Afghanistan after 1998, the IMU supported Taliban efforts to fight the Afghan Northern Alliance. It recruited Kyrgyz, Tajiks, Chechens, and Uighurs and trained them in Afghan-based camps alongside **Taliban** recruits. IMU leaders have held senior-level positions in **Al Qaeda**.

Additionally, the IMU has operated camps in Waziristan, Pakistan, with an abundance of German and Swedish recruits.

Its presence extends from Pakistan to Afghanistan, with leaders in the two countries acting autonomously. Splinter terror groups have formed from IMU factions, including the **Islamic Jihad Union**.

A video released in 2009 by the IMU shows its leader meeting and firing guns with **Tehrik-i-Taliban Pakistan** leader Hakimullah Mahsud.

A September 2014 statement released online by IMU leader Usman Gazi reads:

> I declare that we are in the same ranks with the **Islamic State** in this continued war between Islam and [non-Muslims]. The Islamic State is free from a patriotic or nationalist agenda...you can see Arabs, Chechens, Uzbeks, Tajiks, Kyrgyz, Russians and many English-speaking Muslim mujahidin in its ranks.[1]

Experts predict that **Islamic State** funding and support could allow the IMU to make a substantial resurgence.

FUNDING

Funding is reportedly provided by sympathetic Uzbek Muslims from around Uzbekistan and as far away as Saudi Arabia (where 300,000 Uzbeks ended a forced migration). Additionally, various Turkish entities offer financial support. The IMU also commits criminal activities for financial sustenance, including participating in the drug trade and racketeering, and solicits money from abroad.

NOTES

[1] Daly, John C.K. "Islamic Movement of Uzbekistan Flirts with ISIS." Silk Road Reporters. 13 Oct. 2014. <http://www.silkroadreporters.com/2014/10/13/islamic-movement-uzbekistan-flirts-isis/>.

THE ISLAMIC STATE (IS)

THE ISLAMIC STATE (IS)

Main Area(s) of Operation	Iraq, Syria, Libya, Egypt, Turkey, various other parts of northern Africa, various parts of Southeast Asia
Founder or Spiritual Leader	Abu Ayyub al-Masri
Known or Suspected Leader	Abu Bakr al-Baghdadi
Approximate Year Founded	2006–2009
Approximate Size	60,000 worldwide
Alliances & Cooperations	al-Nusra, Boko Haram, Jeemah Islamiyah, Islamic Movement of Uzbekistan
Enemies/Rivals	Al Qaeda (at times)
Ideological Sect/Affiliation	Salafism, Wahhabism
Flag	

THE ISLAMIC STATE (IS) is a shorthand notation, for the purposes of this encyclopedia, for the group known as ISIS (the Islamic State in Iraq and Syria), ISIL (the Islamic State in the Levant), or Daesh. It is a Sunni jihadist terrorist group that has exhibited unprecedented brutality in its efforts to establish a transnational caliphate in Iraq, in Syria, and across the region known to some as the Levant. The IS's conquests have been quicker, harsher, and more devastating than those of any other Islamic militant group listed in this book. Additionally, considering the IS's current holdings of lands, cities, and infrastructure, it may have more cash and resources on hand than any other militant group in the world.

Using various websites and Twitter, the Islamic State declared itself an established caliphate in July 2014. The group's barbaric leader, Abu Bakr al-Baghdadi, was declared caliph.

> It is incumbent upon all Muslims to pledge allegiance and support him....The legality of all emirates, groups, states, and organizations becomes null by the expansion of the caliph's authority and arrival of its troops to their areas.[1]

The IS controls large portions of territory in Iraq and Syria, and has holdings in Libya, Egypt, Turkey, North Africa, and Southeast Asia. At least 60 countries are engaged in some form of conflict with the IS. It has been involved as a militant force in the Iraq war, the Syrian civil war, and the Libyan civil war. It has engaged in open conflict in Afghanistan and Pakistan, and has assisted militant extremist insurgency efforts in Yemen, the Philippines, and Morocco.

The IS is estimated to have 20,000 to 31,500 members at any given time, and the group now controls land equivalent in size to the United Kingdom.

FOUNDING

The IS grew out of **Al Qaeda in Iraq** (**AQI**). AQI leader Abu Musab al-Zarqawi led a concerted campaign of militants in Iraq that fought U.S. security forces from 2003 to 2011. Al-Zarqawi had developed an extensive network of fighters and supporters in Pakistan, Afghanistan, Syria, and Iraq. Many of these networks were developed during al-Zarqawi's time as the head of the Muslim contingent of a militant separatist group called Ansar al-Islam.

AQI grew under al-Zawahiri's leadership, and attacks intensified against indiscriminate civilian populations. According to letters archived by the Council on Foreign Relations between al-Zarqawi and al-Zawahiri, al-Zawahiri's massive campaign of death and destruction was questioned even by the mastermind of the September 11, 2001, attacks on the World Trade Center in New York City. Particularly, Osama bin Laden feared that AQI's indiscriminate campaign, which targeted as many Muslims as it did nonbelievers, would cause reputational damage to the group internationally.

Al-Zarqawi was killed in a June 2006 U.S. airstrike. Abu Ayyub al-Masri, likely supported by his former friend al-Zawahiri, gained control of the group. He rebranded it under the new name the Islamic State of Iraq to regain local support, and as the group became more involved in the ongoing civil war in Syria, the name was expanded to the Islamic State in Iraq and Syria.

According to analyst Charles Lister of the Brookings Doha Center, the IS's relocation to Mosul, Iraq, in 2009 allowed the group to "dramatically increase the frequency of its bombings across the country, particularly in urban areas." From this point, the group waged a series of campaigns and increased its presence across northern Iraq and into Syria. The IS leadership works to establish relationships with other militant groups as it enters new areas, and is often successful at merging smaller groups into its fold. For example, the Baathists, the ousted Iraqi ethnic group that largely held power under the Saddam Hussein regime in Iraq, are used to provide legitimacy to IS operations in Sunni parts of Iraq.

In Iraq, the IS:

> Spark[ed] the perceptions of sectarian conflict within Iraqi dynamics and worked to transfer what were existing sectarian tensions within the political system, for example, back into the tribal thinking, back into societal thinking. That, in effect, created a vacuum which the Islamic State felt it would be able to step into, and in many respects that is what it has managed to do.[2]

In Syria, the IS has effectively integrated itself into the civil conflict to bolster its legitimacy among susceptible insurgent groups; **Al Nusra** pledged allegiance to the IS in 2013. It knows how to manipulate conflict for its own gains, and does so with great benefit to its own efforts.

As the IS and **Al Qaeda** compete for dominance in the region, the groups often find themselves at odds. In Syria, the groups are considered by some to be at war. But the IS has taken the **Al Qaeda** model and improved upon it. Charles Lister of the Brookings Institute posits:

> The Islamic State has so far succeeded in doing essentially everything that Al Qaeda had previously done, and done it better, except for carrying out a foreign attack.[3]

The IS's propaganda branch is an extensive operation. It produces videos, posters, pamphlets, and web content through its media outlet, the I'tisaam Media Foundation. It also controls the Western-oriented al-Hayat Media Center, producing materials in foreign languages. It produces a magazine, *Dabiq*, and audio chant recordings through its Anjad Media Foundation, and releases regular numerical reports on its activities. By some accounts, the IS's social media presence is greater than that of any other militant Islamic group. IS Twitter hashtags are designed to lead an audience "down a rabbit hole of propaganda," and many Westerners, including Americans and British citizens, have been arrested trying to travel to the Middle East to join its ranks.[22] Among these were "Jihadi John," a recruit from Britain who delighted in appearing in numerous videos beheading IS's prisoners, killed in a drone strike in Syria in 2015.

LEADERSHIP

In 2006, Al-Zarqawi was killed by a U.S. air raid while attending a meeting with some of his command staff in a safe house outside of the city of Baqubah, Iraq. Leadership of the IS passed to Abu Ayyub al-Masri, who was also killed, in 2010, by a joint U.S.-Iraqi ground operation. After him, Abu Bakr al-Baghdadi became the new face of the IS, and he retains control of the group as of early 2016.

Even when addressing his commanders, al-Baghdadi supposedly wears a mask. Only two photos of him are known to exist, and to some in the IS he is known as "the invisible sheikh."

Al-Baghdadi was proclaimed caliph by the IS on June, 29, 2014. Caliph, a position higher than emir, is a title bestowed on a successor of Muhammad. In this capacity, he is the top commander and political figurehead of the group. Al-Baghdadi has a $10 million bounty on his head from the United States.

Al-Baghdadi was born Ibrahim Awad Ibrahim al-Badri in 1971 in the town of Samarra, to the north of Baghdad. He moved to Baghdad for his education, and received a PhD in education from the University of Baghdad. Through al-Zarqawi, he was introduced to Al Qaeda and quickly climbed the ranks. Eventually, he was named emir of the town of Rawa, Iraq. He became notorious for overseeing a brutal Sharia court in this emirate, and was soon offered a position on Al Qaeda's Shura Council, a top-tier advisory organization that produces many of the group's leaders. He stepped into his role as commander of the IS in 2010.

Al-Baghdadi's reputation has led to his being called "the new Bin Laden" in some media outlets.

VIOLENCE

The exact size of the IS death toll is difficult to state because of the vast areas of land, and the large population of civilians susceptible to IS brutality. Over 24,000 Iraqis are estimated to have been victims of the IS in 2014, and 1.8 million in Iraq have been displaced due to IS fighting. An estimated 10,000 have been executed by the IS since they gained power. The IS publicly executes native tribesmen, religious minorities (mostly Christians and Jews), Sunni Muslims, and those who simply refuse to swear allegiance to the IS.

IS violence is both retributive and utilitarian. To punish the "unfaithful" or "impure," the IS uses group executions, beheadings, amputations, live burnings, stoning, torture, and crucifixions. Violence on behalf of the IS is also used to impose fear and obedience. Thus, many of the most depraved acts of violence are videotaped by the group and uploaded to the Internet. This has a chilling effect on the group's regional adversaries. According to the *Washington Post*:

> That fear, evidenced in fleeing Iraqi soldiers and 500,000 Mosul residents, has played a vital role in the group's march toward Baghdad. In many cases, police and soldiers literally ran,

shedding their uniforms as they went, abandoning large caches of weapons.[4]

Termed "terror marketing," the IS's tactics, such as grotesque public executions, are designed to intimidate. Executions take the horrid forms of burnings, drownings, and beheadings. Some of the prominent IS public beheading examples, from just late 2014 to early 2015, include:

— American journalist James Foley
— Lebanese Army sergeant Ali al-Sayyed
— Israeli-American journalist Steven Sotloff
— Humanitarian aid workers David Haines and Alan Henning
— French hiker Hervé Gourdel
— Iraqi reporter and cameraman Raad al-Azzawi
— American Peter Kassig
— Japanese nationals Haruna Yukawa and Kenji Goto

On June 9, 2014, the IS captured one of its largest cities to date, Mosul, Iraq. More than 500,000 of the predominantly Christian population fled, with substantial casualties. Police headquarters were burned, and the black standard of the IS was hoisted over buildings as the group used loudspeakers to declare the city "liberated." The next day, 670 Shia inmates in Mosul's Badush prison were executed.

Minority religious and ethnic groups are targeted by the IS, and systematically attacked. Take, for example, the Yazidis. On August 4, 2014, the IS attacked Jaba Sinjar and killed 60 Yazidi men, thereafter abducting their wives and children. The next day, around 50,000 Yazidis were forced to flee their homes for the mountains. Events like this throughout the month happened with increasing frequency. A total of 5,000 Yazidis were killed in August alone, and 5,000 more abducted. The U.S. declared the persecution of the Yazidis a genocide on August 8, 2014.

The IS tool chest of killing and torture methods knows no limits. On February 3, 2015, the group released a video of Jordanian pilot Muath al-Kasasbeh being burned alive inside a small metal cage. In October,

2015, a Russian passenger plane exploded over the Sinai Peninsula in Egypt, killing all 224 people aboard. In an article in the IS's official magazine, the group bragged about using a Schweppes soft drink can to house the explosive that brought down the plane. On November 12, 2015, two IS suicide bombers in Beirut, Lebanon, killed 43 and injured 239 others. A third would-be bomber was captured and revealed that he was an IS recruit from Syria. On November 14, 2015, the IS publicly celebrated one of its deadliest attacks on foreign soil to date. Eight gunmen, outfitted with explosives and armed with high-caliber rifles, attacked tourist-populous sites around Paris, France. Deaths throughout the evening totaled 129. Targets included the France-Germany soccer match and a concert at the Bataclan concert hall, wherein disabled concertgoers were systematically executed and hostages including children were held for hours.

TIES

The IS evolved from **Al Qaeda** in Iraq, but the two organizations now compete for control in the region.

In April 2013, **Jabhat al-Nusra** pledged loyalty to the IS. On May 12, 2014, **Boko Haram** senior leader Abubakar Shekau released a video pledging **Boko Haram**'s support of the IS and its goals. **Jemaah Islamiyah**, the **Islamic Movement of Uzbekistan**, and various branches of Ansar al-Sharia have also vocalized support for the IS.

The Terrorism Research and Analysis Consortium released research in 2014 that included a list of 60 militant Islamic groups that have vowed either allegiance or support to the IS.

We at TRAC are constantly adding to the list (nearly daily). As of today, there are at least 30 separate regions that have active militant organizations that have pledged support to Islamic State; a total of 60 distinct groups worldwide.[5]

The IS recognizes the following it commands and intends to make use of it. Baghdadi has been quick to capitalize on his group's global support, issuing commands and calls to jihad to groups across the globe through videos and social media.

FUNDING

The IS is well-practiced at manipulating its perceived objective to gather support and resources as it may need. It initially drew funding from wealthy private donors in the Middle East who supported its efforts against the Bashar al-Assad regime in Syria. In 2006, the IS even managed to obtain financial support from the Shiite **Iranian Revolutionary Guard Corps** for its efforts against the United States, though by 2014 Iran offered to fund U.S. efforts against the ever-expanding IS.

The IS also uses criminal activities such as smuggling and extortion to self-finance, and draws money from local charities and communities in which it has been able to legitimize its efforts.

As it expanded, the IS captured cultural sites, oil fields, and infrastructure—all of which proved profitable. The oil fields it controls in Syria are so extensive that even the Bashar Al-Assad government, at war with the IS, is forced to buy oil from them. The IS has a production capacity of 80,000 barrels per day. It also sells antiquities and cultural artifacts to bolster its funding. An estimated $36 million was earned from antiques and artifacts from one region of Syria. In Mosul, the IS helped itself to the reserves of the Iraqi central bank and Iraqi army supplies after it captured the city.

The IS's cash and assets are estimated to be $2 billion, with an estimated revenue of $3 million from oil sales each day.

With its substantial assets, regular income, and cash on hand, the IS has expanded its social services offerings as a means of strengthening its regional legitimacy, and of ensuring that the populations under its control are completely dependent upon the Islamic State. This affords the group control.

According to Charles Lister of the Brookings Institute in a *Frontline* interview:

> It is noticeable, for example, that in Raqqa in Syria, the Islamic State's control of the city, and its ability to provide fairly extensive services to the civilian population, has resulted in at least a tacit acceptance of the group's control of the city by the civilian population. That is a successful example of exactly what the

Islamic State is trying to replicate across other areas of Syria and now also in Iraq, and in Mosul, for example.[6]

Finally, such substantial funding equates to substantial recruiting capacities. Intelligence agencies have reported that the IS pays fighters approximately $400 a month, in addition to providing military equipment, which makes fighting for them more lucrative than joining any other militant group in the region.

NOTES

[1] "Iraq Conflict: ISIS Declares a 'Caliphate', Calls for Muslims to Pledge Allegiance." ABC. 2 July 2014. <http://www.abc.net.au/news/2014-06-30/isis-declares-islamic-caliphate/5558508>.

[2] Collins, Robert. "Inside the Rise of ISIS." PBS. 7 Aug. 2014. <http://www.pbs.org/wgbh/pages/frontline/iraq-war-on-terror/losing-iraq/inside-the-rise-of-isis/>.

[3] Ibid.

[4] McCoy, Terrence. "ISIS, Beheadings and the Success of Horrifying Violence." The Washington Post. 13 June 2014. <http://www.washingtonpost.com/news/morning-mix/wp/2014/06/13/isis-beheadings-and-the-success-of-horrifying-violence/>.

[5] Mohammed, Riyadh. "ISIS Beheads Another American as 60 New Terror Groups Join." The Fiscal Times. 16 Nov. 2014. <http://www.thefiscaltimes.com/2014/11/16/ISIS-Doubles-Down-Infidels-Boosted-60-New-Terror-Groups>.

[6] Collins, "Inside the Rise of ISIS."

JAISH-E-MUHAMMED (JEM)

JAISH-E-MUHAMMED (JEM)

Main Area(s) of Operation	Kashmir
Founder or Spiritual Leader	Maulana Masood Azhar
Known or Suspected Leader	Maulana Masood Azhar
Approximate Year Founded	2000
Approximate Size	Several hundred
Alliances & Cooperations	Al Qaeda, Taliban, Lashkar-e-Taiba, Harkat-ul-Jihad al-Islami, Harkat-ul-Mujahideen al-Islami, Lashkar-e-Jhangvi, Sipah-e-Sahaba Pakistan
Enemies/Rivals	Tehrik-e-Taliban Pakistan
Ideological Sect/Affiliation	Deobandi Islam
Name Meaning	"Army of Mohammed"
Flag	

JAISH-E-MUHAMMED (JEM), translated as "Army of Mohammed," is a militant organization based in Kashmir aimed at separating the region from Indian control. In 2011, the group was named "one of the most violent active terrorist organizations in Pakistan." JeM's preferred modus operandi is to use suicide attacks to assassinate high-level government officials in India and Kashmir. JeM has a wide-reaching network of cooperation and support from other terrorist groups in the region, including **Al Qaeda** and the **Taliban**.

The group is a Deobandi organization that also advocates for the destruction of both America and India. It targets primarily Christians and Shiite Muslims.

The group has renamed itself multiple times to maintain operations in the region. After Pakistan banned it in 2001, the group took up the name Tehrik-ul-Furqan, only to later change its name again to Khuddam-ul-Islam. Both Tehrik-ul-Furqan and Khuddam-ul-Islam are often commonly referred to as JeM.

The group is estimated to have several hundred armed supporters.

FOUNDING

JeM was founded by Maulana Masood Azhar, who studied among and taught followers of the Deobandi movement. Like the spiritual leaders of many other militant Islamic groups in the region, his first exposure to jihadist methodologies was during the Afghan-Soviet war. Azhar became widely known for his extremist Islamic rhetoric and speeches, and is believed to have spent time with Osama bin Laden in the 1990s. He was jailed in India in 1994, but released in 1999 in exchange for Indian hostages taken by **Harkat-ul-Mujahideen al-Islami**. Since Azhar's release, he and a handful of other militant Islamic figureheads have continued to grow the organization, recruiting from among Pakistani, Indian, and Afghani low-income civilians, and networking with other terrorist organizations in the region.

LEADERSHIP

Maulana Masood Azhar has maintained a leadership role in JeM since he founded the group following his release from prison in 1999. Released along with Azhar was Sheikh Omar, an English native who studied at the London School of Economics. Omar is also an active leader of JeM, and is believed to have kidnapped *Wall Street Journal* reporter Daniel Pearl. Azhar and Omar are two of India's most wanted men.

Azhar was arrested again in 2001 by the Pakistani government in connection with attacks on the Indian Parliament, only to be released in 2002.

VIOLENCE

JeM targets primarily high-level government officials. This includes multiple suicide car bombings of Indian army bases and government buildings, an attempted assassination of Pakistani president Musharraf in 2003, an attack on the divisional commander of Kashmir in 2003, a suicide car bomb attack on Indian Kashmiri chief minister Mufti Mohammed Sayeed in 2005, and a grenade attack on a Human Rights Commission escort vehicle in 2006. JeM gunmen have attacked Pakistani-based Christian schools and hospitals.

JeM worked closely with **Lashkar-e-Taiba** to carry out a bombing attack on December 13, 2001, at the Indian Parliament compound, which killed nine. It is suspected of providing support and personnel to deadly anti-Christian attacks in Islamabad, Murree, and Taxila, Pakistan, in 2002.

In 2009, a New York bombing plot was foiled by the FBI and NYPD. Four individuals had planned to detonate explosives in a New York City Jewish community center, and then shoot at military planes at New York's Air National Guard base at Stewart Airport with stinger missile launchers. The arrested individuals admitted in captivity to a desire to fulfill the mission of JeM.

TIES

JeM is known to cultivate relationships and foster cooperation among militant Islamic groups. Its network includes **Al Qaeda**, the **Taliban**, **Lashkar-e-Taiba**, and **Lashkar-e-Jhangvi**. It operates training camps throughout Afghanistan. Additionally, it was reportedly supported by the Pakistani Inter-Services Intelligence agency prior to 2002. JeM is also believed to be supported by wealthy Pakistani and Kashmiri expatriates living in Britain.

In 2002, when the Pakistani government officially banned JeM, many of its members became soldiers for **Al Qaeda** in Pakistan. The group is known to engage in Pakistani politics through the radical political party Jaimat-e-Ulema-e-Islam Fazul Rehman.

JeM's ties to the **Taliban** are numerous; a JeM-produced newspaper has often served as an outlet for **Taliban** initiatives. JeM also overtly associates with **Sipah-e-Sahaba Pakistan** (SSP). At a pro-JeM rally organized in 2000, **SSP** publicly announced, "One hundred thousand Sipah-e-Sahaba workers will join Jaish-e-Muhammed to fight the infidels."

FUNDING
Most of the financial backing (and members) for JeM's activities have been provided by neighboring militant groups **Harkat-ul-Jihad al-Islami** and **Harkat-ul-Mujahideen al-Islami**. The group has also received assistance from the **Taliban** and, before 2002, the Pakistani ISI. Additionally, reports have been made of low-level Pakistani military officials' providing financial and logistical support. Though JeM has been officially banned in Pakistan, it still fundraises there through front groups, notably the Islamic charitable organization Al-Rashid Trust.

JEMAAH ISLAMIYAH (JI)

JEMAAH ISLAMIYAH (JI)

Main Area(s) of Operation	Philippines, Indonesia, Singapore, Thailand, Malaysia
Founder or Spiritual Leader	Abdullah Sungkar, Abu Bakar Bashir
Approximate Year Founded	1991
Approximate Size	1,000+
Alliances & Cooperations	Lashkar-e-Taiba, Al Qaeda
Ideological Sect/Affiliation	Darul Islam
Name Meaning	"Islamic Congregation"

JEMAAH ISLAMIYAH (JI) is a multinational terrorist group active in Southeast Asia with a mission of establishing an Islamic caliphate in the region. Jemaah Islamiyah uses violence and terror to destabilize governments and target Western influences and interests. The group is most active in the Philippines, Indonesia, and Singapore, and cells of Jemaah Islamiyah also operate in Cambodia, Thailand, and Malaysia. The U.S. State Department estimates that membership in Jemaah Islamiyah is over 1,000, while Australian intelligence estimates it as possibly being closer to several thousand.

The group was formed in 1991, initially recruiting trained operatives from the wars in Afghanistan and the Philippines. Jemaah Islamiyah is responsible for a series of deadly bombings from 2000 to 2009 across Indonesia. Since 2009, local authorities have increased arrests of its members, but numerous splinter groups have formed to covertly continue Jemaah Islamiyah's work in the region.

FOUNDING

Jemaah Islamiyah follows the practices of Darul Islam, a movement dedicated to establishing Islamic law and rule in Indonesia, which began around 1940 as the country began to gain independence from the Dutch. Some accounts have the group forming from a handful of radicals exiled from Indonesia into neighboring Malaysia. In the 1980s, JI was reportedly peaceful, but it became radical and violent in the 1990s after the group's spiritual leader and founder, Abu Bakar Bashir, became close with Abdullah Sungkar, a radical operating in Malaysia with ties to **Al Qaeda** and, while he was alive, Osama bin Laden.

LEADERSHIP

Abu Bakar Ba'asyir (Bashir) is the spiritual leader of Jemaah Islamiyah. He was imprisoned in Indonesia in 1975 and later joined a group dedicated to Darul Islam in the 1980s. In 1985, he fled from Indonesia to Malaysia to escape a warrant for his arrest, and formed a group of Muslims from Southeast Asia and Afghanistan to fight the Soviets, with Saudi Arabian financial backing. He allied closely with Abdullah Sungkar in Malaysia, and the two steadily built a network of support and followers to carry out the practices of Darul Islam.

In 1992, Sungkar had a major disagreement with the leaders of the Darul Islam movement, and split off to form Jemaah Islamiyah. Eventually, JI formed four branches, or mantiqis, in Singapore and Malaysia (branch 1), Indonesia (branch 2), the islands of Mindana, Sabah, and Sulawesi (branch 3), and Papua New Guinea and Australia (branch 4). Training camps were formed in Pakistan and Afghanistan. One Jemaah Islamiyah cell in Pakistan reportedly received training from local terrorist group **Lashkar-e-Taiba**.

Bashir and Sungkar returned to Indonesia in 1998, and Bashir took a leadership role in an umbrella group called the Indonesian Mujahideen Council; but Sungkar died of natural causes soon afterward.

For years, Bashir denied his connection to Jemaah Islamiyah's violent activities. He was arrested at least twice for involvement in the JI attacks in 2000 to 2009, but his prison sentences were cut short.

However, in 2014 Bashir publicly declared allegiance to the leader of the **Islamic State**.

Others associated with the leadership of Jemaah Islamiyah include Azhari Husin and Mohammed Noordin Top. Husin is an engineer and explosives expert. Both are connected to leadership roles in JI bombings in 2003 and 2004.

VIOLENCE

In 2002, Jemaah Islamiyah detonated three bombs in Bali, Indonesia. Bali is an international tourist destination with numerous beachfront communities. The bombs were planted in nightclubs and took 202 lives. The group also bombed a Marriott hotel in Jakarta (2003), killing 12; the Australian embassy in Indonesia (2004), killing 11; and three establishments in Bali (2005), killing 22. The 2002 attacks in Bali were suicide bombings.

The group has also specifically targeted Americans and American interests. Plans to attack a U.S. Naval facility in 2001 were foiled by authorities in Singapore. Since 2002, officials in Singapore have been mounting an increasingly successful crackdown on JI, resulting in more than 300 arrests and a major decline in the number of attacks. However, in 2009, splinter groups bombed hotels in Jakarta twice, and more splinter groups have formed since authorities dismantled the core Jemaah Islamiyah group.

TIES

On Christmas Eve in 2000, Jemaah Islamiyah and **Al Qaeda** operatives, working together, bombed churches in the Indonesian capital of Jakarta and eight other cities, killing 18 and injuring many. Bashir expressed support for Osama bin Laden while bin Laden was alive but denies direct ties to **Al Qaeda**. Though many disagree on the extent of cooperation between Jemaah Islamiyah and **Al Qaeda**, some U.S. officials and experts believe JI to be **Al Qaeda**'s "Southeast Asian wing." Factions within Jemaah Islamiyah have made stronger statements of support for **Al Qaeda**'s global goals.

As previously noted, JI leader Abu Bakar Bashir has publicly declared allegiance to the head of the **Islamic State**, Abu Bakr Al-Baghdadi.

FUNDING

Currently, Jemaah Islamiyah is believed to be regrouping. They are recruiting through personal contacts, prisons, religious groups, and schools. Through outreach and infiltration strategies, JI has become involved in the ownership and operation of regional charities and NGOs. The group became actively involved in the tsunami relief efforts of 2004 and 2006. According to the *Middle East Quarterly*, JI has adopted a "Hezbollah model of social organization," in which it engages openly in charity work and social services provision, while secretly supporting and pursuing terrorist activities. This rebranding scheme is an attempt to divert focus and gain public support in light of increasing arrests by local authorities.

JUND AL-SHAM

JUND AL-SHAM

Main Area(s) of Operation	Syria (predominantly), Jordan, Israel, Lebanon, Palestine
Founder or Spiritual Leader	Abu Musab al-Zarqawi, Osama bin Laden
Approximate Year Founded	1999
Approximate Size	Hundreds
Alliances & Cooperations	Al Qaeda
Name Meaning	"Soldiers from the Sham"

JUND AL-SHAM TRANSLATES as "Soldiers from the Sham." The Sham is another name for the Levant (mainly Syria, but it also includes Jordan, Israel, Lebanon, and Palestinian territories). The group was a project of Osama bin Laden's, a militia of Islamic fundamentalists designed to aid the efforts of **Al Qaeda** where its membership presence was low. The mission of Jund al-Sham is that of **Al Qaeda**: to attack Western targets, spread Islam, and establish a regional Islamic caliphate.

Mostly active in Syria, it has been regarded by Syrian officials as "the most active militant group in the country." The group is thought to be targeting the Syrian government for its secular nature and the Shiite ties of Syrian president Bashar Assad. Jund al-Sham is a Sunni group.

The group has publicly announced that its primary targets are Americans, the British, Italians, and Christians in Lebanon. It is believed to have membership levels in the hundreds, with many more potential recruits with **Al Qaeda** support.

FOUNDING

Jund al-Sham was formed in Afghanistan in 1999. Its initial operations were largely interrupted by the 2001 U.S. efforts in Afghanistan. After the U.S. invasion, many members remained to fight in Iraq and Afghanistan, while others fled throughout the Middle East and Europe.

LEADERSHIP

The founding members of Jund al-Sham were recruited and trained by Abu Musab al-Zarqawi, who ran a paramilitary militant Islamic training camp in Afghanistan. He later joined **Al Qaeda** and pledged his allegiance to Osama bin Laden. Al-Zarqawi was a leader of **Al Qaeda** in Iraq and actively organized efforts to fight American troops in Iraq and Afghanistan until he was killed by a U.S. airstrike in 2006.

VIOLENCE

The first reported attack by Jund al-Sham was a suicide car bombing targeting **Hezbollah** in Lebanon in 2004.

In 2005, the group took responsibility for three bombs detonated in Christian Lebanese neighborhoods. It also attempted to take responsibility for a Texas-based oil refinery explosion in 2005, but the claim was disputed. Likewise, a handful of other attacks were falsely claimed by Jund al-Sham, including attacks on Israeli citizens in the Sinai Peninsula in 2004 and 2005.

TIES

Jund al-Sham was created by **Al Qaeda**. Numerous groups have organized under Jund al-Sham since its emergence, including a militant Palestinian group based in Lebanon.

FUNDING

Jund al-Sham was reportedly started by al-Zarqawi with $200,000 in seed money from Osama bin Laden. It is believed to have received financial or operational support from **Al Qaeda**, and allegedly has received support from **Hizb ut-Tahrir** and Iran.

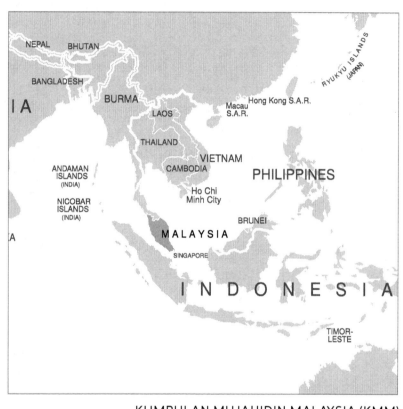

KUMPULAN MUJAHIDIN MALAYSIA (KMM)

KUMPULAN MUJAHIDIN MALAYSIA (KMM)

Main Area(s) of Operation	Malaysia
Founder or Spiritual Leader	Zainon Ismail
Known or Suspected Leader	Nik Adli Nik Abdul Aziz
Approximate Year Founded	1995
Approximate Size	70+
Alliances & Cooperations	Jemaah Islamiyah
Name Meaning	"Malaysian Mujahideen Movement"

KUMPULAN MUJAHIDIN MALAYSIA IS DEDICATED to overthrowing the Malaysian government and creating an Islamic caliphate that also includes Indonesia, the Philippines, and Thailand. KMM maintains a large network of terrorist cells across Southeast Asia, and groups frequently splinter off to independently perpetrate more violent attacks.

KMM networks are known to operate in six Malaysian states and the federal district of Kuala Lumpur. KMM has also sent members to Indonesia to attack Christians.

The Malaysian government believes that KMM has 70 to 80 members. However, this estimate is likely low and correlates only to known suspects and captives. The group may have hundreds working at any given time to execute attacks, and many have splintered from KMM to form smaller, even more extremist subgroups.

FOUNDING

Many KMM members initially worked alongside Maoists in Nepal to overthrow the government in the eastern part of the country and form an independent tribal state. The group disassociated from that cause in 2002, but re-formed in 2011 in Malaysia.

KMM was established in 1995 by Zainon Ismail, a combatant in the Soviet-Afghan war. Ismail, like many having returned from the struggle with the Soviets in Afghanistan and Pakistan in the 1990s, brought the idea of jihad and mujahideen back to Malaysia with a fervor. As a separatist group, KMM sought political influence in Malaysia in 1995 under the leadership of Ismail, but was defeated overwhelmingly in the 1995 national elections. Thus, KMM resorted to covert operations and terror activities to grow its influence.

LEADERSHIP

Leadership passed to Nik Adli Nik Abdul Aziz, an Islamic school teacher, in 1999, four years after the group's founding. Abdul Aziz is the son of the now-deceased former chief minister of Kelantan (a Malaysian state) and former spiritual leader of the Pan-Malaysian Islamic Party. In 2001, the Malaysian government captured and held Abdul Aziz without trial, but he was released in 2006. During his captivity, Abdul Aziz's father was one of many political figures who fiercely criticized the law under which Abdul Aziz was held, the controversial Internal Security Act. Along with Abdul Aziz, 10 other suspected militant group members were released, including four from KMM and six from Jemaah Islamiyah. The Malaysian government has arrested 48 other KMM members, many with former training in Afghan mujahideen camps.

VIOLENCE

After losing in national political elections in the 1990s, KMM turned to subversive tactics. It was one of the first prominent domestic terror groups to force the Malaysian government to develop a strategy to deal with modern extremism and terrorist activities. The Malaysian government has arrested an estimated 50 under the controversial

Internal Security Act (ISA), but with provisions for captivity without trial or charge, many have been released. The ISA itself was repealed and replaced in 2012. Still, the Malaysian government is working to adequately, and appropriately, confront the extremist threat within its borders.

Underground cells of KMM were foiled from committing a massive bombing of a shopping mall in Jakarta, as well as several assassinations, bank robberies, and the bombing of a Hindu temple. In 2000, the group detonated an explosive in the Malaysian city of Klang and assassinated a provincial assembly legislator in the northern part of the country. Since 2001, the Malaysian government has managed to mostly remain ahead of KMM in domestic terror plots, allegedly preventing numerous attacks on civilians. KMM's members have splintered, and many have traveled to the Philippines or Indonesia to aid in terrorist activities working toward a pan-Islamic state.

TIES

KMM is believed to have close ties to **Jemaah Islamiyah** in Indonesia and has supported its terrorist attacks.

FUNDING

KMM is believed to be significantly self-financed through robberies and other criminal activities. **Jemaah Islamiyah** may also contribute funding.

LASHKAR-E-JHANGVI (LEJ)

LASHKAR-E-JHANGVI (LEJ)

Main Area(s) of Operation	Pakistan
Founder or Spiritual Leader	Akram Lahori, Malik Ishaque, Riaz Basra
Known or Suspected Leader	Akram Lahori, Malik Ishaque
Approximate Year Founded	1996
Approximate Size	300
Alliances & Cooperations	Jaish-e-Muhammed, Harkat-ul-Mujahideen al-Islami, Tehrik-e-Taliban Pakistan, Lashkar-e-Taiba, Harkat-ul-Jihad al-Islami, Al Qaeda, Sipah-e-Sahaba Pakistan
Ideological Sect/Affiliation	Deobandi
Name Meaning	"Army of Jhangvi"
Flag	

LASHKAR-E-JHANGVI (LEJ) seeks to establish an Islamic caliphate in Pakistan by any means necessary. It also aims for the implementation of Sharia, the labeling of all Shiite Muslims as "non-believers," and the elimination of Christians, Jews, and Hindus. The group frequently targets Iranian interests and citizens, because the Iranian population is largely Shiite.

LeJ follows a Sunni Deobandi ideology. It operates out of the Punjab region of Pakistan.

It is known as one of the most violent Sunni militant groups in Pakistan, and has killed hundreds. The group operates covertly and utilizes a complex subgroup structure, with an estimated 300 members.

FOUNDING

LeJ was formed as a splinter group of **Sipah-e-Sahaba Pakistan** (SSP) in 1996, when three members—Akram Lahori, Malik Ishaq, and Riaz Basra—accused SSP of abandoning the ideals of cofounder Maulana Haq Nawaz Jhangvi.

LEADERSHIP

Lahori and Ishaq were LeJ's leaders for some of its most violent operations. Basra, who was involved in more than 300 terror attacks prior to starting LeJ, was killed in 2002. LeJ operational commander Qari Zafar was killed by a U.S. drone strike in 2010.

Ishaq was held in long-term Pakistani custody but released in 2014, despite having been tried for the murder of 12 and having 40 pending murder cases against him. In 1997 he stated, "I have been instrumental in the killing of 102 human beings."[1] Lahori remained in Pakistani custody until he was executed in 2015.

LeJ is composed of many autonomous sub-groups that operate in cells of five to eight. This allows it to avoid Pakistani authorities. LeJ maintains two training camps in the Muridke and Kabirwal districts of Pakistan, and one in Afghanistan near the capital city of Kabul.

VIOLENCE

LeJ attacks with rockets, land mines, and suicide bombings. It often films its most violent attacks, or the aftermath, and posts the videos to the Internet to gather followers and prompt similar attacks.

LeJ has assassinated hundreds of prominent and professional Pakistani Shiite Muslims, particularly targeting doctors, lawyers, religious scholars, teachers, students, and politicians. It offered a $135 million bounty in 1999 to anyone who assassinated Pakistani prime minister Nawaz Sharief, and a close attempt was made on his motorcade that same year.

The U.S. State Department believes that LeJ was behind a 1995 attack on U.S. consulate members that killed two.

Since 2008, LeJ has been involved in timed explosive or suicide bombing attacks with targets including the Sri Lankan cricket team, refugee camps, the deputy inspector general of police operations in

Pakistan, American oil workers, Iranian diplomats, and the Pakistani Sports Board director general. In 2010, it detonated a bomb in a busy bazaar in Lahore, Pakistan, killing 57 and injuring 90. In 2011, members of LeJ drove motorcycles by a passenger bus terminal in Quetta and fired on the building, killing 11 and injuring three. Also in 2011, its coordinated bombing in Kabul claimed 60 lives.

LeJ is believed to have taken part in the kidnapping of American journalist Daniel Pearl in 2002.

TIES

Many of the terror groups in the region, including LeJ, the **Taliban**, **SSP**, and the **Islamic Movement of Uzbekistan**, fought alongside each other in the Afghan-Soviet war in the 1990s.

Many members of LeJ belong to other terror outfits, including **Jaish-e-Muhammed** and **Harkat-ul-Mujahideen**. LeJ operates recruiting and training camps for various regional militant groups. Many LeJ members have trained at **Harkat-ul-Mujahideen** camps in Afghanistan, where they received specialized instruction on the use and assembly of improvised explosive devices (IEDs) and hit-and-run tactics.

LeJ has conducted terror attacks with **Tehrik-i-Taliban Pakistan** and maintains ties with **Lashkar-e-Taiba, Harkat-ul-Jihad al-Islami**, and the **Taliban**. On numerous occasions, the **Taliban** has offered safe haven to LeJ fugitives from Pakistan. LeJ is also reported to be integrated, in some capacities, with **Al Qaeda**. LeJ and **SSP**, together, are described as a "mainstay of **Al Qaeda** planning in Pakistan."

Despite LeJ's being the product of a split with **SSP**, analysts believe the two groups routinely support each other's efforts, and cooperate to facilitate terror attacks.

FUNDING

LeJ has wealthy donors in Karachi, Pakistan, and Saudi Arabia, and utilizes kidnappings, extortion, and bank robberies to fund its activities.

NOTES

[1] Lashkar-e Jhangvi section on Australian government website. 3 Mar. 2015. <http://www.nationalsecurity.gov.au/Listedterroristorganisations/Pages/Lashkar-e-Jhangvi.aspx>.

LASHKAR-E-TAIBA (LET)

LASHKAR-E-TAIBA (LET)

Main Area(s) of Operation	Pakistan and India, focused on Jammu and Kashmir
Founder or Spiritual Leader	Abdullah Azzam
Known or Suspected Leader	Hafiz Muhammed Saeed
Approximate Year Founded	1985
Approximate Size	50,000+
Alliances & Cooperations	Harkat-ul-Jihad al-Islami, Jaish-e-Muhammed, Harkat-ul-Mujahideen al-Islami, Al Qaeda, Taliban
Enemies/Rivals	Tehrik-e-Taliban Pakistan
Ideological Sect/Affiliation	Wahhabism
Name Meaning	"Army of the Pure"
Flag	

LASHKAR-E-TAIBA (LET) IS ONE of the largest militant Islamic groups in South Asia. The name translates to "Army of the Pure," and the group's mission is to establish a worldwide Islamic caliphate through jihad. LeT is known for its extensive infrastructure and operational capabilities, and has become a leader among the numerous terrorist groups operating in Pakistan. It offers protection, training, operational assistance, and funding to other terrorist organizations; actively cooperates with organized crime syndicates; and supports the activities of international terror groups like **Al Qaeda**. LeT's strength, much like **Al Qaeda**'s, is in large-scale organization: establishing terror networks.

The group is based out of Pakistan, and for more than 20 years has waged war in India over the disputed territories of Jammu and Kashmir. Though LeT follows Wahhabi beliefs, it has a unique ideology that justifies collaboration with other militant Islamic groups—even those of different denominations and beliefs—for the sake of achieving its objectives. In his book *Call for Transnational Jihad: Lashkar-e-Taiba 1985-2014, New York Times* contributor Arif Jamal claims the organization has a presence in more than 100 countries and ties to other militant Islamic groups across the globe. This makes LeT particularly dangerous and formidable.

LeT is in many ways the fountainhead of terrorist activity on the subcontinent and throughout Asia. Using its vast financial and organizational resources, it supports attacks and operations conducted by dozens of other groups in Pakistan, including **Jaish-e-Muhammed**, **Al Qaeda**, and the **Taliban**.

Lashkar-e-Taiba formed in Pakistan in conjunction with other large jihadist groups, including **Harkat-ul-Jihad al-Islami, Jaish-e-Muhammed, and Harkat-ul-Mujahideen al-Islami**. These groups, though having their own distinct internal agendas, share origins, motivations, objectives, and recruitment techniques. Many of these groups began as paramilitary organizations to counter Soviet objectives in Afghanistan and the region. Additionally, all of these groups at some point received favorable treatment from the state of Pakistan and the Pakistani Inter-Services Intelligence (ISI) agency.

LeT has stated that its goals of "liberating" Jammu and Kashmir from Indian control are about more than just territory. The group wants the Kashmir region to serve as a base to restore Islamic ideology to the entire subcontinent. The Carnegie Endowment for International Peace published a 2012 report on Lashkar-e-Taiba, labeling it "after **Al Qaeda**...the most dangerous group operating in South Asia."[1]

FOUNDING

In 1985, Hafiz Muhammad Saeed and Abdullah Azzam, two professors at Lahore University in Pakistan, formed a missionary group called Jamat ud Dawah (JuD). This group soon teamed up with militant groups involved in the Soviet-Afghan war to create Markaz al-Dawa-wal-Irshad (MDI). One of the cofounders of MDI was Azzam, mentor of Osama bin Laden and regarded by some sources as the father of modern global jihad. The other cofounder, Saeed, now serves as the group commander. Initially, the group received support from the Pakistani ISI and the U.S. (through the CIA), in its efforts against the Soviets. However, after the war ended and America withdrew support, Pakistani financial assistance helped the group fight for the return of Indian-controlled Jammu and Kashmir to Pakistan. In 1990, a military wing of MDI splintered off to become Lashkar-e-Taiba, with a commitment to global jihad. LeT's efforts have since been allegedly supported by the Pakistani ISI, by some estimates to the tune of $50 million.

LEADERSHIP

LeT acts as the military component of MDI. The two groups share resources and finances. The combined LeT/MDI holdings are estimated at over 2,000 offices or bases of operation throughout Pakistan and the region. LeT has several thousand members and a highly organized, hierarchical leadership. Members are supplied with assault weapons, rocket-propelled grenades, and advanced communications equipment.

Saeed, as previously noted, is commander of the group. In 2009, Indian officials demanded that Pakistan turn over Saeed for connection to a 2008 attack, but the Pakistani government instead chose to prosecute a separate, lower-ranking member of LeT, refusing to hand over Saeed for lack of evidence.

The location of the LeT headquarters is known, and the group operates openly in the Kashmir region. The complex is comparable to a small city. Located outside of Lahore, the capital city of the Pakistani province of Punjab, it includes a hospital, a market, a residential area, a fish farm, and agricultural tracts. Additionally, the group operates over 135 schools and 16 Islamic seminaries in Pakistan, in addition to various health clinics, through an entity called Jamat'ut'Dawah, which operates and communicates its mission through a website (http://jamat-dawa.com) and publishes several magazines.

VIOLENCE

While LeT typically outsources violence to other groups, they are not above launching their own operations when they see an opportunity. The most notorious instance of direct LeT violence occurred in 2008, when 10 agents traveled to Mumbai, India, and attacked two five-star hotels, a railway terminal, a Western-frequented café, and a Jewish community center. They killed 174 people, including six Americans.

LeT is also blamed for bombings in Delhi in 2005 that killed over 60 people, and financing attacks carried out by other local terrorist groups on the Indian Parliament complex. LeT has claimed responsibility for attacking one of India's most famous landmarks, the army barracks at the Red Fort, Delhi, in 2000, killing three and damaging the landmark.

After an attack on security forces in Kashmir, a 20-year-old LeT militant was captured. "I came to kill Hindus," he stated once captured. "It's fun doing this."[2]

TIES

LeT's extensive financial resources allow it to sponsor the terrorist activities of other militant Islamic groups. It frequently lends training camps, operational bases, recruitment networks, and media platforms to other terror groups in the region, such as **Hizbul-Mujahideen, Jaish-e-Muhammad, Harkat-ul-Jihad-ul-Islami, Tehrik-i-Taliban Pakistan**, and **Lashkar-e-Jhangvi**. Aside from sharing physical assets, LeT directly contributes to financing acts of terror, including reportedly funding a portion of the **Jaish-e-Muhammed** attack on India's Parliament building in December 2001.

In 2002, an **Al Qaeda** senior member was captured by the United States in a LeT safe house in Pakistan.

LeT is believed to network and fundraise in cooperation with various terrorist groups internationally, and has played a part in terrorist activities in Russia and Iraq. It has shared recruitment facilities and training infrastructure and techniques with the Afghanistan **Taliban**.

LeT is also a member of the International Islamic Front organization, formerly led by Osama bin Laden.

FUNDING

LeT funds its operations through a variety of Pakistan-based charities and businesses. The bulk of the group's spending is on spreading its ideology, providing social services, and recruiting for their jihadist efforts.

Various sources indicate that LeT also receives funding from the Pakistani military and Pakistani ISI. Pakistan has officially denied supporting or funding the group, and the international community has very little evidence of support beyond reports of inside sources. However, the Pakistani government still allows LeT to overtly operate its extensive network of compounds, offices, and businesses.

LeT involves itself in Pakistani social welfare programs to assert influence and maintain a steady pool of dedicated citizens from which to recruit, the most notable example being Jamat ud Dawah (JuD). In Islam, da'wah is the practice of proselytizing Islam. From JuD's website:

> [JuD] is a Pakistan based organization that is blessed with billions of followers in each village and city who share the same vision and follow the same direction that Islam has enlightened us with, and JUD helps facilitate the process called Dawah.[3]

JuD led "humanitarian" relief efforts after a 2005 earthquake in Kashmir, and is believed to be a major front for the activities of LeT. There are LeT donation boxes and money collection sites in JuD offices throughout the country. LeT also receives contributions from wealthy donors in Arab Gulf states.

LeT controls numerous businesses in the health industry (ambulance services, hospitals, etc.) and the farming industry (markets, agricultural plots, livestock facilities, etc.). It collects an estimated 1.2 million animal hides per year at state-sponsored holy festivals and sells them for a sizable profit.

Finally, LeT is believed to get the remainder of its operational financing from counterfeiting, extortion, and the opium trade.

NOTES

[1] Tellis, Ashley J. "The Menace That Is Lashkar-e-Taiba." *Policy Outlook*. Carnegie Endowment for International Peace. Mar. 2012. <http://carnegieendowment.org/files/let_menace.pdf>.

[2] Upadhyay, Tarun. "I Came to Kill Indians, It's Fun: Captured Pak Militant Naved." *Hindustan Times*. 8 Aug. 2015. <http://www.hindustantimes.com/india/i-came-to-kill-indians-it-s-fun-captured-pak-militant-naved/story-cxxFxBAjvfdZ3wWAuxziON.html>.

[3] About Us section on Jamat ud Dawah official blog. <https://judofficial.wordpress.com/about/>.

LIBYAN ISLAMIC FIGHTING GROUP (LIFG)

LIBYAN ISLAMIC
FIGHTING GROUP (LIFG)

Main Area(s) of Operation	Libya
Founder or Spiritual Leader	Sami al Saadi
Known or Suspected Leader	Anas Sebai
Approximate Year Founded	1995
Approximate Size	1,000-2,500
Alliances & Cooperations	Al Qaeda, Moroccan Islamic Combatant Group, Salafia Jihadia, Tunisian Combatant Group

THE LIBYAN ISLAMIC FIGHTING GROUP (LIFG) was formed to overthrow the Muammar Gaddafi regime in Libya and replace it with a fundamentalist Islamic state. In addition to its local objectives, the group is also committed to aiding in global jihad. In 2007, the LIFG formally merged with **Al Qaeda**.

For 42 years, Gaddafi ruled over multiple forms of Libyan governments. He initially seized power in a military coup (he was formerly a colonel) in 1969, and when Libya shifted to a socialist "Jamahiriya" state in 1977, he stepped into the role of "brotherly leader." Despite Gaddafi's affiliation with the Arab Socialist Union party and his implementation of Sharia practices in Libya, he was still the target of the LIFG's efforts since he engaged in trade and acted diplomatically with the West. In 2011, a revolt led by the National Transition Council (NTC), a Libyan rebel alliance, successfully removed Gaddafi's regime from power. Gaddafi was subsequently executed. The LIFG partnered with the NTC in the overthrow, but the new Libyan government is still not the desired caliphate.

At its peak, the LIFG had by some estimates 1,000 active members, and by other estimates nearly 2,500.

FOUNDING

The LIFG was founded in 1995 by Islamic Libyans who were returning to the country after the Soviet-Afghan war. It was formed in Afghanistan, but Libya was announced as its base of operations in 1995. The group worked to build an insurgency within the country, and made three attempts on the life of Gaddafi. The Gaddafi regime retaliated with a powerful crackdown that forced the group to flee the country in 1998. Some members went south to Sudan, and hundreds moved back to the Middle East to join **Al Qaeda**. Terrorist activities were continued in exile.

Back in Libya, members of the LIFG who remained participated in uprisings in Benghazi. Many were imprisoned. Around 200 LIFG members were eventually released from prison when they organized and officially renounced violence in a 417-page theological document.

After Gaddafi's regime fell, some LIFG members began publicly pushing for peaceful Islamic revolts, but many others joined the growing **Al Qaeda in the Islamic Maghreb** to continue the campaign of jihad against the West.

LEADERSHIP

The LIFG's commanders include spiritual leader Sami al Saadi and top commander Anas Sebai.

VIOLENCE

The LIFG helped coordinate serial bombings by the **Moroccan Islamic Combatant Group** (GICM) in Casablanca in 2003, which killed 40 and injured over a hundred more. Similarly, the group was linked to the **GICM**'s and **Salafia Jihadia**'s bombing of busy commuter trains in Madrid, Spain, in 2004.

LIFG members were involved in the September 11, 2011, attack on the U.S. diplomatic compound in Benghazi, Libya. An information manager and CIA contractors were killed. U.S. ambassador to Libya J. Christopher Stevens was dragged from the compound, stripped, and beaten to death in the streets.

Other attacks include a multitude of violent skirmishes with Benghazi police and Libyan security forces in the 1990s and 2000s, and involvement in riots at the Abu Salim prison in 1996 that killed over 1,200 prisoners.

Along with continued attacks perpetrated under the **Al Qaeda** banner, LIFG members have dispersed to other parts of Africa, the Middle East, Asia, Europe, and notably, the United Kingdom. The UN Security Council believes that an LIFG group in eastern Libya has helped supply jihadist groups in Iraq with fighters.

TIES

The hierarchy of Libyan militant groups is complex. The LIFG maintains itself as a group and acts under the LIFG banner, but also has integrated into other terrorist networks. Some reports insist that the group was disbanded in 2010, but LIFG leaders are active and hold high ranks in various other militant Islamic groups in Libya.

Ansar al-Sharia, an umbrella name developed in 2011 for Libyan militant Islamic groups to work cohesively, claims the LIFG as a member. It was under this banner that the attack on the U.S. consulate in Benghazi was carried out. Despite the clear implications in the attack, the LIFG and Ansar al-Sharia have been allowed by the Libyan government to maintain some degree of authority over Benghazi.

The LIFG was quickly identified as an **Al Qaeda** affiliate after the September 11 attacks in New York City. In 2007, **Al Qaeda**'s then-second-in-command, Ayman al-Zawahiri, officially announced the LIFG's merger with **Al Qaeda**. LIFG commander Zawahiri released the following statement:

> Today, with grace from God, the Muslim nation witnesses a blessed step....Honorable members of the Fighting Islamic Group in Libya announce that they are joining the al Qaeda group to continue the march of their brothers...[against the] infidel of the West.[1]

The LIFG joined **Al Qaeda** in the Islamic Maghreb in conjunction with the **Moroccan Islamic Combatant Group** and the **Tunisian Combatant Group**. According to *The Long War Journal*, "The official joining of the Libyan Islamic Fighting Group with Al Qaeda represents the terror group's strategy to united allied Islamist terror groups under a single banner."

FUNDING

According to former LIFG commander Noman Benotman, the LIFG has a network of financial supporters throughout Libya, the Middle East, and Europe.

NOTES

[1] Roggio, Bill. "Libyan Islamic Fighting Group Joins Al Qaeda." *The Long War Journal*. 3 Nov. 2007. <http://www.longwarjournal.org/archives/2007/11/libyan_islamic_fight.php>.

MORO ISLAMIC LIBERATION FRONT (MILF)

MORO ISLAMIC LIBERATION FRONT (MILF)

Main Area(s) of Operation	Philippines
Founder or Spiritual Leader	Hashim Salamat
Known or Suspected Leader	Ibrahim al Haj Murad
Approximate Year Founded	1984
Approximate Size	15,000
Alliances & Cooperations	Abu Sayyaf, Al Qaeda, Jemaah Islamiyah
Flag	

THE MORO ISLAMIC LIBERATION FRONT (MILF) seeks to establish an independent Muslim state in the southern Philippines. They are a part of a long-term separatist movement conducted against the largely Catholic nation. The movement, which includes other separatist rebel groups, has claimed 120,000 lives and displaced 2 million residents.

The MILF had an estimated 90,000 members in 1998, but more recent estimates are 2,500 to 15,000. Most estimates are closer to the upper figure.

The MILF's attacks, in combination with other separatist efforts, led the Philippine government in 1989 to grant them semi-political autonomy over a region of the country referred to as the Autonomous Region of Muslim Mindanao (ARMM). Though formally required to "remain an…inseparable part of the national territory of the Republic [of the Philippines]," the ARMM has a regional governor, a legislative body, and the power to levy taxes and collect revenue.[1]

Since 1989, the southern region of the Philippines under ARMM jurisdiction has seen widespread poverty, conflict, and lawlessness. Extremists there continue to demand more from the Philippine government, and groups like the MILF and Abu Sayyaf use violence and terror to underscore these demands.

In 2012, political talks began about replacing the ARMM with a larger, more autonomous region known as Bangsamoro. Many in the country have expressed concern with the plan, especially given that the Bangsamoro justice system follows Sharia practices. Minorities living in the southern region of the Philippines fear persecution; others see the region as compromising the unity and strength of the Philippine nation. The office of the president of the Philippines, likely inundated with inquiries from concerned citizens, has posted FAQs on the proposed territory and independence plan at http://www.opapp.gov.ph/milf/news/frequently-asked-questions-draft-bangsamoro-basic-law.

FOUNDING

The MILF was founded in 1984 by Hashim Salamat. Salamat was a member of the Moro National Liberation Front (MNLF), a secessionist group in the Philippines with a Marxist orientation. He split to form the MILF to reorient the cause to Islamic goals, including the establishment of an independent Islamic state.

In a public interview, Salamat described the separatist movement as a "liberation" from the Philippines, which refers to the southern islands that were "illegally and immorally annexed" by the Philippine government into the boundaries of the new nation after the United States granted the Philippines independence in 1946. Salamat says his followers and their attacks are not criminal, because they "strictly follow the teachings of Islam."[2] He has issued a call to Muslims worldwide to help aid the Bangsamoro movement both materially and spiritually.

LEADERSHIP

Hashim Salamat led the group after founding it in 1984. In 2000, another MNLF detractor, Ibrahim al Haj Murad, gained control when Salamat was forced to go into hiding.

Salamat has stated that the primary goal of the MILF is to "make the word of Allah supreme."[3] The group has published a 20-year, four-point plan to achieve this objective and to create and maintain a large Muslim state in the southern Philippines.

MILF recruits are trained in the Mindanao region of the Philippines, but training is also outsourced to camps in Pakistan and Libya. Its main bases are in Mindanao; bases also exist on the islands of Basilan, Jolo, Tawi-tawi, and Palawan.

VIOLENCE

The MILF's first bombing targeted a Catholic wedding party in Salvador, Philippines, killing one and injuring 90. Violent activities increased after the Philippine government's initial refusal to grant autonomy to Bangsamoro in 1987.

In 1995, the MILF massacred 50 civilians in the town of Ipil, Philippines. In 1997, it killed 14 people in a movie theater in Iligan; in 2000, 13 Christians were killed on a bus; and later that year a bombing in Manila killed 22 and injured over 100. Other attacks include a 2008 bombing of a local police force and an attack against the corporate board of Toyota. From 1985 to 2008, the MILF committed 276 attacks or other acts of terror.

Throughout the three decades that the MILF has sought an independent Muslim state, it has had numerous battles and heated skirmishes with the Armed Forces of the Philippines (AFP).

Though various peace agreements have been made and broken, the group declared an official jihad against the Philippine government in 2000.

In 1987, the Philippine government refused the MILF's demands for land to self-govern as a Muslim state. In response, the group resorted to terrorism. In 2012, the Philippine government conceded, and negotiated a new region in the pre-existing Autonomous Region of Muslim Mindanao, to be called Bangsamoro, to have autonomy and an independent police force, and to be governed according to Sharia. Resource sharing negotiations ended in 2013, and the MILF has agreed in return to cease violent activities. In 2015, the MILF began seeking to engage in the Bangsamoro political process as an official political party.

TIES

The MILF is believed to receive operational support, recruits, and financial aid from **Abu Sayyaf, Al Qaeda**, and **Jemaah Islamiyah**. It is also known to harbor Islamic extremists from the broader Indonesian region.

The group officially denies ties to **Abu Sayyaf** and **Al Qaeda**. On various occasions, it has accused **Abu Sayyaf** of perpetrating attacks that the MILF was accused of orchestrating. However, evidence suggests that hundreds of MILF members were trained in **Al Qaeda**-linked camps in Afghanistan with ties to Osama bin Laden. Other evidence suggests that **Al Qaeda** has sent recruits to training camps in Mindanao, Philippines.

A **Jemaah Islamiyah** explosives expert was arrested in 2013 for aiding and consulting the MILF. Nine JI members arrested later that year admitted to receiving training at MILF camps.

FUNDING

Much of the MILF's funding is provided by its own members and wealthy regional residents. Additionally, since the group has autonomous governing control over the region, it uses tax revenues. It also has received donations from local charity groups, including Zakat, MERC International, Islamic Wisdom Worldwide Mission, and the Daw'l Immam al Shafee Center.

Criminal activities, including kidnappings, drug trafficking, and extortion, also provide financial support. MILF members often target high-profile victims with large potential ransoms to kidnap, continuing even after semi-autonomy concessions by the Philippine government.

Perhaps not even the expanded autonomy of the Bangsamoro plan or anything short of a completely independent, self-governed nation will quell their demands.

The MILF has used a front organization to channel funds, the International Islamic Relief Organization, which was led by Muhammed Jamal Khalifa, Osama bin Laden's brother-in-law. Other terrorist groups, including **Jemaah Islamiyah** and **Al Qaeda**, have contributed as well.

NOTES

[1] Republic of the Philippines, Congress of the Philippines, Eighth Congress. *An Act Providing for an Organic Act for the Autonomous Region in Muslim Mindanao.* 1989. Republic Act No. 6734. Available online at: http://www.lawphil.net/statutes/repacts/ra1989/ra_6734_1989.html.

[2] "Perhaps the Moro Struggle for Freedom and Self-Determination Is the Longest and Bloodiest in the Entire History of Mankind." FAS Intelligence Research Program. <http://fas.org/irp/world/para/docs/ph2.htm>.

[3] Moro Islamic Liberation Front section in Mapping Militant Organizations on Stanford University website. 24 Aug. 2015. <http://stanford.edu/group/mappingmilitants/cgi-bin/groups/view/309>.

MOROCCAN ISLAMIC COMBATANT GROUP (GICM)

MOROCCAN ISLAMIC COMBATANT GROUP (GICM)

Main Area(s) of Operation	Morocco, Britain, Belgium, Italy, Netherlands, Egypt, Denmark, France, Spain, Turkey
Founder or Spiritual Leader	Abdelkarim el-Mejjati and Nourredine Nafia
Known or Suspected Leader	Numerous
Approximate Year Founded	1998
Approximate Size	Thousands
Alliances & Cooperations	Al Qaeda
Ideological Sect/Affiliation	Salafism

THE MOROCCAN ISLAMIC COMBATANT GROUP (GICM) is an international militant group composed of Moroccan diaspora communities throughout Europe. Its main branches are in Morocco and Britain, but it has cells in Belgium, Italy, the Netherlands, Egypt, Denmark, France, Spain, Turkey, and Scandinavia.

The goals of the GICM are to establish an Islamic caliphate in Morocco and to support **Al Qaeda** in its pursuit of global jihad. The GICM subscribes to Salafi ideology.

FOUNDING

The GICM was founded in 1998 by numerous recruits training in radical militant camps in Afghanistan, many of whom had recently fought in the Afghan-Soviet war. They included Abdelkarim el-Mejjati and Nourredine Nafia. Nafia helped compose one of the group's early organizational charters, and was later captured by Moroccan security forces and imprisoned for his role in a 2003 terror attack in Casablanca. El-Mejjati later became a commander in **Al Qaeda** in Saudi Arabia, and was killed in 2004.

The GICM maintains a propaganda magazine called *Sada al-Maghrabi*, which translates to "Reign of Morocco" and is dedicated to overthrowing the Moroccan king for an Islamic state.

LEADERSHIP

After the GICM was linked to 2003 bombings in Casablanca, among various other conspiracies to help **Al Qaeda** operatives, the Moroccan government made a phenomenal effort to bring the group to justice, with the aid of Interpol. Most GICM leaders and operatives have been arrested, and leadership of the group is currently uncertain.

The leader of the GICM cell in Belgium that facilitated the transportation of suicide bombers into Iraq was arrested in 2004. Another GICM operative, Saad al-Houssaini, also known as "The Chemist," designed and created the bombs used in the 2003 Casablanca bombings. He was apprehended in 2007 and sentenced in 2009.

In 2010, the U.S. State Department stated that most of the GICM leaders had been imprisoned or killed.

VIOLENCE

On May 16, 2003, GICM and GICM-supported **Salafia Jihadia** suicide bombers killed 45 people in a busy civilian area in Casablanca. The attack involved 14 simultaneous suicide bomb detonations, and was the largest terrorist attack in Moroccan history.

GICM members also helped facilitate the coordinated bombings of crowded commuter trains in Madrid, Spain, in March 2004, which killed 191 people and injured 1,800. The bombs, which were improvised explosive devices (IEDs), were smuggled onto the trains in 13 pieces of luggage. This has been the largest terror attack to ever take place in Spain, and is known as the "11-M" incident.

TIES

The GICM and **Salafia Jihadia** are the two major terror groups active in Morocco. **Salafia Jihadia** is considered an offshoot of the GICM, and, as noted above, the two organizations worked together to execute the 2003 Casablanca suicide bombings.

One of the GICM's stated objectives is to assist **Al Qaeda**'s global jihad movement. The group has various high-ranking personnel with direct ties to **Al Qaeda** in Saudi Arabia. In August 2001, GICM members met with Osama bin Laden in Kandahar, Afghanistan, to reach an agreement concerning shared use of **Al Qaeda** training camps.

The GICM facilitates **Al Qaeda** in Saudi Arabia's assimilation into Morocco and Europe. In 2002, GICM members arranged a wedding between three Moroccan women and members of **Al Qaeda** in Saudi Arabia to help the group establish a presence in Morocco. Another GICM operative helped one of the 2004 Madrid bombers get back to Iraq while avoiding arrest by coordinating his trip through Belgium.

FUNDING

A portion of the GICM's funding comes from illegal activities, including trafficking false documents and illegal arms, and participating in the drug trade in Morocco. The GICM also self-finances through international crime syndicates throughout Europe and northern Africa. Gunrunning and counterfeit currency operations are some of its most lucrative financing efforts in northern Africa.

MUSLIM BROTHERHOOD

MUSLIM BROTHERHOOD

Main Area(s) of Operation	Egypt, Iraq, Jordan, Lebanon, Syria, Palestine, Kuwait, Bahrain, Saudi Arabia, Tunisia, Algeria, Libya, Sudan, Yemen, Iran, Morocco, Somalia, Mauritana
Founder or Spiritual Leader	Hasan Al Banna
Known or Suspected Leader	Numerous
Approximate Year Founded	1928
Approximate Size	500,000+

THE MUSLIM BROTHERHOOD is the oldest international Islamist group in existence. Its slogan is "Islam is the solution." The group renounced violence in the 1970s, and recently constituted the largest independent bloc of elected representatives in the Egyptian Parliament. The Muslim Brotherhood is also not listed on the U.S. Foreign Terrorist Organizations list. However, it maintains ties to numerous militant Islamic terror groups, and with its size, funding, and network, militarization would be easy if it decided to reinstate its former tactics.

The Muslim Brotherhood has had numerous reincarnations throughout its 80-year history. Leaders of the present Muslim Brotherhood support democratic governments with Islamic underpinnings. According to senior member Isam Al Aryan in 1995:

> The Brothers consider constitutional rule to be the closest to Islamic rule....We are the first to call for and apply democracy. We are devoted to it until death.[1]

In 2011, protests across Egypt led by the Muslim Brotherhood ousted President Hosni Mubarak. Various members of the group were elected to Parliament, and the Muslim Brotherhood's candidate, Mohammed Morsi, was elected president. While in office, Morsi gave himself widely unchecked power, and proclaimed his actions to be immune from judicial review and legal challenges. Allegations of corruption and economic mismanagement plagued his administration. In 2013, protests erupted again across Egypt, and a military-led coup replaced Morsi with a new Egyptian president.

FOUNDING

The Muslim Brotherhood was founded in 1928 by Hasan Al Banna. Al Banna was a native Egyptian and the son of an Islamic imam. He grew up receiving an Islamic education from his father, and participated in pro-Islam and anti-Christian advocacy from early adolescence. In 1920, Al Banna moved to Cairo to teach Arabic. He moved to Ismailiya, Egypt, in 1927, and shortly thereafter began organizing the first Muslim Brotherhood.

Originally, the Muslim Brotherhood's ideology was incompatible with democracy. "Banna completely rejected the Western model of secular, democratic government, which contradicted his notion of universal Islamic rule."[2]

From its inception, the group recognized the potential for expanding Islamic influence through social welfare programs and political activism. It initially operated social programs and charities, and ran youth education centers, all aimed at the middle to low classes. Between 1936 and 1938, membership in the group rose from 800 to 200,000. In 1939, the Muslim Brotherhood became a political party. In the 1940s, it produced "the secret apparatus," a paramilitary group given autonomy to act on matters of domestic and foreign affairs. In 1948, members of the secret apparatus assassinated Egyptian prime minister Mahmud Fahmi Nokrashi and fought in the Arab-Israeli war.

The Muslim Brotherhood maintained various ties to the Nazis throughout the 1930s. Its main foes at that time were colonial Britain and the newly forming state of Israel. The group organized mass anti-Semitic demonstrations throughout Egypt between 1936 and 1938, and maintained anti-Jew propaganda outlets. Its demonstration and propaganda techniques resembled Nazi tactics and were supported by Nazi funding.

According to some scholars, the Muslim Brotherhood was the first militant Islamic group to establish Islamic jihad as a global movement, and embrace the concept of death and violence as a means to an end. According to Al Banna in an article written in 1938 titled "The Industry of Death," "To a nation that perfects the industry of death and which knows how to die nobly, Allah gives proud life in this world, and eternal grace in the world to come."[3]

In 1952 the king of Egypt abdicated the throne. Gamel Abdul Nasser, first prime minister and then president, advocated for secular solutions to Egypt's economic and domestic challenges, which the Muslim Brotherhood opposed. In 1954, the group attempted to assassinate Nasser with gunfire while he was giving a speech in Alexandria. Nasser survived. In response, the government banned the Muslim Brotherhood from operating in Egypt, and government officials allegedly shot and killed Al Banna in 1948. Many Muslim Brotherhood members were subsequently imprisoned and executed.

LEADERSHIP

The Muslim Brotherhood continued to operate as an alternative to Egypt's secular government throughout the second half of the 20th century. Membership rose to 500,000 or more.

Nasser's successor was Anwar al-Sadat, who was willing to publicly recognize the Muslim Brotherhood in exchange for an oath from the group to refrain from violence. A splinter cell of the Muslim Brotherhood played a part in the assassination of al-Sadat in 1981. From there, Hosni Mubarak controlled the Egyptian state, until Muslim Brotherhood-backed protests ousted him in 2011.

The group began political participation in 1984. Its greatest victories and strongest majority followed the 2011 regime change that made Muslim Brotherhood candidate Muhammed Morsi president.

Following the demise of the Morsi administration in 2013, **Al Qaeda** committed to "renewed violence by Islamists who feel short-changed by democracy and secularism."

VIOLENCE

The Muslim Brotherhood's earliest violent activities were typically political assassinations or assassination attempts. The group has not taken responsibility for any large-scale civilian attacks, but the Egyptian government has accused it of detonating a car bomb at Egyptian security forces headquarters in 2013. Muslim Brotherhood leaders in Syria and elsewhere have called for anti-Israel and anti-Western actions on the part of Islamists.

TIES

The Muslim Brotherhood has branches in Egypt, Iraq, Jordan, Lebanon, Syria, Palestine, Kuwait, Bahrain, Saudi Arabia, Tunisia, Algeria, Libya, Sudan, Yemen, Iran, Morocco, Somalia, and Mauritania, and has supporting organizations in Russia, the United Kingdom, Indonesia, and the United States. Those organizations played significant roles in many of the 2011 democratic uprisings, protests, and revolutions that swept the Middle East.

Following the failed 1954 attempt to assassinate President Nasser, imprisoned Muslim Brotherhood leader Sayyid Qutb wrote a manifesto titled *Milestones* that would later be used and cited by both **Al Qaeda** and **Hamas**. *Milestones* argues that non-Sharia governments are illegitimate and valid targets of jihadist objectives. The work is said to have inspired many of today's radical Islamic groups.

Article II of the charter of **Hamas** describes the group as a wing of the Muslim Brotherhood in Palestine.

FUNDING

According to the Council on Foreign Relations, "Though establishing an Islamic state based on Sharia was at the core of the Brotherhood's agenda [in the 1960s], the group gained prominence by effectively providing social services where the security state failed."[4]

The Muslim Brotherhood has always taken advantage of the lower socioeconomic classes of Egypt with social programs to gain credibility and favor. As a by-product, lucrative charities and public service entities have allowed the Muslim Brotherhood to self-finance.

NOTES

[1] Zalman, Amy. "Muslim Brotherhood: Roots of Modern Jihad?" About News. <http://terrorism.about.com/od/politicalislamterrorism/a/MuslimBrothers.htm>.

[2] Wright, Lawrence. *The Looming Tower: Al-Qaeda and the Road to 9/11*. New York: Knopf, 2006. p. 25.

[3] Aminoff, Gary. "Islamic Fascism: The Nazi Connection." American Thinker. 11 Dec. 2012. <http://www.americanthinker.com/articles/2012/12/islamic_fascism_the_nazi_connection.html>.

[4] Laub, Zachary. Egypt's Muslim Brotherhood. Backgrounder section on Council on Foreign Relations website. 15 Jan. 2014. <http://www.cfr.org/egypt/egypts-muslim-brotherhood/p23991>.

PALESTINIAN ISLAMIC JIHAD (PIJ)

PALESTINIAN ISLAMIC JIHAD (PIJ)

Main Area(s) of Operation	Israel/Palestine
Founder or Spiritual Leader	Fathi abd al-Aziz Shaqaqi, Shayk Abd al-Aziz Awda
Known or Suspected Leader	Dr. Ramadan Abdullah Shallah
Approximate Year Founded	1979
Approximate Size	Less than 1,000
Alliances & Cooperations	Muslim Brotherhood, Iranian Revolutionary Guard, Hezbollah
Enemies/Rivals	Hamas (formerly)
Ideological Sect/Affiliation	Palestinian nationalism
Flag	

THE PALESTINIAN ISLAMIC JIHAD (PIJ) is a Sunni Islamic militant group dedicated to the destruction of Israel. The organization is composed of a leadership council and a military wing. The military wing is called the al-Quds Brigade, and the PIJ leadership has claimed responsibility for all terrorist activities and attacks committed by the al-Quds Brigade.

Playing a role in the assassination of Egyptian president Anwar Sadat in 1981, the group, along with its brother organization, the **Egyptian Islamic Jihad,** was expelled from Egypt. Though they have since focused on terror in the Palestinian territories, they occasionally find time to torment innocent civilians in Egypt.

The PIJ seeks to replace Israel with an Islamic state and refuses to recognize any scenario or peace offering that includes a compromise with Israel. Only the complete destruction of the state of Israel will satisfy the mission of the PIJ. Thus, unlike **Hamas** and other militant Palestinian groups, the PIJ refuses to participate in any political process or peace negotiation, opting instead for action through violence and terror alone. It is believed that the PIJ has worked to foil peace agreements, such as the 1993 Oslo accords, through a series of concerted terror attacks.

The PIJ has continued terrorist activities even when Palestinian political leaders like Mahmoud Abbas have agreed to cease-fire agreements in Israel, illustrating the lack of control the Palestinian leadership has over many of the radical organizations that operate under the same banner or cause.

The PIJ is believed to have around 1,000 members.

FOUNDING

Fathi abd al-Aziz Shaqaqi and Abd al-Aziz Awda broke away from the **Muslim Brotherhood** to found the PIJ in 1979.

Shaqaqi and Awda believed the **Muslim Brotherhood** organization was too moderate in its mission of Palestinian statehood. The PIJ has always considered itself a "radical alternative." Some sources consider it to be one of the most radical militant Islamic groups in the region.

The PIJ began its terror operations in Egypt as a branch of the **Egyptian Islamic Jihad**, called the Islamic Jihad-Shaqaqi Faction, but was expelled to Gaza by the Egyptian government for involvement in the 1981 assassination of Egyptian president Anwar Sadat. The PIJ has since maintained some activities in Egypt, however; its 1990 bus bombing of Israeli tourists in Egypt killed 11.

After a series of Gaza-based terrorist activities in 1987, Shaqaqi and Awda were exiled to Lebanon. Awda was added to the FBI's Most Wanted Terrorists list in February 2006. PIJ operations are now orchestrated from Syria, where Awda is likely still in hiding.

LEADERSHIP

Fathi abd al-Aziz Shaqaqi was killed by Israeli intelligence forces in 1995 while traveling under an alias. After Shaqaqi's death, Dr. Ramadan Abdullah Shallah took leadership of the organization. Shallah controls operations and fundraising for al-Quds Brigade terror activities in the West Bank, Gaza, and Lebanon from his base in Damascus. Before assuming control of the PIJ, Shallah was a professor of Middle Eastern studies at the University of South Florida from 1990 to 1995.

PIJ recruits come mostly from Palestinian refugee camps in Gaza and the West Bank.

The PIJ has tried to organize in the United States, but in 2003, U.S.-based PIJ leader Sami al-Arian and three of his lieutenants were arrested. U.S. PIJ branches are still actively engaged in fundraising and spreading propaganda. Organizations like the Tampa, Florida-based Islamic Committee for Palestine and the World and Islam Studies Enterprise are believed to be U.S. front organizations for the PIJ.

VIOLENCE

The PIJ attacks Israelis indiscriminately, with the sole objective of maximizing casualties. It has claimed responsibility for over 30 suicide bombings from 1987 to 2006, and has participated in even larger numbers of rocket attacks from Gaza into Israel.

In 1996, the PIJ executed a suicide bombing in the Dizengoff Center in downtown Tel Aviv that killed 20 and injured over 75 more.

In 2006, despite a cease-fire agreement between Israel and Hamas, the PIJ carried out two suicide bombings in central Tel Aviv. In 2007, it fired rockets at schools in the Israeli city of Sderot. The PIJ played a large role in facilitating the firing of 2,300 rockets into Israel from Gaza in 2012 alone. A PIJ bus bombing in Israel in 2012 resulted in at least 29 civilians injured.

TIES

According to Australian National Security, the PIJ, though Sunni, is "inspired by and remains ideologically supportive of Iran's Islamic

Revolution and maintains close ties with the **Iranian Revolutionary Guards Corps** and **Hezbollah**."

The PIJ and **Hamas** were considered enemies until around 1994. **Hamas** began adopting violent actions similar to the PIJ at that time, and the two groups worked together to execute a suicide bombing in Beit-Lid, the West Bank, in 1995 that killed 20 and wounded over 75 civilians. After the PIJ bus bombings of 2012, **Hamas** called the attack "welcomed." However, **Hamas**'s political leadership does not control the PIJ's terrorist activities, which makes the organization dangerously unpredictable.

FUNDING

The Iranian and Syrian governments, as well as Palestinian sources, have provided financial assistance to the PIJ. It maintains offices in Beirut, Lebanon; Tehran, Iran; and Khartoum, Sudan.

POPULAR FRONT FOR THE
LIBERATION OF PALESTINE (PFLP)

POPULAR FRONT FOR THE LIBERATION OF PALESTINE (PFLP)

Main Area(s) of Operation	Israel/Palestine
Founder or Spiritual Leader	Wadi Haddad, George Habash
Known or Suspected Leader	Ahmad Sadat
Approximate Year Founded	1968
Approximate Size	800+
Ideological Sect/Affiliation	Palestinian nationalism, socialism

THE POPULAR FRONT FOR THE LIBERATION OF PALESTINE (PFLP) publicly calls for armed insurrection and high-profile media attacks to bring international attention to its cause of establishing a Palestinian nation in place of Israel.

The group formed in response to the Arab states' loss in the 1967 Six Day War with Israel.

It is believed that the PFLP has over 800 members.

FOUNDING

The PFLP was founded on December 11, 1967, as the convergence of two preexisting left-wing Palestinian groups. Its founding ideology is closely linked with Marxism and Leninism, and one of the group's leaders claims the "liberation" of Palestine is "an integral part of the world Communist revolution."[1] The PFLP is also committed to toppling conservative Arab states and destroying the nation of Israel.

LEADERSHIP

The PFLP was founded by Wadi Haddad (later PFLP commander of terrorist operations) and George Habash (later PFLP general secretary), with the support of then-Egyptian president Gamal Abdul Nasser. Habash was arrested by the Syrian government in 1968 under speculation of supporting an overthrow of the Syrian Baath regime, but was rescued by the PFLP in the same year. Haddad, however, had the backing of the KGB, which supplied him with the arms to carry out his attacks. In 1970, Haddad was made a KGB agent, and that same year carried out a hijacking that would define his penchant for violence. In fact, the KGB's involvement in militant Islam was not unique to Haddad. The Soviets were known and suspected of supplying various militant Palestinian national groups with weapons and specialized training through the KGB. Some believe post-Soviet covert Russian operations still support various facets of militant Islam when beneficial to the country's political agenda.

The group was formerly closely associated with the Palestinian Liberation Organization until 1970. In that year, Habash made the organization distance itself when the PLO adopted the June 1974 Stage Strategy, because it partly recognized the state of Israel and opposed the Oslo accords of 1993 and 1995. The group later reconciled with PLO leader Yasser Arafat and renewed allegiance with the PLO. The group has, to date, never recognized the state of Israel or its right to exist.

In 2000, Habash resigned for health reasons, to be replaced by Abu Ali Mustafa, who ushered the group to commit more frequent and deadly attacks on Israeli citizens. Mustafa was killed in 2001 and replaced by Ahmad Sadat, who orchestrated the assassination of the Israeli minister of tourism. Pressure from this attack led the PLO to arrest Sadat shortly after the attack in 2002. By 2006, Sadat had been elected to the Palestinian Parliament. Two months later, he was captured and arrested by Israeli forces.

VIOLENCE

Terrorist activities conducted by the PFLP are typically aimed at garnering international media attention. Hundreds of terrorist activities and attacks were attributed to the PFLP shortly after its formation. The PFLP hijacked an Israeli aircraft in 1968; 16 prisoners were eventually released. Three more aircraft were hijacked in the 1970s, and each of them was blown up after passengers were evacuated. In 1981, the group kidnapped journalists from *The New York Times*, *The Washington Post*, and *Newsweek* in Beirut, Lebanon.

In 2001, the PFLP assassinated Rehavam Ze'evi, an Israeli politician, party leader, and minister of tourism. Suicide bombings in 2002 and 2003 claimed three lives each and wounded dozens in the West Bank and the Israeli city of Tel Aviv, respectively.

The PFLP facilitated rocket attacks on Israel in 2008 and 2009 and claimed to have a part in several attacks on IDF forces, including a deadly ambush in Gaza. Additional PFLP rocket attacks took place in 2010 and 2011.

A 2012 kidnapping attempt was foiled by the IDF, wherein the PFLP planned to take Israeli soldiers hostage in order to negotiate the release of their incarcerated leader, Ahmad Sadat.

On November 18, 2014, two PFLP affiliates attacked a synagogue in the Har Nof neighborhood of Jerusalem. Four of the five victims (three Americans and a British citizen) were rabbis, and the fifth was an Israeli police officer. The rabbis were sliced to pieces with meat cleavers. The attack and the PFLP were praised by the **Al-Aqsa Martyrs Brigade**, who called it a "heroic operation."

TIES

The PFLP was a founding member of the Palestinian Liberation Organization. It has since split and re-formed an allegiance with the group.

In the 1970s, the PFLP worked with members of the Japanese Red Army (JRA) to carry out a hijacking of a Japan Airlines flight, a terror attack in Singapore, and a massacre at the Lod Airport in Tel Aviv that killed 26 and injured 80. JRA leader Shingenobu Fusako is known to have contacted the PFLP on numerous occasions, and helped produce a film with the group called *The PFLP and Red Army Declare World War* in 1971. The PFLP is also known to have associated with the Baader Meinhof organization, a left-wing militant group in Germany, in the 1970s.

FUNDING

The PFLP received financial support from the Soviet Union, and has received financial support from China. Syria and Libya have provided operational support and havens. It is believed that the PFLP's head-quarters is located in the Syrian capital of Damascus. The PFLP have sided with the Assad regime in Syria in the Syrian civil war, likely in exchange for the continued funding and arms provisions that Assad has provided the group throughout its history of violent attacks against Israel. However, Assad's interests lie in winning the civil war and main-taining control in Syria at seemingly endless costs. Various Palestinian groups have been pitted against each other over the course of the war, and an estimated 90,000 Palestinian refugees in Syria are caught in the middle of the conflicts between the militant groups in the region vying for power.

NOTES

[1] Popular Front for the Liberation of Palestine (PFLP) section on Jewish Virtual Library website. <http://www.jewishvirtuallibrary.org/jsource/Terrorism/pflp.html>.

SALAFIA JIHADIA

SALAFIA JIHADIA

Main Area(s) of Operation	Morocco, Spain
Known or Suspected Leader	Mohammed Fizazi
Approximate Year Founded	Late 1990s
Approximate Size	700+
Alliances & Cooperations	Moroccan Islamic Combatant Group, Al Qaeda
Ideological Sect/Affiliation	Salafism
Name Meaning	"Forefathers" or "First-Generation Fighters"

SALAFIA JIHADIA, or the "First Generation Fighters," is a network of smaller Salafist groups in Morocco, including Hijra Wattakfir, Attakfir Bidum Hijra, Assirat al Mustaqim, Ansar al Islam, and the Moroccan Afghans. The collective group's goals are to overthrow "impious" Arabic governments, including Morocco's, and counter other "corrupt" Arab governments through violent Jihad. Salafia Jihadia ideology also supports a violent jihad against Israel and the U.S. It is one of the largest terrorist groups in Morocco.

Salafia Jihadia is a decentralized collection of Moroccan fundamentalist groups affiliated by a common ideology. The Salafia Jihadia ideology is considered by some to be the most militant and uncompromising kind of Islamic fundamentalism. Salafia Jihadia cells spread ideological propaganda through the Internet, including jihadist forums and blogs, many of which include instructions on how to make improvised explosive devices (IEDs).

The group has an estimated 700 members.

FOUNDING

Salafia Jihadia was established in the late 1990s. Some believe the name was given by the Moroccan government to classify the network of Salafi groups that comprise the organization.

LEADERSHIP

Salafia Jihadia's leader is Mohamed Fizazi. He taught at the Al Quds Islamic center in Hamburg, Germany, and his talks were frequently attended by Mohammed Atta, an operational leader in the September 11 terrorist attacks in New York City.

VIOLENCE

Thirty-one Salafia Jihadia suicide bombers killed 45 people in Casablanca on May 16, 2003. The attack involved 14 simultaneous suicide bomb detonations, and was the largest terrorist attack in Moroccan history. The bombs were detonated in a Spanish club, an Israeli Alliance club, a Jewish cemetery, the Belgian consulate, and a hotel.

Salafia Jihadia publicly took responsibility for the coordinated bombings of crowded commuter trains in Madrid, Spain, in March 2004. The attack killed 191 people and injured 1,800. IEDs were smuggled onto public trains in 13 pieces of luggage. It was the largest terror attack to ever take place in Spain, known as the "11–M" incident.

A 2009 statement by the Moroccan government following the arrest of several Salafia Jihadia members indicates that the group was conspiring to commit further acts of 'instability'. Tapes released by Salafia Jihadia and seized by Moroccan authorities depict members calling for a continued violent jihad and executing partner terror group **AQIM**'s hostages.

A 2011 bombing by Salafia Jihadia in a restaurant in Marrakesh, Morocco, killed 15 and injured 20, mostly tourists.

TIES

Salafia Jihadia is an offshoot of the **Moroccan Islamic Combatant Group** (GICM). The two organizations worked together to execute the 2003 Casablanca attacks and the 2004 Madrid attacks.

According to a U.S. Senate Armed Services Committee hearing, Salafia Jihadia receives "operational help" from **Al Qaeda in the Islamic Maghreb**.

Jamal Zougam, a prominent member of **Al Qaeda**'s Spanish cell who was seen on the trains in Madrid in 2004 shortly before the bombings, shared a safe house with Salafia Jihadia members and met on occasion with Salafia Jihadia leader Mohamed Fizazi in 2001.

FUNDING

Salafia Jihadia's activities are supported through the criminal activities of its member groups, mainly gun and drug trafficking. **Al Qaeda in the Islamic Maghreb** has ties with many of these groups and is another likely source of substantial funding.

SIPAH-E-SAHABA PAKISTAN (SSP)

SIPAH-E-SAHABA PAKISTAN (SSP)

Main Area(s) of Operation	Pakistan
Founder or Spiritual Leader	Maulana Haq Nawaz Jhangvi, Maulana Zia-ur-Rehman Farooqi, Maulana Eesar-ul-Haq Qasmi, Maulana Azam Raiq
Known or Suspected Leader	Muhammad Ahmad Ludhianvi
Approximate Year Founded	1985
Approximate Size	2,000–10,000
Alliances & Cooperations	Jaish-e-Mohammed, Lashkar-e-Taiba, Harkat-ul-Mujahideen al-Islami, Islamic Movemebt of Uzbekistan, Al Qaeda
Ideological Sect/Affiliation	Deobandi, takfiri

SIPAH-E-SAHABA PAKISTAN (SSP) is a Sunni Deobandi militant Islamic group that targets primarily Shiite Muslims in Pakistan. According to SSP leader Azam Tariq, "If Islam is to be established in Pakistan, then Shias must be declared infidels."

SSP is a takfiri group. Any non-Sunni believers are considered enemies. SSP also has attacked Pakistani and Iranian government interests, Westerners and business professionals.

The group is believed to be associated with Ramzi Ahmed Yousuf, the extremist who was responsible for planning the 1993 World Trade Center bombing in New York City.

After SSP was formally banned in Pakistan in 2001, it was renamed the Millat-e-Islamia Party, and then switched to Ahle Sunnat Wal Jamaat. Size estimates of the group range from 2,000 to 10,000.

FOUNDING

SSP was founded in 1985 in the Punjab province of Pakistan by Maulana Haq Nawaz Jhangvi, Maulana Zia-ur-Rehman Farooqi, Maulana Eesar-ul-Haq Qasmi, and Maulana Azam Tariq. It was originally named Anjman-e-Sipah-Sahaba.

At its founding, many parts of Punjab and the region were controlled by large, wealthy landowning Shia. Additionally, the 1979 Iranian revolution was a Shiite-led Islamic political movement. SSP was created as a Sunni extremist response to Shia feudalism and Iranian counter-influences.

One cofounder and leader, Jhangvi, was a political figure in the Pakistani Deobandi party Jamaat Ulema-e-Islami (JUI). Many SSP leaders ran for public office in Pakistan as members of JUI. Other factions traveled to Afghanistan to aid and fight alongside the **Talban**.

On February 22, 1990, Jhangvi was assassinated outside of his home. In 1996, members of SSP unhappy with the group's divergence from Jhangvi's ideals split to form **Lashkar-e-Jhangvi**.

LEADERSHIP

After Jhangvi's assassination, leadership of SSP passed to cofounder Maulana Eesar-ul-Haq Qasmi (Eesar Qasmi). Like many other SSP members, he was involved in Punjab politics. He was elected to both the provincial assembly and the national Pakistani parliament. Qasmi was assassinated in January 1991, and leadership passed to cofounder Maulana Zia-ul-Rehman Farooqi, who helped expand the reach and influence of SSP from provincial to national prominence in Pakistan. From 1993 to 1996, Farooqi allied the SSP with the Pakistani People's Party, the party of then-Prime Minister Benazir Bhutto. During Farooqi's period of leadership, factionalization was rampant within SSP.

Farooqi was killed on January 18, 1997, by a motorcycle bomb, as he arrived at a Pakistani courthouse to stand trial for murder. Farooqi's second-in-command, Azam Tariq, was injured in the bombing but survived to become SSP's next leader. In retaliation, Tariq led the group to set fire to numerous Iranian cultural centers and assassinate 75 prominent Shia citizens.

Previously, Tariq had won election to Qasmi's vacated seat in Parliament in 1991 and used the position to institute anti-Shia legislation. After assuming leadership of SSP, he focused efforts on strengthening SSP's network with various regional terror groups, including **Al Qaeda**.

In 2001, Tariq was arrested by Pakistani authorities. He won reelection to the Pakistani Parliament from his jail cell in 2002 but was killed in a 2003 shootout allegedly executed by Shia militants. Leadership then passed to Ali Sher Hyderi until he was killed in 2009, and then to Muhammad Ahmad Ludhianvi, who is still one of the leaders.

In 2001, Pakistan formally banned Sipah-e-Sahaba, so leadership at this point is covert and includes many provincial senior members.

VIOLENCE

SSP massacred hundreds of Shias in Afghanistan in 1998 while fighting alongside the Taliban.

Most of its terrorist activities focus on worshippers at mosques operated by opposing Muslim sects, and prominent Shia figures. In 1994, SSP killed approximately 300 worshippers by indiscriminate gunfire aimed at crowds in mosques. A similar attack in 1998 on Shia mourners at a funeral service killed 27 and injured 34.

In 2001, SSP gunmen open-fired on worshippers in a Catholic church in Bahawalpur, Punjab, killing 18 and injuring nine. A 2002 mosque attack in Rawalpindi killed 11 and injured 14. In 2004, SSP launched grenades at a procession of Shias observing Ashura in the city of Quetta, killing 40 and injuring 150.

TIES

Lashkar-e-Jhangvi was created as an offshoot of SSP. Other, smaller groups formed as splinter groups are run by senior SSP officers, including Jhangvi Tigers, Al Haq Tigers, Tanzeemul Haq, Al Farooq, Al Badr Foundation, and Allah Akbar.

SSP maintains training facilities across Punjab and shares recruits with various terrorist cells and militant outfits. It has ties to **Jaish-e-Mohammad, Lashkar-e-Taiba, Harkat ul-Mujahideen**, the **Islamic Movement of Uzbekistan**, and **Al Qaeda**. Together with **LeJ**, SSP has been called "a mainstay of **Al Qaeda** planning in Pakistan." According to a statement made in 2000 by **Jaish-e-Muhammed** chief Maulana Masood Azhar, "Sipah-e-Sahaba stands shoulder to shoulder with **Jaish-e-Muhammed** in Jihad." By some analysts' accounts, the SSP, LeJ, and **JeM** constitute the "Punjab Taliban."

SSP recruits have trained at **Taliban**-operated camps in Khost, Afghanistan, formerly associated with Osama bin Laden.

A former chief commander of SSP, Yusuf Ludhianvi, was named supreme leader of the terror group **Jaish-e-Muhammed** until he was killed in 2000.

FUNDING

Like other similar Deobandi groups in the region, SSP received initial funding from the Pakistani government to operate madrassas around the nation. Madrassas in Pakistan numbered 17,000 in 2010, with more than 1 million students.

SSP has over 500 branch offices across Pakistan and 1 million associated workers. It runs welfare programs for its workers in Punjab.

The group has financial networks with Persian Gulf countries interested in containing Iranian influence, including Saudi Arabia and the UAE. It also participates in criminal activities to raise funds, including the narcotics trade.

THE TALIBAN

THE TALIBAN

Main Area(s) of Operation	Afghanistan
Founder or Spiritual Leader	Mullah Mohammed Omar
Known or Suspected Leader	Mullah Mohammed Omar
Approximate Year Founded	1994
Approximate Size	35,000 average
Alliances & Cooperations	Haqqani Network, Tehrik-i-Taliban Pakistan, Islamic Movement of Uzbekistan, Al Qaeda (mainly, but offers support to many)
Ideological Sect/Affiliation	Deobandi
Name Meaning	"Students"
Flag	

THE TALIBAN IS A MILITANT ISLAMIC organization that controlled Afghanistan from 1994 to 2001. During its rule, the group implemented "the strictest interpretation of Sharia law ever seen in the Muslim world."[1] While in power, the Taliban were criticized internationally for their cruel treatment of women and children, and for refusing aid and food offered from the international community for those Afghan citizens that the Taliban considered "unworthy."

The word "taliban" translates to "students" in the Pashtun dialect. The Pashtun are an ethnic tribe native to Afghanistan that had controlled Afghan politics for many years before the arrival of the Taliban. Many of the Taliban members are Pashtun. The group emerged around the leadership of Mullah Mohammed Omar, who traveled the country recruiting students to his cause and organizing a militia that would later dominate the country.

After U.S. efforts in Afghanistan beginning in 2001 ousted the Taliban from formal control, they fled to Pakistan, where they were able to operate, regroup, and rebuild. They currently operate from Pakistan, supporting other militant Islamic groups in campaigns of terror and further destabilizing the region.

The Taliban ideology is Deobandi, with influences from native Pashtun interpretations of Islam and Osama bin Laden's global jihadist agenda.

The group has around 35,000 members, based on the average of many estimates. It is believed to have 200 to 1,000 various leaders.

FOUNDING

Members of the Afghan mujahideen that had fought in the Soviet-Afghan war formed the Taliban in the early 1990s. Unlike other groups that carved out a position of political or militant opposition to the nations they operate within, the Taliban seized complete control of Afghanistan in 1994, after it overthrew Afghan president Najibullah. Najibullah's regime had been weakened by persistent conflict since the Soviet withdrawal from the country in 1989. According to Ahmed Rashid's work book *Taliban*:

> Afghanistan was in a state of virtual disintegration just before the Taliban emerged at the end of 1994. The country was divided into warlord fiefdoms and all the warlords had fought, switched sides, and fought again in a bewildering array of alliances, betrayals, and bloodshed.[2]

The Taliban capitalized on Afghanistan's exhausted and disorganized state and took control after organizing behind Omar. They instituted strict Sharia, closing down schools for girls, forbidding women from holding jobs or engaging in any type of recreational sport, and even destroying televisions in peoples' homes.

The Taliban are reluctant to participate in peace negotiations and diplomacy, because they shun politics and political parties as an un-Islamic practice. The group has stated that they intend to "recreate the time of the Prophet" in Afghanistan, referring to Mohammed, who lived approximately 1,400 years ago.

While the Taliban ruled Afghanistan from 1994 to 2001, no elections or political parties were allowed. Omar had complete and final veto power for any decision made in the country. Since the group's removal from power in 2001, some members have called for participation in the political process, specifically peace talks. Afghan president Hamid Karzai invited members of the Taliban and Al Qaeda to engage in peace negotiations, and to participate in the Afghan government to a limited degree. Omar consistently opposed any such engagement while he was alive.

Taliban propaganda tactics are targeted and effective. The group uses social media and modern news outlets to exploit the specific religious, social, and political needs of the various tribes in Afghanistan to gain favor and support.

While controlling Afghanistan, the Taliban banned all media except their own "Voice of Sharia" radio program and a few heavily controlled newspapers. Formal spokesmen were appointed by Omar, and because they have largely centralized control over the group's outreach, messaging is unified and effective. In local villages, the Taliban uses propaganda in mosques, schools, and clinics to gain recruits and undermine the efforts of the Afghanistan government. If a village does something disliked by the Taliban, residents are warned by "night letters," threatening messages dropped all over the village, to conform to the Taliban's wishes or face violent reprisal.

LEADERSHIP

From Ahmed Rashid's book *Taliban*, (published in 2010 while Omar was still alive):

> No leader in the world today is surrounded by as much secrecy and mystery as Mullah Mohammed Omar. Aged 39, he has never been photographed or met with Western diplomats and journalists.[3]

Mullah Mohammed Omar was the spiritual leader and highest commander in the Taliban. He presided over Taliban operations in southern Afghanistan. Under him sat the executive leadership council, known as the Quetta Shura Taliban, based out of Quetta, Pakistan. The **Haqqani Network** also takes part in organizing Taliban operations around the country.

Omar became prominent in Taliban circles as a fighter in the Soviet-Afghan war. He lost his right eye in battle in 1989. He was "chosen" among the other fighters to lead a militia against the tribal warlords who fought within the power vacuum in the country after the Soviets withdrew. He gathered widespread support from tribes across the country, and led the charge to overthrow the Afghan government, claiming the country as "the Islamic Emirate of Afghanistan." When the U.S. deposed Taliban rule in 2001, he fled. From his secluded base of operations, he continued to denounce the Afghan government and control Taliban military operations. While in hiding, he aided in assisting Osama bin Laden and other members of Al Qaeda to evade United States forces. Although it wasn't confirmed until 2015, Omar died while hiding in Afghanistan in 2013. There are reports of a possible assassination by splinter groups, but they are unconfirmed. Omar was succeeded by his deputy, (Mullah) Akhtar Mansour. Mansour was formerly the Civil Aviation Minister in the Taliban's Afghan government. Unlike Omar, Mansour lives and operates publicly, suggesting a favorable treatment, or at least a blind eye, from the Pakistani government. He is reported as a ruthless opportunist. He is pragmatic, and willing to engage in capitalistic trade (there are reports of him owning a cell phone company) and peace talks when to his benefit. By other accounts, he is also merciless. "[He is] the kind of person who doesn't care much about how destruction occurs....If he is told to destroy one road he will destroy 10, if he is told to kill one person, he will kill 100," reported fellow Taliban leader Salaam Alizai in a 2015 *New York Times* interview.[4] Mansour retains control of the group despite occasional challenges to the legitimacy of his ascension from within. He has presided over militant territorial victories against the Afghan government since taking over, most notably in northern Afghanistan.

VIOLENCE

The Taliban employs suicide bombings, improvised explosive devices (IEDs), armed assaults, grenade attacks, and kidnappings. It has a specialized assassinations unit, called the Jihad Kandahar, which it uses to influence the political landscape.

The group targets civilian aid workers in addition to security forces. In a well-known incident in 2008, the Taliban killed Gayle Williams, a U.K. aid worker and volunteer with the Christian organization Serve Afghanistan.

According to UN estimates, the Taliban was responsible for 76 percent of all civilian deaths in Afghanistan in 2009, 75 percent in 2010, and 80 percent in 2011. It uses civilian homes and town centers to hide snipers and militants. Many of the Taliban's suicide bombers are women. Since 2007, it has detonated IEDs at 15 all-female educational facilities.

In 2006, a suicide car bomber at the U.S. embassy killed 16 and injured 29. In 2007, a suicide bomber killed 23 and injured 12 outside of a compound where U.S. vice president Dick Cheney was visiting troops. In a 2011 offensive, the group organized seven separate suicide bombings, killing four civilians and injuring 40. A similar campaign in 2012 killed 15. Another attack in 2012 involved Taliban members open-firing on a crowd of tourists in a hotel in Kabul and taking many hostages. Eighteen were killed. In 2013, a suicide bomber outside of the Afghanistan Supreme Court building killed 17 and injured 40.

A 2013 report published by the United Nations Assistance Mission in Afghanistan estimated Taliban-related civilian deaths and injuries at 8,615, the highest number since it began recording such figures in 2009.

In 2014, the Afghan national elections resulted in a deadlock between two political entities, forcing the country to form a unity government comprised of the two different groups. Seizing on the divided leadership, the Taliban showed a militaristic resurgence in 2014 and 2015 that is proving to be a significant issue for the precarious functionality of the national Afghan government. In 2015 the group raided and captured the northern Afghanistan city of Kunduz, despite opposition from the Afghan Armed Forces.

TIES

The Afghanistan-based Taliban is a separate organization from the Pakistan-based **Tehrik-i-Taliban Pakistan (TTP)**. Both are composed of a majority of Pashtun members and share Deobandi ideology, although they differ in mission, strategy, and intended targets. However, "it is clear that there is much overlap in both the backgrounds of the militants recruited into fighting, as well as many aspects of the ideological background of both organizations."[5]

The Taliban is closely allied with the **Islamic Movement of Uzbekistan (IMU)**; the groups share recruits and bases of operations. The **IMU** provides the Taliban with arms, and in return the Taliban supplies financial aid. In 2001, 600 IMU members were provided to aid Taliban combat efforts. In a similar arrangement, the Taliban is aligned with the **Haqqani Network**, sharing troops and operational support.

The Taliban and **Al Qaeda** supported each other in the mid-1990s, but Omar worked to separate the Taliban from Osama bin Laden's influence. However, Omar and the Taliban provided shelter and refuge for Osama bin Laden and **Al Qaeda** during U.S. efforts in Afghanistan.

Reportedly, the Taliban claims to avoid killing Afghan civilians, although in practice this is far from the truth. **Al Qaeda** and **TTP** don't make this claim, and frame civilian deaths as acceptable, since they believe all civilians should either be fighting Western influence and the "illegitimate" government in Afghanistan or be killed in the process.

FUNDING

When the Taliban was founded, it was mostly against Soviet efforts in Afghanistan in the 1980s. At the time, the United States provided arms to the group to combat Soviet forces, under a buyback program whose terms were largely ignored by the Taliban. Additionally, the Pakistani government and the Pakistani ISI supported the group when it sought influence over Afghanistan and worked to control the country for nearly five years. Money, and training camp construction and maintenance, were provided by the ISI. Early training and recruitment gatherings were reportedly funded by Saudi Arabia.

When the Taliban no longer had the Soviet Union to contend with, they began the effort to self-finance. From 1996 to 1999 they controlled 96 percent of Afghanistan's agricultural lands dedicated to the harvest of poppies, and used heroin and opium profits to finance most of their activities. In 2007, a UN report estimated that 93 percent of the world's heroin came from Afghanistan. In addition to the drug trade, illegal mining activities earn the Taliban an estimated $400 million per year.

NOTES

[1] Rashid, Ahmed. *Taliban: Militant Islam, Oil and Fundamentalism in Central Asia*. New Haven, CT: Yale University Press, 2010.

[2] Ibid.

[3] Ibid.

[4] Goldstein, Joseph. "Taliban's New Leader Strengthens His Hold With Intrigue and Battlefield Victory." *The New York Times*. 4 Oct. 2015. <http://www.nytimes.com/2015/10/05/world/asia/kunduz-fall-validates-mullah-akhtar-muhammad-mansour-talibans-new-leader.html?_r=1>.

[5] The Taliban section in Mapping Militant Organizations on Stanford University website. 20 July 2014. <http://stanford.edu/group/mappingmilitants/cgi-bin/groups/view/367>.

TEHRIK-I-TALIBAN PAKISTAN (TTP)

TEHRIK-I-TALIBAN PAKISTAN (TTP)

Main Area(s) of Operation	Pakistan
Founder or Spiritual Leader	Baitullah Mehsud
Known or Suspected Leader	Maulana Fazlullah
Approximate Year Founded	2007
Approximate Size	20,000–50,000
Alliances & Cooperations	Taliban, Al Qaeda, Sipah-e-Sahaba Pakistan, Harkat-ul-Jihad al-Islami, Lashkar-e-Jhangvi
Enemies/Rivals	Lashkar-e-Taiba, Jaish-e-Muhammed
Ideological Sect/Affiliation	Deobandi
Name Meaning	"Taliban Movement of Pakistan"
Flag	

IMAGE BY ARNOLDPLATON (OWN WORK, BASED ON THIS IMAGE) [CC BY-SA 4.0 (HTTP://CREATIVECOMMONS.ORG/LICENSES/BY-SA/4.0)], VIA WIKIMEDIA COMMONS

TEHRIK-I-TALIBAN PAKISTAN (TTP), founded as an extension of the Taliban, is the largest (and perhaps most bloodthirsty) militant Islamic group in Pakistan. It was created to combine all of the cells of the unofficial "Pakistani Taliban," to impose Sharia across the nation, to wage jihad on the Pakistani Army, and to attack the United States and Britain. TTP's main targets have been Pakistani government interests and security forces, but the group has recently expanded operations to perform attacks internationally and against Pakistani civilians, including schoolchildren.

TTP is a Sunni Deobandi group. It is an independent entity from the Afghanistan-based **Taliban**, although it previously declared itself an extension of the larger Taliban movement. The Pakistani government suspects TTP involvement in the assassination of Pakistani prime minister Benazir Bhutto in 2007.

In January 2014, peace negotiations opened between the Pakistani government and TTP. TTP demanded the application of strict Islamic law, the release of TTP prisoners, and the removal of Pakistani security forces from the FATA region. They were halted within a month when TTP claimed responsibility for the beheadings of 23 Pakistani security personnel.

The group is estimated to have 20,000 to 50,000 members.

FOUNDING

TTP was founded on December 13, 2007, at a meeting of Pakistani tribal elders and senior militant commanders. Attendees represented 24 Pakistani districts, seven tribes, and six frontier regions. When the group was formed, it released a statement that indicated it was uniting Pakistani Taliban cells to organize synchronized attacks on Pakistani and NATO security forces.

Groups absorbed into TTP when it was formed include Tehrik-e-Islami, Islami Taliban, Jaish-e-Islami, and Al Hizb.

LEADERSHIP

TTP's first appointed emir was Baitullah Mehsud, who had previously pledged his allegiance to Afghanistan-based **Taliban** leader Mullah Omar. Mehsud's selection as commander and emir effectively declared TTP to be an extension of the Taliban.

TTP's senior leaders are also representatives from the tribes associated with the group's membership. The group recruits from the tribes and clans associated with them, often targeting young men through missions, mosques, and radio broadcasts.

According to Mehsud, TTP works to "impose Islamic law in Pakistan and the entire world, to fight imperial powers fighting against Muslims in Afghanistan and around the world, to fight disbelievers and to wage jihad against the Pakistani state and Pakistani Army."[1]

Since its founding, TTP has had a history of internal factions. Two of Mehsud's senior commanders, Hakimullah Mehsud and Waliur Rehman, led opposing movements within the group. In 2009, Baitullah Mehsud was killed in a U.S. drone strike, and the **Taliban** appointed Hakimullah Mehsud to replace him as emir, with Waliur Rehman as his deputy. Another drone strike in 2013 killed Hakimullah Mehsud. The tribal elements of TTP voted to replace Mehsud with Waliur Rehman, and then Khan Said after Rehman's death in 2013. The larger **Taliban**, however, appointed Maulana Fazlullah to lead the group instead of Said. A rift emerged between those in TTP with tribal alliances, and those with more radically ideological ties to the greater worldwide militant Islamic movement. In May 2014, Said and many tribal TTP members split and formed a separate group, which is now reportedly engaged in peace talks with the Pakistani government. Violent clashes have occurred between the factions, including one in 2014 that claimed the lives of 35 TTP members.

Maulana Fazlullah, now leader of TTP, is nicknamed "The Radio Mullah" for his regular radio broadcasts. His penchant for radio is derived from his previous work operating an illegal radio station calling for the implementation of Sharia. He has supported the destruction of shops that sell "sinful" goods, such as electronics, and has supported attacks on medical teams administering polio vaccinations. Fazlullah also supports the destruction of schools that are willing to educate girls. In 2012 he authorized the assassination attempt of activist Malala Yousafzai, who lived despite being shot in the face and would later receive the Nobel Peace Prize in 2014 for her work on behalf of women's rights.

VIOLENCE

TTP has been known to commit kidnappings, grenade and IED attacks, and bombings of civilian areas. It often posts videos of its attacks online to draw recruits.

TTP sent a suicide bomber to a Marriott hotel in Islamabad in 2008, who killed 57 people. In 2009, it committed three major attacks. In March, members dressed as police officers and infiltrated a Pakistani police academy, killing eight and injuring 95 new police recruits. In October, a suicide bomber attacked Pakistan Army headquarters and killed 14. And in December, a TTP suicide bomber attacked a U.S. CIA base in Khost, Afghanistan, killing nine and injuring eight. That attack was the second-largest attack on CIA personnel in history, and was facilitated with support from both the **Taliban** and **Al Qaeda**.

In 2010, TTP attacked two mosques in Lahore, Pakistan, killing 86 and injuring 120. During the same year, it bombed a political rally in Pakistan, killing 45. In 2011, TTP members drove a truck rigged with explosives into a Pakistani police station, killing six and injuring 30. In 2012, TTP gunmen attacked a Pakistani army camp, killing eight.

TTP claimed responsibility for a car bombing attempt in Times Square, New York, in 2010.

On December 16, 2014, nine armed members of TTP, robed in suicide vests, entered a public school in Peshawar, Pakistan. They massacred 132 schoolchildren and 10 teachers. During the eight-hour siege of the school, three soldiers were also killed. In one classroom, the group burned a teacher alive in front of the students. They entered other classrooms and shot children one by one. Children who tried to hide, or cried excessively, were killed by example. In an auditorium where an exam was being administered, a TTP militant burst through the door and fired on the children. Over 100 others were injured in the attack. Most of the children killed were between the ages of 12 and 16. In a 12-minute video released by the group following the attack, a TTP spokesman said the attack was retaliation for the government's detention and killing of TTP members, and threatened, "You will forget the Peshawar school attack when you face more deadly attacks."[2]

TIES
TTP leader Baitullah Mehsud has proclaimed formal allegiance to the Afghanistan-based **Taliban**. According to the Mapping Militant Orga-

nizations project, TTP emulates the Afghanistan **Taliban** in its mission and organization.

TTP maintains close ties with **Al Qaeda**. In an interview with Al Jazeera, Mehsud acknowledged that **Al Qaeda** played a role in the group's formation.

According to the U.S. State Department:

> TTP and **Al Qaeda** have a symbiotic relationship; TTP draws ideological guidance from **Al Qaeda**, while **Al Qaeda** relies on TTP safe havens in the Pashtun areas along the Afghan-Pakistani border. This mutual cooperation gives TTP access to both **Al Qaeda**'s global terrorist network and the operational experience of its members. Given the proximity of the two groups and the nature of their relationship, TTP is a force multiplier for **Al Qaeda**.[3]

TTP is also known to work in tandem with **Sipah-e-Sahaba Pakistan** and **Harkat-ul-Jihad al-Islami**. Although TTP has previously been at odds with **Lashkar-e-Jhangvi** in its mission, it is now known to cooperate with the group to facilitate international attacks.

Because of TTP's anti-Pakistani objectives, groups that have ties to the Pakistani ISI, including **Lashkar-e-Taiba** and **Jaish-e-Muhammed**, are considered rivals.

TTP is also known to be closely affiliated with political parties in Pakistan, including Jamaat-e-Ulema Islami Fazal-ur-Rehman (JUI-F). JUI-F frequently works on behalf of TTP in negotiations with the Pakistani government.

FUNDING

Funding for TTP initiatives has been provided by **Al Qaeda**. Allegedly, the group also receives funding from foreign intelligence agencies with the motive of destabilizing the Pakistani government.

TTP also uses extortion, kidnapping, and the drug trade to make money, and collects donations from sympathizers in Pakistan.

NOTES

[1] Tehreek-e-Taliban Islami Pakistan (TTIP / TTP) section on Terrorism Research and Analysis Consortium website. <http://www.trackingterrorism.org/group/tehreek-e-taliban-islami-pakistan-ttip-ttp>.

[2] Yusufzai, Mushtaq. "Taliban Chief Behind Pakistan School Massacre Promises More Attacks." NBC News. 16 Jan. 2015. <http://www.nbcnews.com/storyline/paki-stan-school-massacre/taliban-chief-behind-pakistan-school-massacre-promises-more-attacks-n280786>.

[3] Tehreek-e-Taliban Pakistan section in Mapping Militant Organizations on Stanford University website. 7 Aug. 2012. <http://stanford.edu/group/mappingmilitants/cgi-bin/groups/view/105>.

THE TUNISIAN COMBATANT GROUP (TCG)

THE TUNISIAN
COMBATANT GROUP (TCG)

Main Area(s) of Operation	Tunisia, cells in the Middle East and Western Europe
Founder or Spiritual Leader	Sayf Allah bin Hussayn, Tarek Ben Habib Maaroufi
Known or Suspected Leader	Sami ben Khermais Essid, Sayf Allah bin Hussayn, Tarek Ben Habib Maaroufi
Approximate Year Founded	2000
Approximate Size	Dozens to hundreds among multiple cells
Alliances & Cooperations	Al Qaeda, Armed Islamic Group of Algeria, Libyan Islamic Fighting Group
Ideological Sect/Affiliation	Salafist

THE TUNISIAN COMBATANT GROUP (TCG) is dedicated to forming an Islamic state in Tunisia. TCG cells operate in the Middle East and Western Europe. The TCG targets and attacks Western and, in particular, U.S. interests. The group is considered by many accounts to be a "loose" network of terrorists operating in tandem.

The TCG is part of the international Salafist movement.

FOUNDING

TCG was cofounded by Sayf Allah bin Hussayn and Tarek Ben Habib Maaroufi in 2000. It was an offshoot of the Tunisian Islamist movement, which was officially banned in Tunisia. The group consists mostly of Tunisian expatriates, members of the Tunisian diaspora community, living in Europe.

In 2001, Belgian authorities arrested Maaroufi following the group's assassination attempts in Afghanistan, and he was sentenced to six years in prison.

According to the U.S. Department of State, TCG cells that have not joined **Al Qaeda** in the Islamic Maghreb maintain operations in Western Europe.

LEADERSHIP

TCG maintains, in addition to its Tunisian base, large branches in Italy and Belgium. The Italian branch is led by Sami ben Khermais Essid. The Belgian branch is led by TCG cofounder Maaroufi.

VIOLENCE

In 2001, TCG was suspected of playing a role in attacks on U.S., Algerian, and Tunisian diplomatic missions in Rome, which were eventually foiled. The group provided falsified Belgian passports that aided the travel of two assassins in 2001 who successfully killed Ahmed Shah Massoud, leader of the Afghan Northern Alliance that resisted the **Taliban** in Afghanistan.

A 2002 TCG suicide bombing killed 20 in the el-Ghriba synagogue in Djerba, Tunisia.

Members of the coalition of terrorists that attacked the U.S. diplomatic embassy in Benghazi in 2011, killing U.S. ambassador J. Christopher Stevens and three others, had links to TCG.

TIES

TCG cofounder Maaroufi plays a senior role in the umbrella organization under which Maghreb terror groups are coalescing, called Ansar al-Sharia. Ansar al-Sharia has committed political assassinations, and in 2013 the Tunisian government confirmed the group is stockpiling large quantities of weapons to distribute to jihadists throughout the Maghreb. In September 2012, Ansar al-Sharia ransacked the U.S. embassy in Tunisia.

The TCG runs recruitment campaigns and traffics falsified documents for **Al Qaeda** and other groups in Afghanistan. It has ties to the

Salafist Group for Preaching and Combat, an offshoot of the **Armed Islamic Group of Algeria**.

By many reports, most of the TCG, the **Moroccan Islamic Combatant Group**, the **Armed Islamic Group of Algeria**, and the **Libyan Islamic Fighting Group** have amalgamated into **Al Qaeda in the Islamic Maghreb**.

FUNDING
Funding for the group is self-supplied through working to recruit and traffic false documents throughout Europe on behalf of other terrorist groups, including **Al Qaeda**.

EPILOGUE

AFTER THE 9/11 ATTACKS, common wisdom proclaimed that we were in a new kind of war that required a new strategy to defeat terrorist networks and the nations that support them.

We were so consumed by the supposed newness of militant Islam that we forgot America has faced it almost since its founding.

America's first encounter with Islamic holy war—jihad—was in 1785. In London, Thomas Jefferson and John Adams met with the ambassador of the Tripolitan pirates. When they asked why Tripoli was making war on a country that had done them no harm, one account has the Tripoli ambassador replying that "it was written in their Koran, that all nations which had not acknowledged the Prophet were sinners, whom it was the right and duty of the faithful to plunder and enslave; and that every [Muslim] who was slain in this warfare was sure to go to paradise."

Since then, we have never come to grips with the real basis of Islamic extremism. In that failure is the reason we have lost the wars in Iraq and Afghanistan despite our military's ability to overwhelm any enemy.

We have lost because we refuse to recognize that, at its heart, this is an ideological war. We cannot defeat Islamic extremism until we defeat its ideology, and we haven't yet attempted that.

Webster's dictionary defines "ideology" as "the integrated assertions, theories and aims that constitute a sociopolitical program." The mission and objectives held and sold by militant Islamic groups and extremists are precisely that. They prescribe every aspect of how people are allowed to live and govern themselves.

David Galula was a French officer who served in China at the time of Mao's communist insurgency. He also observed or fought against insurgencies in Greece, Vietnam, and Algeria. In 1964, he wrote the most important book on the subject, *Counterinsurgency Warfare: Theory and Practice*. In it, he explains the two points that made our failures in Iraq and Afghanistan inevitable.

First, Galula writes that the objective in any counterinsurgency war is the people, and thus political action remains foremost throughout such wars. Second, the insurgent—as we believed our enemies to be in post-Saddam Iraq and Afghanistan—has to offer a cause that the counterinsurgent cannot. They did: Islamic fundamentalism. Its ideology can take so powerful a hold over their societies that democracy and freedom—which some Muslim imams, sheiks, and other authority figures have declared were a substitute for Islam that invaders were trying to impose—could not possibly win in competition with their ideology.

If you read the memoirs of the Iraq and Afghanistan wars by George W. Bush, Richard Cheney, and Tony Blair, only Blair evidences any understanding that the ideological war is important.

The man who most clearly understood was Marine general Peter Pace, who served as chairman of the Joint Chiefs of Staff from 2005 to 2007.

In Pace's guidance to the Joint Chiefs of Staff, published right after he took the job, he wrote, "Our enemies are violent extremists who would deny us, and all mankind, the freedom to choose our own destiny. Finding this distributed, loosely networked enemy is the greatest challenge we face. We must find and defeat them in an environment where information, perception, and how and what we communicate are every bit as critical as the application of traditional kinetic effects."

Pace understood that what we say and write is just as important as how well we shoot. Because of our experiences in Iraq and Afghanistan, fighting the kinetic war without fighting the ideological war—Pace's argument—is no longer disputable. If we are ever going to defeat the terrorist networks and nations that support them, we have to defeat their ideology.

It is not at all clear that we are willing to do so.

In our last ideological war—the Cold War against Soviet communism—it became fashionable to criticize the West and its culture. Too many politicians, activists, and pundits chose to conflate healthy criticism of our own system of government with praise for our Soviet adversaries. They were willing to deny the horrific repressions, mass murders, and subjugation by force of other peoples.

The Soviet ideology was defeated by the facts. It became neither fashionable nor even polite to say, as Ronald Reagan and Margaret Thatcher did relentlessly, that Soviet enslavement of people was inferior to our freedoms. Their words made clear that Western freedom was objectively superior to Soviet oppression. That constant ideological pounding, coupled with the physical courage and intellectual mastery of Alexander Solzhenitsyn and Lech Walesa, won the ideological battle of the Cold War. We have to do the same in this war, and in the very same way.

The first step toward winning this ideological war is to recover confidence in our culture and its values. We have to cure the cultural malaise that has beset America and Western Europe. We have to both regain the courage to label oppression and extremism for what it is, and condemn it.

The next step is for us to speak out eagerly, strongly, and continuously. We must make a habit of comparisons between our constitutional system of government and the violence and hatred of human freedom required by Sharia and Islamic fundamentalist ideology. We can, and must, make it clear to the world that Sharia as a political system is bankrupt and an utter failure. If we speak the obvious truths about the failure of the nations that ascribe to hard-line Sharia to protect their peoples against that violence and oppression, they—like the Soviets before them—can have no answer.

Despite the best efforts of too many faux defenders of freedom, there are strong glimmers of hope.

The most important strategic statement in the ideological war has come not from any Western leader. On New Year's Day 2015, Egyptian president Abdel Fattah al-Sisi called for a "revolution" among Islam and said the whole world was waiting for it. Addressing a gathering of Islamic clerics, he said:

> It's inconceivable that the thinking that we hold most sacred should cause the entire Islamic world to be a source of anxiety, danger, killing and destruction for the rest of the world. Impossible!
>
> That thinking—I am not saying "religion" but "thinking"— that corpus of texts and ideas that we have made sacred over the centuries, to the point that departing from them has become almost impossible, is antagonizing the entire world. It's antagonizing the entire world!
>
> Is it possible that 1.6 billion people should want to kill the rest of the world's inhabitants—that is 7 billion—so that they themselves may live? Impossible!

It is essential that we understand that the religious revolution al-Sisi called for can only be brought about by Muslims themselves. But it is the duty of us all—the president, congressional leaders, and the media—to support al-Sisi and other like-minded revolutionaries in their statements and writings. Almost no one has.

Nearly six months before al-Sisi's remarks, a July 2014 editorial in *The Economist* entitled "The Tragedy of the Arabs" claimed that the Arabs are in a civilizational decline. It said the fruit of the "Arab spring" had rotted into new autocracy and war, and that "only the Arabs can reverse their civilizational decline."

Most important, the writer said that "Islam, or at least modern interpretations of it, is at the core of some of the Arabs' deepest troubles. The faith's claim, promoted by many of its leading lights, to combine spiritual and earthly authority, with no separation of mosque and state, has stunted the development of independent political institutions. A militant minority of Muslims are caught up in a search for legitimacy through even more fanatical interpretations of the Koran."

There is no excuse for us to lack the courage of *The Economist*. There is no need for us to apologize for our beliefs, our culture, or our values. If we fail to engage the enemy in the ideological war, we cannot win it. And if we do not, as General Pace argued, we cannot win the kinetic war. It is not a vital national security interest of the United States to free the Arab nations or Iran from the ideology of Sharia that enslaves them. But it is a vital national security interest of the United States to defend our system of government, our culture, and our values from those who would oppress us if they could.

In times of war, the president of the United States has to be the boldest spokesperson for freedom in the world. In the Cold War, Ronald Reagan and Margaret Thatcher stood fast and spoke clearly without fear of offending the enemy, because they knew that a war between ideologies cannot be fought with soft words and euphemisms.

What was true for the Cold War is no less true today. It's not enough to say that we fight tyranny. It is essential to say that we fight for what is right, and what is by any measure better than that which the enemy will ever deliver, to even its most loyal followers.

—JED BABBIN

GLOSSARY

ANSAR AL-SHARIA—Translates as "supporters of Sharia." The name has been adopted by various terror groups independently to emphasize a common ideology to support the establishment of an Islamic caliphate ruled under strict Sharia. The groups that have adopted the name are largely independent and have no common command structure. However, the Ansar al-Sharia trend indicates an acknowledgement of globally shared ideologies of militant Islamic groups, which is a significant development in the cohesion of international jihadist efforts. Currently, the name Ansar al-Sharia is used by groups in Yemen, Libya, Tunisia, Mali, Egypt, Mauritania, Morocco, and Syria.

BASHAR AL-ASSAD REGIME AND THE SYRIAN CIVIL WAR—The Syrian civil war began in early 2011 along with the Arab Spring protests. The conflict emerged from armed insurgent opposition against the harsh and violent Syrian regime led by Bashar al-Assad. Assad's regime has used chemical weapons, mass arrests, and beatings, among other violent tactics, to maintain control over the Syrian population and restrict freedom of speech and assembly. The conflict is ongoing, and the Syrian government now controls only approximately 30 to 40 percent of the country geographically. Other groups controlling substantial amounts of Syrian land as of 2015 include the Free Syrian Army (indigenous coalition of insurgents), the Kurds, the Islamic State, the al-Nusra Front, and Hezbollah.

CALIPHATE—An Islamic state government headed by a caliph, who is considered a Muslim political and religious successor to the prophet Mohammed.

CAUCASUS—The region around the Caucasus Mountains on the border of Europe and Asia. The Caucasus includes parts of Russia in the north, and the countries of Armenia, Azerbaijan, and Georgia and parts of Iran and Turkey in the south. The Caucasus region is one of the most ethnic and linguistically diverse regions in the world.

DARUL—An Islamic movement in Indonesia that calls for the creation of an Islamic caliphate there. The movement was founded in 1949 during the Indonesian National Revolution. Many Indonesian terrorist groups are part of the Darul Islam movement. "Darul" means "state."

DAWA (da'wah)—The act of proselytizing or preaching Islam, including engaging in dialogue and inviting others to prayer.

DEOBANDI—A Sunni Islamic movement that originated in India but has practitioners throughout Pakistan, Afghanistan, Bangladesh, and South Africa, as well as a strong following in the United Kingdom. Deobandi ideology promotes a strict adherence to one of four Sunni Islamic schools of law, or madhhabs. The movement is based on the work of Shah Waliullah Dehlvi, and the main Deobandi school, the Darul Uloom Deoband, is located in Deobandi, India.

EMIR (position)—A title bestowed upon a Muslim ruler.

EMIRATE—Lands and assets under the control of an emir, in a sovereign Muslim kingdom or state.

FATAH—A secular Palestinian political organization that is the largest represented group in the Palestinian Liberation Organization, a confederation of Palestinian political parties. Fatah was founded in 1965 by Yasser Arafat and is currently led by Mahmoud Abbas, who is also considered the second president of the State of Palestine. Fatah maintains political leadership and control over the West Bank territory.

FATA REGION OF PAKISTAN—Or the Federally Administered Tribal Areas of Pakistan, maintain semi-autonomy and include seven tribal agencies and six frontier regions. The region is in northern Pakistan along the border with Afghanistan. In its modern history, it has been used largely as a base of operations by militant Islamic groups to conduct operations without Pakistani government reprisal.

FATWA—An Islamic legal ruling or decree made by an Islamic authority (plural "fatawa").

FIRST INTIFADA—A Palestinian uprising against Israel that began with the signing of the Oslo Accords. It lasted from December 1987 to September 1993 and included Palestinian-led efforts to boycott Israel, as well as increased attacks against Israeli security forces.

FIRST, SECOND, AND THIRD INTIFADAS—"Intifada" is an Arabic word that translates as "shaking off" and refers to an uprising or a rebellion.

HADITH—A collection of teachings, sayings, and deeds that reflect Islamic teachings. Different Muslim sects differ regarding hadith authority in comparison to the Quran, and the compositions of hadith.

HEJAZ—A region that runs along the west coast of Saudi Arabia and the Red Sea. The Hejaz was historically an independent kingdom until it was incorporated into Saudi Arabia in 1925. It contains the majority of the country's population and the Islamic holy site Mecca.

IDF—The Israel Defense Forces, the combined ground, air, and naval forces of the Israeli military. They were formed in 1948 and are considered one of the most advanced military forces in the world. Israeli citizens, including women, must serve in the IDF for a period of time.

IED—An improvised explosive device is a bomb constructed and used in ways outside of conventional military usage. It is often composed of an improvised explosive agent combined with a unit housing various types of shrapnel to maximize damage and injury.

JAMMU & KASHMIR—A region contested by China, India, and Pakistan. It includes Ladakh and has two capitals: Srinagar (in summer) and Jammu (in winter). Previously an independent kingdom, the region was divided by the British in 1947 between India and Pakistan. Both countries continue to claim sovereignty over the portion of the region held by the other country. The region has semi-autonomous authority according to the constitution of India.

JIHAD—An Islamic term meaning "struggle" or "resistance." The term "jihad" occurs in the Quran 164 times. In most interpretations, it means an internal struggle for piety. Militant Islamists often interpret it to mean an offensive call to fight any who do not submit to the ways of Islam or do not believe in the Islamic God, Allah.

LEVANT—A region that includes Cyprus, parts of Turkey, Israel, Jordan, Lebanon, Syria, and the Palestinian territories. The term is used to reference the region typically in the context of ancient or medieval times, which included large populations of Jews, Muslims, and Christians.

MADRASSA—An Islamic religious school.

MAGHREB—A region in North Africa consisting of parts of Morocco, Algeria, Tunisia, Libya, Mauritania, Western Sahara, and the Atlas Mountains. The name "Maghreb" is derived from the Arabic word for "west," "maghrib." The region was conquered by Islamists in the seventh century.

MUJAHID/MUJAHIDEEN—A mujahid is a person engaged in Jihad (plural "mujahideen").

1996 FATWA—"Declaration of War Against the Americans Occupying the Land of the Two Holy Places." A statement denouncing American foreign policy in the Middle East.

1998 FATWA—A statement denouncing American foreign policy in the Middle East and the Jewish people as a whole. It was designed to impart legal authority to mujahideen killing Americans and Jews in jihad. The signatories included Osama bin Laden, Ayman al-Zawahiri (leader of the Islamic Jihad in Egypt), Ahmed Refai Taha, Mir Hamzah, and Fazul Rahman (leader of the Harkat ul-Jihad-e-Islami in Bangladesh). The group called itself The World Islamic Front for Jihad Against Jews and Crusaders.

OSAMA BIN LADEN'S FATAWA—Lengthy statements issued by Osama bin Laden in the late 1990s to advance his political agenda and promote the mission of Al Qaeda.

OSLO ACCORDS—Agreements signed between Israel and the Palestine Liberation Organization in 1993 and 1995 as part of a peace process that began as covert negotiations in Oslo, Norway. The accords acknowledged recognition of the PLO as the representative Palestinian political authority and recognition of the State of Israel by the PLO. They also granted the PLO limited governance of the Gaza Strip and West Bank, and addressed various other contested issues between the two entities.

PAKISTANI ISI—Or the Pakistani Inter-Services Intelligence agency, is the largest of three intelligence agencies that serve the government of Pakistan. It was founded in 1948. The ISI has a history of active involvement in Pakistani and international affairs, and of supporting various terror groups to achieve a political agenda.

PAKISTAN WAZIRISTAN OPERATION ZARB-E-AZB—An offensive led by the government of Pakistan in the FATA region and various districts along the Afghan border to counter growing militant Islamic operations.

The initiative was launched in June 2014 after the attack by Tehrik-i-Taliban Pakistan and the Islamic Movement of Uzbekistan on Jinnah International Airport in Karachi. Pakistan has committed as many as 30,000 troops to the offensive to date.

SALAFIST—A fundamentalist doctrine of Islam that has ideological roots in Wahhabism, but developed in the late 19th century as a reaction to globalization and the spread of European and Western ideas. Salafists interpret the Quran literally and encourage global jihad. The Salafist movement is regarded by some scholars as the fastest-growing Islamic movement in the world.

SECOND INTIFADA—A second Palestinian uprising that lasted from September 2000 to February 2005. It began after Israeli prime minister Ariel Sharon visited the Temple Mount, a Jewish and Muslim holy site. The period was marked by increased violence and attacks on Israeli security forces and civilians. After this intifada, Israel constructed a wall around the West Bank (which reduced violent attacks) and withdrew from the Gaza Strip.

SHARIA—An Islamic political agenda, touted as a "body of law," that regulates life under Islamic interpretation. It addresses politics, economics, banking, law, sexuality, and social issues. Hard-line interpretations dictate a theocracy and legitimize jihad against any non-Islamic entity, including forced conversions by violent means. It allows for slavery, includes harsh restrictions for the daily lives of women, allows for the betrothal of prepubescent girls, and encourages violent beatings and executions for blasphemous activities, gambling, drinking, fornication, homosexuality, petty and major crimes, and adultery.

SHIA AND SUNNI—Sunni and Shia are the two main sects of Islam, with Sunni having the dominant following, approximately 85 percent of the world's Islamic population. The divide between the two sects reflects a historic dispute over the rightful successor to the prophet Mohammed upon his death in A.D. 632. Since Muhammad was a caliph, the divide over his successor was largely political. The Sunnis believe that the father of Muhammad's wife Aisha is the rightful heir, while the Shia believe the next in line was his cousin and son-in-law Ali Ibn Talib. A number of wars following the succession split exaggerated the polarity between the groups. The groups have since developed a number of different political and religious ideals, including interpretations about the end of the world and the powers and role of Islamic leaders.

SOVIET-AFGHAN WAR—Fought between the Soviet Union and an internationally backed insurgency in Afghanistan from December 1979 to February 1989. The insurgents consisted of mujahideen from various countries in the Middle East, Southeast Asia, and beyond. The insurgents were backed financially by Western countries interested in defeating the Soviet Union, including the U.S., the United Kingdom, and Saudi Arabia. The Afghan PDPA government was largely defeated early in the war, so the majority of the conflict was fought by international mujahideen recruits. In 1987 the Soviet Union began to withdraw troops, and the war ended two years later. The conflict took an estimated 850,000 to 1.5 million lives.

TAKFIRI—A Muslim who accuses another Muslim of impiety, disobedience to Islam, or apostasy. "Takfir" is derived from the Arabic word for "infidel."

THIRD INTIFADA—A third Palestinian uprising that began in 2014 and is marked by increased violent attacks in Jerusalem and the Hamas government's calling for a "day of rage" against Israel. It is also called the "Silent Intifada." The Third Intifada is ongoing, having manifested in lasting anti-Israeli propaganda movements such as the Boycott, Divest, and Sanction (BDS) effort.

U.S. FOREIGN TERRORIST ORGANIZATIONS LIST—The official list by which the United States State Department designates foreign entities as terrorist organizations involved in terrorist activities. Most of it names militant Islamic groups, separatist groups, and militant Marxist groups.

WAHHABISM—A fundamentalist sect of Sunni Islam, in which believers seek to return Islamic practices to those at the time of the first three generations of Sunni Muslims, known as the Salaf. It includes strict and literal interpretations of the Quran; hard-line opposition to the Shiite and Sufi Islamic doctrines, as well to as any other religion; and a rejection of any modern interpretation of Islamic texts. The doctrine is named after Muhammad ibn Abd al-Wahhab, who lived and taught in the 18th century.

XINJIANG PROVINCE—A large territory in western China that borders eight countries, including Afghanistan and Pakistan. It has a very low population density and is populated mostly by indigenous Uighurs. Originally called East Turkestan, it was a territory independent of China but a protectorate of it, until the Qing Dynasty incorporated it as the Xinjiang province (officially recognized later in 1884). The region was home to both Russians and Chinese, and the ethnic tensions played into a series of Sino-Soviet power plays in the region. Eventually, the Russians conceded the territory to China, but conflict among the various ethnic groups there remains.

BIBLIOGRAPHY

INTRODUCTION

"From Sydney to Rome, until Islam Rules the World." Ynetnews.com.
16 Dec. 2014.

ABDULLAH AZZAM BRIGADES

Abdullah Azzam Brigades (AAB) section on Terrorism Research and
Analysis Consortium website. <http://www.trackingterrorism.org/
group/abdullah-azzam-brigades-aab>.

Abdullah Azzam Brigades section on GlobalSecurity.com. <http://
www.globalsecurity.org/military/world/para/aab.htm>.

"Profile: Abdullah Azzam Brigades." BBC. 19 Nov. 2013. <http://
www.bbc.com/news/world-middle-east-25005417>.

"Terrorist Designations of the Abdallah Azzam Brigades." U.S. Department of State. 24 May 2012. <http://www.state.gov/r/pa/prs/ps/
2012/05/190810.htm>.

Adaki, Oren. "Abdullah Azzam Brigades Launches Rocket Attacks
from Gaza." Threat Matrix blog on *The Long War Journal* website.
15 July 2014. <http://www.longwarjournal.org/archives/2014/07/
abdullah_azzam_brigades_launch.php?a_aid=3598aabf>.

Baker, Aryn. "The Abdullah Azzam Brigades: Behind the Terrorist
Group That Bombed Iran's Beirut Embassy." *Time.* 20 Nov. 2013.
<http://world.time.com/2013/11/20/the-abdullah-azzam-brigades-
behind-the-group-that-bombed-irans-beirut-embassy/>.

ABU SAYYAF

Abu Sayyaf Group (ASG) entry on The National Counterterrorism
Center website. <http://www.nctc.gov/site/groups/asg.html>.

Abu Sayyaf Group (Philippines, Islamist Separatists). Backgrounder section on Council on Foreign Relations Backgrounders website. 27 May 2009. <http://www.cfr.org/philippines/abu-sayyaf-group-philippines-islamist-separatists/p9235>.

Abu Sayyaf Group section on Australian government website. 12 July 2013. <http://www.nationalsecurity.gov.au/Listedterroristorganisations/Pages/AbuSayyafGroup.aspx>.

"Swiss Hostages [sic] Escapes Abu Sayyaf Captors in Philippines." BBC. 6 Dec. 2014. <http://www.bbc.com/news/world-asia-30358073>.

Dominguez, Gabriel. "Abu Sayyaf 'Seeking Global Attention' with Hostage Kill Threat." Deutsche Welle. 25 Sept. 2014. <http://www.dw.de/abu-sayyaf-seeking-global-attention-with-hostage-kill-threat/a-17954921>.

Romero, Alexis. "Abu Sayyaf Strengthens in 2014." *The Philippine Star*. 30 Dec. 2014. <http://www.philstar.com/headlines/2014/12/30/1407911/abu-sayyaf-strengthens-2014>.

ADEN-ABYAN ISLAMIC ARMY

Aden-Abyan Islamic Army section on GlobalSecurity.org. <http://www.globalsecurity.org/military/world/para/aden-abyan.htm>.

Aden-Abyan Islamic Army section on Terrorism Research and Analysis Consortium website. <http://www.trackingterrorism.org/group/aden-abyan-islamic-army>.

Al Qaeda in Yemen section in Mapping Militant Organizations on Stanford University website. 8 July 2015. <http://stanford.edu/group/mappingmilitants/cgi-bin/groups/view/23>.

"Al-Qaeda Usurps Yemen's Aden-Abyan Army." *Terrorism Monitor* 8.41 (2010). The Jamestown Foundation. <http://www.jamestown.org/programs/tm/single/?tx_ttnews[tt_news]=37162&cHash=59f68d9779#.VN_yivnF9ds>.

"Islamic Army of Aden." Australian Security Intelligence Operation, 27 Mar. 2007. <www.aphref.aph.gov.au-house-committee-pjcis-grouped-iaa.pdf>.

"Islamic Army of Aden." FAS Intelligence Resource Program. 28 May 2004. <http://fas.org/irp/world/para/iaa.htm>.

Carapico, Sheila. "Yemen and the Aden-Abyan Islamic Army." Middle East Research and Information Project. 18 Oct. 2000. <http://

www.merip.org/mero/mero101800?ip_login_no_cache=d5e7237e3
729463ff3fea0537e85d431>.

Johnsen, Gregory D. "The Resiliency of Yemen's Aden-
Abyan Islamic Army." *Terrorism Monitor*. The Jamestown
Foundation. 13 July 2006. <http://www.jamestown.org/
programs/tm/single/?tx_ttnews%5Btt_news%5D=838&tx_
ttnews%5BbackPid%5D=181&no_cache=1#.VPU0YvnF98E>.

Sallam, Mohamed Bin. "Yemen Caught Between Ansar Allah and
Ansar Al-Shariah." *Yemen Times*. 5 Apr. 2012. <http://www.
yementimes.com/en/1561/report/678/Yemen-caught-between-
Ansar-Allah-and-Ansar-Al-Shariah.htm>.

Swift, Christopher. "Arc of Convergence: AQAP, Ansar Al-Shari'a and
the Struggle for Yemen." Combating Terrorism Center. 21 June
2012. <https://www.ctc.usma.edu/posts/arc-of-convergence-aqap-
ansar-al-sharia-and-the-struggle-for-yemen>.

AL-AQSA MARTYRS BRIGADE

Al Aqsa Martyrs Brigade (AAMB) section on *Terrorism Research and
Analysis Consortium* website. <http://www.trackingterrorism.org/
group/al-aqsa-martyrs-brigade-aamb>.

Al-Aqsa Martyrs Brigade section on The National Counterterrorism
Center website. <http://www.nctc.gov/site/groups/al_aqsa.html>.

Al Aqsa Martyrs Brigades section on *Anti-Defamation League* website.
<http://archive.adl.org/terrorism/symbols/al_aqsa_martyrs_2.html>.

Fletcher, Holly. "Al-Aqsa Martyrs Brigade." Backgrounder section on
Council on Foreign Relations website. 2 Apr. 2008. <http://www.
cfr.org/israel/al-aqsa-martyrs-brigade/p9127>.

Halevi, Jonathan D. "The Al-Aqsa Martyrs Brigades, the Military
Wing of Fatah, Is Officially Returning to Armed Struggle and Terror." Jerusalem Center for Public Affairs. <http://jcpa.org/al-aqsa-
martyrs-brigades-military-wing-fatah/>.

AL QAEDA

Al Qaeda section in *World Almanac of Islam*. The American Foreign Policy Council. 13 Oct. 2014. <http://almanac.afpc.org/al-
qaeda>.

Al Qaeda section on Counter Extremism Project website. <http://
www.counterextremism.com/threat/al-qaeda>.

"The American Face of Foreign Terror Recruits." Anti-Defamation League. 5 Sept. 2014. <http://blog.adl.org/extremism/american-recruits-to-terror-abroad-isis>.

"Osama Bin Laden." *The Economist*. 5 May 2011. <http://www.economist.com/node/18648254>.

Bajoria, Jayshree, and Greg Bruno. Al-Qaeda section on Council on Foreign Relations website. 6 June 2012. <http://www.cfr.org/terrorist-organizations-and-networks/al-qaeda-k-al-qaida-al-qaida/p9126>.

Bergen, Peter, and Jennifer Rowland. "Al Qaeda Controls More Territory than Ever in Middle East." CNN. N.p., 8 Jan. 2014. Web. <http://edition.cnn.com/2014/01/07/opinion/bergen-al-qaeda-terrority-gains/>.

Byman, Daniel L. "The History of Al Qaeda." Brookings. 1 Sept. 2011. <http://www.brookings.edu/research/opinions/2011/09/01-al-qaeda-history-byman>.

Farrall, Leah. "How Al Qaeda Works." Foreign Affairs. 16 Sept. 2011. <https://www.foreignaffairs.com/articles/south-asia/2011-02-20/how-al-qaeda-works>.

Katzman, Kenneth. "Al Qaeda: Profile Threat and Assessment" report. The Congressional Research Service, 17 Aug. 2005.

McCormick, Ty. "Al Qaeda Core: A Short History." Foreign Policy. 17 Mar. 2014. <http://foreignpolicy.com/2014/03/17/al-qaeda-core-a-short-history/>.

Musharbash, Yassin. "Surprising Study on Terrorism: Al-Qaida Kills Eight Times More Muslims Than Non-Muslims." Spiegel Online International. 3 Dec. 2009. <http://www.spiegel.de/international/world/surprising-study-on-terrorism-al-qaida-kills-eight-times-more-muslims-than-non-muslims-a-660619.html>.

Whitlock, Craig, and Munir Ladaa. "Mustafa Abu Al-Yazid, Liaison to Taliban Nationality: Egyptian." *The Washington Post*. <http://www.washingtonpost.com/wp-srv/world/specials/terror/yazid.html>.

AL-SHABAAB

"Al Shabaab Leadership Profiles." AEI Critical Threats. <http://www.criticalthreats.org/somalia/al-shabaab-leadership>.

Al-Shabaab section on Australian government website. <http://www.nationalsecurity.gov.au/Listedterroristorganisations/Pages/Al-Shabaab.aspx>.

Al-Shabaab. section on National Counterterrorism Center website. <http://www.nctc.gov/site/groups/al_shabaab.html>.

Iaccino, Ludovica. "Who Is Sheikh Ahmed Umar, Al-Shabaab's Ruthless New Leader?" International Business Times. 8 Sept. 2014. <http://www.ibtimes.co.uk/who-sheikh-ahmed-umar-al-shabaabs-ruthless-new-leader-1464553>.

Masters, Jonathan, and Mohammed Aly Sergie. Al-Shabab section on Council on Foreign Relations website. 13 Mar. 2015. <http://www.cfr.org/somalia/al-shabab/p18650>.

"Who Are Somalia's Al-Shabab?" BBC. 3 Apr. 2015. <http://www.bbc.com/news/world-africa-15336689>.

ANSAR DINE

Ansar Al Din ("Defenders of the Faith") section on GlobalSecurity.org. <http://www.globalsecurity.org/military/world/para/ansar-al-din.htm>.

Ansar Dine section on Terrorism Research and Analysis Consortium website. <http://www.trackingterrorism.org/group/ansar-dine>.

"Mali Crisis: Key Players." BBC. 12 Mar. 2013. <http://www.bbc.com/news/world-africa-17582909>.

"Terrorist Designations of Ansar Al-Dine" media note from the Office of The Spokesperson, U.S. Department of State. 21 Mar. 2013. <http://www.state.gov/r/pa/prs/ps/2013/03/206493.htm>.

Lambert, Michael, and Jason Warner. "Who Is Ansar Dine?" Global Public Square. 14 Aug. 2012. <http://globalpublicsquare.blogs.cnn.com/2012/08/14/who-are-ansar-dine/>.

Sandner, Philipp. "Ansar Dine: Radical Islamists in Northern Mali." Deutsche Welle. 18 Dec. 2014. <http://www.dw.de/ansar-dine-radical-islamists-in-northern-mali/a-18139091>.

ARMED ISLAMIC GROUP OF ALGERIA

Armed Islamic Group (GIA) report by the U.S. Department of State, on The Investigative Project on Terrorism website. 30 Apr. 2006.

<http://www.investigativeproject.org/profile/126/armed-islamic-group-gia>.

Armed Islamic Group (GIA) report. Parliament of Australia House of Representatives. <http://www.aph.gov.au/parliamentary_business/committees/house_of_representatives_committees?url=pjcis/asg_jua_gia_gspc/gia.pdf>.

Armed Islamic Group (GIA) section on Terrorism Research and Analysis Consortium website. <http://www.trackingterrorism.org/group/armed-islamic-group-gia>.

Armed Islamic Group (GIA) section on Terrorism Watch and Warning website. 26 Apr. 2014. <http://www.terrorism.com/2014/04/26/armed-islamic-group-gia/>.

GIA (Armed Islamic Group) section on *MEDEA* (European Institute for Research on Mediterranean and Euro-Arab Cooperation) website. <http://www.medea.be/en/countries/algeria/gia-armed-islamic-group/>.

Pflanz, Mike, Nairobi Laing, and Aislinn Laing. "Kenya Attack: 147 Dead as Islamist Gunmen Target Christian Students." *The Telegraph*. 2 Apr. 2015. <http://www.telegraph.co.uk/news/worldnews/africaandindianocean/kenya/11513626/Kenya-attack-147-dead-as-Islamist-gunmen-target-Christian-students.html>.

Pike, John. Armed Islamic Group (GIA) section on FAS Intelligence Resource Program website. 30 Apr. 2004. <http://fas.org/irp/world/para/gia.htm>.

Vriens, Lauren. Armed Islamic Group (Algeria, Islamists). Backgrounder section on Council on Foreign Relations website. 27 May 2009. <http://www.cfr.org/algeria/armed-islamic-group-algeria-islamists/p9154>.

BOKO HARAM

"50 Killed in Explosion at Nigerian Market." Fox News Latino. 11 Aug. 2015. <http://latino.foxnews.com/latino/news/2015/08/11/50-killed-in-explosion-at-nigerian-market/>.

"Boko Haram Chief Voices Support for IS, Claims Deadly Attacks in New Video." RT. 13 July 2014. <http://rt.com/news/172452-boko-haram-support-is/>.

"Boko Haram Claims Responsibility for Bomb Blasts in Bauchi, Maiduguri." Vanguard. 1 June 2011. <http://www.vanguardngr.com/2011/06/boko-haram-claims-responsibility-for-bomb-blasts-in-bauchi-maiduguri/>.

"Boko Haram Leader, Believed Dead, Appears in New Video." United Press International. 25 Sept. 2013. <http://www.upi.com/Top_News/World-News/2013/09/25/Boko-Haram-leader-believed-dead-appears-in-new-video/UPI-16641380144687>.

"Boko Haram, Not ISIS, Is World's Deadliest, Study Finds." CBS News. 18 Nov. 2015. <http://www.cbsnews.com/news/boko-haram-isis-worlds-deadliest-terrorist-group-study/>.

"Girl, 13, Blows Herself up near Mosque in Suspected Boko Haram Attack." *The Guardian*. 6 July 2015. <http://www.theguardian.com/world/2015/jul/06/girl-13-blows-herself-up-near-mosque-in-suspected-boko-haram-attack>.

"Nigeria and Neighbours Hold Talks on Boko Haram's Rapid Advance." *The Guardian*. 3 Sept. 2014. <http://www.theguardian.com/world/2014/sep/03/nigeria-talks-boko-haram-advance>.

"Nigeria Army Rescues Nearly 300 Females from Boko Haram." Al Jazeera. 29 Apr. 2015. <http://www.aljazeera.com/news/2015/04/nigerian-army-rescues-200-girls-boko-haram-camps-150428195337887.html>.

"Nigeria Blast: Yola Market Explosion Kills 30." BBC. 18 Nov. 2015. <http://www.bbc.com/news/world-africa-34852971>.

"Nigeria Rescues 178 People from Boko Haram." Al Jazeera. 3 Aug. 2015. <http://www.aljazeera.com/news/2015/08/nigeria-rescues-178-people-boko-haram-150803023932607.html>.

Abubakar, Aminu, and Faith Karimi. "2,000 Feared Killed in 'Deadliest' Boko Haram Attack in Nigeria." CNN. 12 Jan. 2015. <http://www.cnn.com/2015/01/09/africa/boko-haram-violence/>.

Boyle, Joe. "Nigeria's 'Taliban' Enigma." BBC. 31 July 2009. <http://news.bbc.co.uk/2/hi/africa/8172270.stm>.

Chothia, Farouk. "Who Are Nigeria's Boko Haram Islamists?" BBC African Service. 11 Jan. 2012. <http://cfec.typepad.com/files/article---boko-haram-background---1-11-12---bbc.pdf>.

Cook, David. "Boko Haram: A Prognosis." James A. Baker III Institute for Public Policy at Rice University, 16 Dec. 2011. <https://bakerinstitute.org/files/735/>.

Cook, David. "The Rise of Boko Haram in Nigeria." Combating Terrorism Center at West Point. 26 Sept. 2011. <https://www.ctc.usma.edu/posts/the-rise-of-boko-haram-in-nigeria>.

Culzac, Natasha. "Boko Haram Releases 27 Hostages Including Deputy PM's Wife, Cameroon Says." *Independent*. 11 Oct. 2014. <http://www.independent.co.uk/news/world/africa/boko-haram-releases-27-hostages-including-deputy-pms-wife-cameroon-says-9788845.html>.

Dixon, Robyn. "Year After Schoolgirls Taken, Report Catalogs Boko Haram Atrocities." *Los Angeles Times*. 12 May 2014. <http://www.latimes.com/world/africa/la-fg-nigeria-boko-haram-20150414-story.html#page=1>.

Forest, James J.F. "Confronting the Terrorism of Boko Haram in Nigeria." Joint Special Operations University. May 2012. <http://jsou.socom.mil/Documents/12-5_Forest_053112_FINAL.pdf>.

Jacinto, Leela. "The Boko Haram Terror Chief Who Came Back from the Dead." France 24. 25 Sept. 2014. <http://www.france24.com/en/20120111-terror-chief-boko-haram-imam-shekau-youtube-nigeria-goodluck-jonathan-al-qaeda-oil>.

Kumar, Anugrah. "Nigeria's Boko Haram Violence Killed as Many People as ISIS in Iraq, New Figures Say." *The Christian Post*. 13 Dec. 2014. <http://www.christianpost.com/news/nigerias-boko-haram-violence-killed-as-many-people-as-isis-in-iraq-new-figures-say-131151/>.

McCoy, Terrence. "This Is How Boko Haram Funds Its Evil." *The Washington Post*. 6 June 2014. <http://www.washingtonpost.com/news/morning-mix/wp/2014/06/06/this-is-how-boko-haram-funds-its-evil/>.

Misketi, Nicholas. "Boko Haram: Nigerian Militant Group's Attacks on the Rise." CBC News. 16 Jan. 2015. <http://www.cbc.ca/news/world/boko-haram-nigerian-militant-group-s-attacks-on-the-rise-1.2912678>.

Nikala, Oscar. "Nigeria Tops World Terror Attack Fatality List." *Defence*. 29 July 2014. <http://www.defenceco.za/index.

php?option=com_content&view=article&id=35643:nigeria-tops-
world-terror-attack-fatality-list&catid=49:National%20Security&
Itemid=115>.

Onouh, Felix. "Nigeria Islamists Better Armed, Motivated
than Army: Governor." Reuters. 17 Feb. 2014. <http://www.
reuters.com/article/2014/02/17/us-nigeria-violence-idUS-
BREA1G1AO20140217>.

Sergie, Mohammed Aly, and Toni Johnson. Boko Haram section on
Council on Foreign Relations website. 5 Mar. 2015. <http://www.
cfr.org/nigeria/boko-haram/p25739>.

Walker, Andrew. "What Is Boko Haram?" *Special Report*. United
States Institute of Peace. 2012. <http://www.xtome.org/docs/
groups/boko-haram/SR308.pdf>.

CAUCASUS EMIRATES

Caucasus Emirate section in Mapping Militant Organizations on
Stanford University website. 11 Apr. 2014. <http://stanford.edu/
group/mappingmilitants/cgi-bin/groups/view/255>.

Caucasus Emirate (CE) section on GlobalSecurity.org. <http://www.
globalsecurity.org/military/world/para/ik.htm>.

Central Asian Terrorism section on The National Counterterrorism
Center website. <http://www.nctc.gov/site/groups/cent_eurasian.
html>.

Caucasus Emirate (CE) section on Terrorism Research and Analysis Consortium website. <http://www.trackingterrorism.org/group/
caucasus-emirate-ce>.

Hahn, Gordon M. "Caucasus Emirate Is a Growing Threat to Russia."
The Moscow Times. 14 Dec. 2014. <http://www.themoscowtimes.
com/opinion/article/caucasus-emirate-is-a-growing-threat-to-
russia/513275.html>.

Joscelyn, Thomas. "New Leader of Islamic Caucasus Emirate Killed
by Russian Forces." The Long War Journal. 11 Aug. 2015. <http://
www.longwarjournal.org/archives/2015/08/new-leader-of-islamic-
caucasus-emirate-killed-by-russian-forces.php>.

Joscelyn, Thomas. "The Unknown in the Boston Bombing." *The
Weekly Standard*. 27 Mar. 2014. <http://www.weeklystandard.com/
blogs/unknown-boston-bombings_786126.html>.

EAST TURKESTAN ISLAMIC MOVEMENT

"China Blames East Turkestan Islamic Movement for Beijing Attack." *The Guardian.* 1 Nov. 2013. <http://www.theguardian.com/world/2013/nov/01/china-blames-east-turkestan-islamic-movement-beijing-attack>.

Eastern Turkistan Islamic Movement (ETIM) section on Terrorism Research and Analysis Consortium website. <http://www.trackingterrorism.org/group/eastern-turkistan-islamic-movement-etim>.

"What Is the East Turkestan Islamic Movement?" *Voice of America.* 3 Aug. 2011. <http://www.voanews.com/content/what-is-the-east-turkestan-islamic-movement-126763973/167829.html>.

Acharya, Arabinda, Rohan Gunaratna, and Wang Pengxin. *Ethnic Identity and National Conflict in China.* Palgrave Macmillan, 2010.

Xu, Beina, Holly Fletcher, and Jayshree Bajoria. The East Turkestan Islamic Movement (ETIM). Backgrounder section on Council on Foreign Relations website. 4 Sept. 2014. <http://www.cfr.org/china/east-turkestan-islamic-movement-etim/p9179>.

EGYPTIAN ISLAMIC JIHAD

Al Jihad (Egyptian Islamic Jihad) section on Terrorism Watch and Warning website. 26 Apr. 2014. <http://www.terrorism.com/2014/04/26/al-jihad-egyptian-islamic-jihad/>.

Egyptian Islamic Jihad (EIJ) section on Terrorism Research and Analysis Consortium website. <http://www.trackingterrorism.org/group/egyptian-islamic-jihad-eij>.

Egyptian Islamic Jihad section in *Encyclopedia of the Middle East.* <http://www.mideastorg/Middle-East-Encyclopedia/egyptian_islamic_jihad.htm>.

Egyptian Islamic Jihad section in Investigating Terror Organisations on BBC website. <http://news.bbc.co.uk/hi/english/static/in_depth/world/2001/war_on_terror/investigation_on_terror/organisation_2.stm>.

Egyptian Islamic Jihad section in Mapping Militant Organizations on Stanford University website. 26 Oct. 2015. <http://stanford.edu/group/mappingmilitants/cgi-bin/groups/view/401>.

Fletcher, Holly. Egyptian Islamic Jihad. Backgrounder section on Council on Foreign Relations website. 30 May 2008. <http://www.cfr.org/egypt/egyptian-islamic-jihad/p16376>.

GREAT EASTERN ISLAMIC RAIDERS' FRONT

"After Meeting Erdogan, Militant Islamist Leader Complains of 'Mind Control'." 1 Dec. 2014. <http://www.hurriyetdailynews.com/after-meeting-erdogan-militant-islamist-leader-complains-of-mind-control.aspx?pageID=238&nID=75044&NewsCatID=338>.

Great East Islamic Raiders' Front (IBDA-C) section on FAS Intelligence Resource Program website. <http://fas.org/irp/world/para/ibda-c.htm>.

Great Eastern Islamic Raiders Front (IBDA-C) section on Terrorism Research and Analysis Consortium website. <http://www.trackingterrorism.org/group/great-eastern-islamic-raiders-front-ibda-c?ip_login_no_cache=760e5d9a9f798264525452766751152c>.

Great Eastern Islamic Raiders' Front (IBDA-C) section on Terrorism Watch and Warning website. 26 Apr. 2014. <http://www.terrorism.com/2014/04/26/great-eastern-islamic-raiders-front-ibda-c/>.

"Great Eastern Islamic Raiders' Front (Turkey)." Flags of the World. 24 Apr. 2009. <http://www.crwflags.com/fotw/flags/tr%7Dibdac.html>.

Islamic Great Eastern Raiders/Front (IBDA/C) section on GlobalSecurity.org. <http://www.globalsecurity.org/military/world/para/eastern-raiders.htm>.

Fighel, Yoni. "The Great East Islamic Raiders Front (IBDA-C)" report, Intelligence and Terrorism Information Center at the Center for Special Studies (C.S.S.). <http://www.terrorism-info.org.il/Data/articles/Art_506/dec_03b_1580673991.pdf>.

HAMAS

"Fatalities and Injuries in the Last Decade." Israeli Security Agency. Dec. 2009. <http://www.shabak.gov.il/English/EnTerrorData/decade/Fatalities/Pages/default.aspx>.

Hamas. Backgrounder section on Council on Foreign Relations website. 1 Aug. 2014. <http://www.cfr.org/israel/hamas/p8968 >.

Hamas section on Terrorism Research and Analysis Consortium website. <http://www.trackingterrorism.org/group/hamas>.

"Profile: Hamas Palestinian Movement." BBC. 11 July 2014. <http://www.bbc.com/news/world-middle-east-13331522>. "The Rise of Hamas: A Timeline of Key Events in the History of the Movement." PBS. 9 May 2006. <http://www.pbs.org/frontlineworld/stories/palestine503/history.html>.

"Rocket Attacks on Israel From Gaza." Israel Defense Forces. <http://www.idfblog.com/facts-figures/rocket-attacks-toward-israel/>.

"UNRWA Strongly Condemns Placement of Rockets in School | UNRWA." UNRWA. 17 July 2014. <http://www.unrwa.org/newsroom/press-releases/unrwa-strongly-condemns-placement-rockets-school>.

Jones, Bryony. "Q&A: What Is Hamas?" CNN. 24 Nov. 2012. <http://www.cnn.com/2012/11/16/world/meast/hamas-explainer/>.

Laub, Zachary. Hamas section on Council on Foreign Relations website. 1 Aug. 2014. <http://www.cfr.org/israel/hamas/p8968>.

Phillips, Moshe, and Benyamin Korn. "Conclusive Proof That Hamas Uses Palestinians as Human Shields." The Algemeiner. 7 Aug. 2014. <http://www.algemeiner.com/2014/08/07/conclusive-proof-that-hamas-uses-palestinians-as-human-shields/#>.

Sherwood, Harriet. "In Gaza, Hamas Fighters Are Among Civilians. There Is Nowhere Else for Them to Go." The Guardian. 24 July 2014. <http%3A%2F%2Fwww.theguardian.com%2Fworld%2F2014%2Fjul%2F24%2Fgaza-hamas-fighters-military-bases-guerrilla-war-civilians-israel-idf>.

HAQQANI NETWORK

"Afghan Militant Leader Jalaluddin Haqqani 'Has Died'" BBC. 31 July 2015. <http://www.bbc.com/news/world-asia-33740337>.

"The Haqqani Network: Blacklisted." The Economist. 15 Sept. 2015. <http://www.economist.com/node/21562974>.

Haqqani Network section in Mapping Militant Organizations on Stanford University website. 15 May 2015. <http://stanford.edu/group/mappingmilitants/cgi-bin/groups/view/363>.

Haqqani Network section on Institute for the Study of War website. <http://www.understandingwar.org/haqqani-network>.

"Haqqanis: Growth of a Militant Network." BBC. 14 Sept. 2011.
<http://www.bbc.com/news/world-south-asia-14912957>.

Fantz, Ashley. "The Haqqani Network, a Family and a Terror Group."
CNN. 7 Sept. 2012. <http://www.cnn.com/2012/09/07/world/who-is-haqqani/>.

Scarborough, Rowan. "Haqqani Network, Pakistan Terror Group,
Grows into Worst Enemy for U.S." *The Washington Times*. 5
June 2014. <http://www.washingtontimes.com/news/2014/jun/5/
haqqani-network-pakistan-terror-group-grows-into-w/?page=all>.

HARKAT-UL-JIHAD AL-ISLAMI

"Country Reports on Terrorism 2013—Foreign Terrorist Organizations: Harakat-ul Jihad Islami." U.S. Department of State. 30 Apr.
2014. <http://www.refworld.org/docid/5362298914.html>.

Harkat-ul-Jihad-al Islami Bangladesh (HuJI-B) section on South
Asian Terrorism Portal website. <http://www.satp.org/satporgtp/
countries/bangladesh/terroristoutfits/Huj.htm>.

Harkat-ul-Jihadi Al-Islami section in Mapping Militant Organizations
on Stanford University website. 28 Nov. 2012. <http://stanford.
edu/group/mappingmilitants/cgi-bin/groups/view/217>.

Harakat Ul-Jihad-I-Islami (HUJI) section on The Investigative Project on Terrorism website. <http://www.investigativeproject.org/pro-
file/147/harakat-ul-jihad-i-islami-huji>.

Harakat Ul-Jihad-i-Islami (HuJI) section on Terrorism Research and
Analysis Consortium website. <http://www.trackingterrorism.org/
group/harakat-ul-jihad-i-islami-huji>.

Harkat-ul-Jihad-al-Islami (HuJI) section on South Asian Terrorism
Portal website. <http://www.satp.org/satporgtp/countries/india/
states/jandk/terrorist_outfits/HuJI.htm>.

Chadhury, Dipanjan Roy. "HuJI Militants Sentencing Comes at Right
Time for New Delhi-Dhaka Ties." *The Economic Times*. 25 June
2014. <http://articles.economictimes.indiatimes.com/2014-06-
25/news/50856167_1_bangladesh-court-bangladesh-government-
sheikh-hasina>.

Cook, David. "The Rise of Boko Haram in Nigeria." Combating Terrorism Center at West Point. 26 Sept. 2011. <https://www.ctc.
usma.edu/posts/the-rise-of-boko-haram-in-nigeria>.

Ramachandran, Sudha. "South Asia Part 1: Bangladesh Treads Fine Terror Line." *Asia Times*. 9 Dec. 2004. <http://www.atimes.com/atimes/South_Asia/FL09Df03.html>.

HARKAT-UL-MUJAHIDEEN AL-ISLAMI

Bureau of Counterterrorism Country Reports on Terrorism 2013. U.S. Department of State. <http://www.state.gov/j/ct/rls/crt/2013/224829.htm>.

Harkat-ul-Mujahedeen section in Mapping Militant Organizations on Stanford University website. 28 Nov. 2012. <http://stanford.edu/group/mappingmilitants/cgi-bin/groups/view/219>.

Harkat-ul-Mujahideen (HUM). section on Civil Effort in Fighting International Terrorism website. <http://www.ceifit.com/?categoryId=26686>.

Harkat-ul-Mujahideen section on *South Asian Terrorism Portal*. <http://www.satp.org/satporgtp/countries/india/states/jandk/terrorist_outfits/harkatul_mujahideen.htm>.

Roggio, Bill. "Harakat-ul-Mujahideen 'Operates Terrorist Training Camps in Eastern Afghanistan'." *The Long War Journal*. 8 Aug. 2014. <http://www.longwarjournal.org/archives/2014/08/harakat-ul-mujahidee.php>.

Roggio, Bill. "US Adds Harakat-ul-Mujahideen's Emir to Terrorism List." *The Long War Journal*. 30 Sept. 2014. <http://www.longwarjournal.org/archives/2014/09/us_adds_harakat-ul-m.php>.

HEZBOLLAH

"Hezbollah's Death Toll in Syrian Civil War Tops 1263." Yalibnan. 29 Oct. 2015. <http://yalibnan.com/2015/10/28/hezbollahs-death-toll-in-syrian-civil-war-tops-1263/>.

Hezbollah section on Terrorism Research and Analysis Consortium website. <http://www.trackingterrorism.org/group/hezbollah>.

"Profile: Lebanon's Hezbollah Movement." BBC. 4 Dec. 2013. <http://www.bbc.com/news/world-middle-east-10814698>.

Addis, Casey L., and Christopher M. Blanchard. "Hezbollah: Background and Issues for Congress." Congressional Research Service, posted on FAS Project on Government Secrecy wesbite. 3 Jan. 2011. <http://fas.org/sgp/crs/mideast/R41446.pdf>.

Cohler, Sarah. "Hezbollah: Analysis of Violence." American Diplomacy. Mar. 2011. <http://www.unc.edu/depts/diplomat/item/2011/
0104/comm/cohler_hezbollah.html>.

Masters, Jonathan, and Zachary Laub. Hezbollah (a.k.a. Hizbollah,
Hizbu'llah). Backgrounder section on Council on Foreign Relations website. 3 Jan. 2014. <http://www.cfr.org/lebanon/hezbollah-
k-hizbollah-hizbullah/p9155>.

Schwartz, Stephen, ed. *Hassan Nasrallah: In His Own Words.* New
York, New York: Pamphleteer, LLC, 2006.

HIZBUL MUJAHIDEEN

Hizb-ul-Mujahideen section on South Asian Terrorism Portal website. <http://www.satp.org/satporgtp/countries/india/states/jandk/
terrorist_outfits/hizbul_mujahideen.htm>.

Hizbul Mujahideen section on Terrorism Research and Analysis Consortium website. <http://www.trackingterrorism.org/group/hizbul-
mujahideen>.

"Pak Supports Militants in Kashmir: Hizbul Mujahideen Chief."
The Times of India. 27 May 2011. <http://timesofindia.indiatimes.
com/world/pakistan/Pak-supports-militants-in-Kashmir-Hizbul-
Mujahideen-chief/articleshow/8594878.cms>.

"Profiles: Armed Groups." *Al Jazeera.* 3 Apr. 2012. <http://www.
aljazeera.com/indepth/spotlight/kashmirtheforgottencon-
flict/2011/07/2011731161726482729.html>.

Ganai, Naseer. "Jihadi Boss Invites Taliban to Kashmir: United Jihad
Council Head Salahuddin Says Terrorists Including Al-Qaeda Are
Welcome to 'Liberate' the Region." *Daily Mail India.* 14 July 2014.
<http://www.dailymail.co.uk/indiahome/indianews/article-2692082/
United-Jihad-Council-head-Syed-Salahuddin-invites-Taliban-
Kashmir.html>.

Sheikh, Zafar Mahmood. "Normalization of Indo-Pak Ties Hurts
Kashmir Cause: Salahuddin." *Arab News.* 31 May 2012. <http://
www.arabnews.com/world/normalization-indo-pak-ties-hurts-
kashmir-cause-salahuddin>.

HIZB-UT TAHRIR

About Us section of Hizb Ut-Tahrir website. <http://english.
hizbuttahrir.org/index.php/about/about-us>.

Gilligan, Andrew. "Council Suspends Funding to Schools Linked to Hizb Ut-Tahrir." *The Telegraph*. 31 Oct. 2009.

Hizb Ut-Tahrir Al-Islami (Islamic Party of Liberation) section on GlobalSecurity.org. <http://www.globalsecurity.org/military/world/para/hizb-ut-tahrir.htm>.

Hizb Ut-Tahrir Australia website <http://www.hizb-australia.org/>.

"The Caliphate in South Asia: A Profile of Hizb-ut Tahrir in Pakistan." *The Long War Journal*. 10 July 2014. <http://www.jamestown.org/programs/tm/single/?tx_ttnews%5Btt_news%5D=42600&cHash=840c6347960273b28f53c542eee386ab#.VQww6o7F9ds>.

"Tony Abbott Condemns Hizb Ut-Tahrir over Beheadings." The Australian. 9 Oct. 2014. <http://www.theaustralian.com.au/in-depth/terror/tony-abbott-condemns-hizb-uttahrir-over-beheadings/story-fnpdbcmu-1227084755026>.

"The Zionist Hatred." Hizb Ut-Tahrir Britain website. 22 July 2006. <http://archive.org/web/20100601033659/http://www.hizb.org.uk/hizb/resources/issues-explained/the-zionist-hatred.html>.

Miazee, Manik. "Hizb-ut-Tahrir Making a Comeback." *Dhaka Tribune*. 18 Oct. 2014. <http://www.dhakatribune.com/bangladesh/2014/oct/18/hizb-ut-tahrir-making-comeback>.

Valentine, Simon Ross. *Fighting Kufr and the American Raj: Hizb-ut-Tahrir in Pakistan*. Rep. no. 56. Pakistan Security Research Unit (PSRU). 12 Feb. 2010. <https://www.dur.ac.uk/resources/psru/briefings/archive/Brief56.pdf>.

HOUTHIS

"Houthis 'Beat and Detain Demonstrators' in Yemen." *Al Jazeera*. 28 Jan. 2015. <http://www.aljazeera.com/news/2015/01/houthis-beat-detain-demonstrators-yemen-150128164708190.html>.

"Houthis' Rise in Yemen Risks Empowering Al-Qaeda." *Time*. 22 Jan. 2015. <http://time.com/3677676/houthis-yemen-al-qaeda/>.

The Houthis section on Islamopedia Online. <http://www.islamopediaonline.org/country-profile/yemen/political-landscape/houthis>.

"How Yemen's Capital Sanaa Was Seized by Houthi Rebels." BBC. 27 Sept. 2014. <http://www.bbc.com/news/world-29380668>.

"Saudi and Arab Allies Bomb Houthi Positions in Yemen." *Al Jazeera*. 26 Mar. 2015. <http://www.aljazeera.com/news/middleeast/2015/03/saudi-ambassador-announces-military-operation-yemen-150325234138956.html>.

"Who Are the Houthis of Yemen?" *The New York Times*. 20 Jan. 2015. <http://www.nytimes.com/2015/01/21/world/middleeast/who-are-the-houthis-of-yemen.html?_r=0>.

"Yemen Crisis: Who Is Fighting Whom?" BBC. 26 Mar. 2015. <http://www.bbc.co.uk/news/world-middle-east-29319423>.

"Yemen: Houthi Rebels and Militia Clash in Sanaa." BBC. 19 Sept. 2014. <http://www.bbc.com/news/world-middle-east-29275891>.

Ghosh, Bobby. "Yemen's Houthis Are a Reminder of Iran's Sectarian Agenda in the Arab World." Quartz. 21 Jan. 2015. <http://qz.com/330498/yemens-houthis-are-a-reminder-of-irans-sectarian-agenda-in-the-arab-world/>.

Zimmerman, Katherine, and Chris Harnisch. "Profile: Al Houthi Movement." AEI Critical Threats. 28 Jan. 2010. <http://www.criticalthreats.org/yemen/profile-al-houthi-movement>.

INDIAN MUJAHIDEEN

Indian Mujahideen section on Terrorism Research and Analysis Consortium website. <http://www.trackingterrorism.org/group/indian-mujahideen>.

"Terrorist Designations of the Indian Mujahideen" media note from the Office of the Spokesperson, U.S. Department of State. 15 Sept. 2011. <http://www.state.gov/r/pa/prs/ps/2011/09/172442.htm>.

Goswami, Namrata. "Who Is the Indian Mujahideen?" Institute for Defence Studies and Analyses. 3 Feb. 2009. <http://www.idsa.in/backgrounder/IndianMujahideen>.

IRANIAN REVOLUTIONARY GUARD CORPS

"Iranian Commander Lets Slip That Revolutionary Guard Is Fighting in Syria." *Time*. 7 May 2014. <http://time.com/90807/iran-syria-revolutionary-guard/>.

Pasdaran - Iranian Revolutionary Guard Corps (IRGC) section on GlobalSecurity.org. <http://www.globalsecurity.org/military/world/iran/pasdaran.htm>.

"Profile: Iran's Revolutionary Guards." BBC. 18 Oct. 2009. <http://news.bbc.co.uk/2/hi/middle_east/7064353.stm>.

Bruno, Greg, Jayshree Bajoria, and Jonathan Masters. Iran's Revolutionary Guards. Backgrounder section on Council on Foreign Relations website. 14 June 2013. <http://www.cfr.org/iran/irans-revolutionary-guards/p14324>.

Madabish, Arafat. "Iranian Revolutionary Guard, Hezbollah Assist Houthis in Sana'a: Intelligence Source." Asharq Al-Awsat. 27 Sept. 2014. <http://www.aawsat.net/2014/09/article55337014/iranian-revolutionary-guard-hezbollah-assist-houthis-in-sanaa-intelligence-source>.

Mass, Warren. "Iran's Revolutionary Guards Fighting ISIS in Iraq." *The New American.* 4 Aug. 2014. <http://www.thenewamerican.com/world-news/asia/item/18852-irans-revolutionary-guards-fighting-isis-in-iraq>.

Rubin, Michael. "Iran's Revolutionary Guards - A Rogue Outfit?" *Middle East Quarterly* Fall 15.4 (2008): 37-48. <http://www.meforum.org/1990/irans-revolutionary-guards-a-rogue-outfit>.

Tabatabai, Ariane. "Where Does the Islamic Revolutionary Guard Corps Stand on Nuclear Negotiations?" Bulletin of the Atomic Scientists. 11 Mar. 2015. <http://thebulletin.org/where-does-islamic-revolutionary-guard-corps-stand-nuclear-negotiations8084>.

ISLAMIC JIHAD UNION

"Country Reports on Terrorism 2013 - Foreign Terrorist Organizations: Islamic Jihad Union." UNHCR. 30 Apr. 2014. <http://www.refworld.org/docid/53622986d.html>.

Islamic Jihad Group (Uzbekistan) section on National Consortium for the Study of Terrorism and Responses to Terrorism (START) website of University of Maryland. <http://www.start.umd.edu/tops/terrorist_organization_profile.asp?id=4582>.

Islamic Jihad Union (IJU) section on Terrorism Research and Analysis Consortium website. <http://www.trackingterrorism.org/group/islamic-jihad-union-iju>.

"Treasury Designates Leadership of the IJU Terrorist Group" press release by U.S. Department of the Treasury. 18 June 2008. <http://www.treasury.gov/press-center/press-releases/Pages/hp1035.aspx>.

Moore, Cerwyn. "The Rise and Fall of the Islamic Jihad Union: What Next for Uzbek Terror Networks?" *Terrorism Monitor* 8.14 (2010). The Jamestown Foundation. <http://www.jamestown.org/programs/tm/single/?tx_ttnews[tt_news]=36251&cHash=05af79606d#.VkvWOfmrRhE>.

Sorcher, Sara. "What Is the Islamic Jihad Union?" *National Journal*. 19 Apr. 2013. <http://news.yahoo.com/islamic-jihad-union-183001458--politics.html >.

ISLAMIC MOVEMENT OF UZBEKISTAN

Islamic Movement of Uzbekistan section on Australian government website. 15 Mar. 2015. <http://www.nationalsecurity.gov.au/Listedterroristorganisations/Pages/IslamicMovementofUzbekistan.aspx>.

Islamic Movement of Uzbekistan section on Berkley Center for Religion, Peace, and World Affairs website. <http://berkleycenter.georgetown.edu/organizations/islamic-movement-of-uzbekistan>.

Daly, John C.K. "Islamic Movement of Uzbekistan Flirts with ISIS." Silk Road Reporters. 13 Oct. 2014. <http://www.silkroadreporters.com/2014/10/13/islamic-movement-uzbekistan-flirts-isis/>.

Ovozi, Qishloq. "The Islamic Movement of Uzbekistan: An Evolving Threat." Radio Free Europe. 20 Nov. 2015. <http://www.rferl.org/content/islamic-movement-uzbekistan-roundtable/25405614.html>.

ISLAMIC STATE

"Boko Haram Chief Voices Support for IS, Claims Deadly Attacks in New Video." RT. 13 July 2014. <http://rt.com/news/172452-boko-haram-support-is/>.

"Iraq Conflict: ISIS Declares a 'Caliphate', Calls for Muslims to Pledge Allegiance." ABC. 2 July 2014. <http://www.abc.net.au/news/2014-06-30/isis-declares-islamic-caliphate/5558508>.

"Iraq Crisis: Islamists Force 500,000 to Flee Mosul." BBC. 11 June 2014. <http://www.bbc.com/news/world-middle-east-27789229>.

"Syria Iraq: The Islamic State Militant Group." BBC. 2 Aug. 2014. <http://www.bbc.com/news/world-middle-east-24179084>.

Aboulenein, Ahmed, and Lin Noueihed. "Islamic State Says 'Schweppes Bomb' Used to Bring Down Russian Plane." Reuters.

19 Nov. 2015. <http://www.reuters.com/article/2015/11/19/us-egypt-crash-islamicstate-photo-idUSKCN0T725Q20151119#OhT GYRbYZaiXxAlE.97>.

Beaumont, Peter. "Abu Bakr Al-Baghdadi: The Isis Chief with the Ambition to Overtake Al-Qaida." *The Guardian*. 12 June 2014. <http://www.theguardian.com/world/2014/jun/12/baghdadi-abu-bakr-iraq-isis-mosul-jihad>.

Bergen, Peter. "Why Does ISIS Keep Making Enemies?" CNN. 18 Feb. 2015. <http://www.cnn.com/2015/02/16/opinion/bergen-isis-enemies/>.

Botelho, Greg, Paul Cruickshank, and Catherine E. Shoichet. "Beirut Suicide Bombings Kill 43; Suspect Claims ISIS Sent Attackers." CNN. 16 Nov. 2015. <http://www.cnn.com/2015/11/12/middleeast/beirut-explosions/>.

Castillo, Mariano, Margot Haddad, Michael Martinez, and Steve Almasy. "Paris Suicide Bomber Identified; ISIS Claims Responsibility for 129 Dead." CNN. 16 Nov. 2015. <http://www.cnn.com/2015/11/14/world/paris-attacks/index.html>.

Collins, Robert. "Inside the Rise of ISIS." PBS. 7 Aug. 2014. <http://www.pbs.org/wgbh/pages/frontline/iraq-war-on-terror/losing-iraq/inside-the-rise-of-isis/>.

Dilanian, Ken. "CIA: Islamic State Group Has up to 31,500 Fighters." The Associated Press. 11 Sept. 2014. <http://bigstory.ap.org/article/cia-islamic-state-group-has-31500-fighters>.

Johnstan, Ian. "The Rise of Isis: Terror Group Now Controls an Area the Size of Britain, Expert Claims." *Independent*. 4 Sept. 2014. <http://www.independent.co.uk/news/world/middle-east/the-rise-of-isis-terror-group-now-controls-an-area-the-size-of-britain-expert-claims-9710198.html>.

Kumar, Anugrah. "Nigeria's Boko Haram Violence Killed as Many People as ISIS in Iraq, New Figures Say." *The Christian Post*. 13 Dec. 2014. <http://www.christianpost.com/news/nigerias-boko-haram-violence-killed-as-many-people-as-isis-in-iraq-new-figures-say-131151/>.

Laub, Zachary, and Jonathan Masters. The Islamic State. Backgrounder section on Council on Foreign Relations website. 16 Nov. 2015. <http://www.cfr.org/iraq/islamic-state-iraq-syria/p14811>.

McCoy, Terrence. "ISIS, Beheadings and the Success of Horrifying Violence." *The Washington Post.* 13 June 2014. <http://www.washingtonpost.com/news/morning-mix/wp/2014/06/13/isis-beheadings-and-the-success-of-horrifying-violence/>.

Mohammed, Riyadh. "ISIS Beheads Another American as 60 New Terror Groups Join." *The Fiscal Times.* 16 Nov. 2014. <http://www.thefiscaltimes.com/2014/11/16/ISIS-Doubles-Down-Infidels-Boosted-60-New-Terror-Groups>.

Mosendz, Polly. "Beheadings as Terror Marketing." *The Atlantic.* 2 Oct. 2014. <http://www.theatlantic.com/international/archive/2014/10/beheadings-as-terror-marketing/381049/>.

Mullen, Jethro. "ISIS' High-Profile Hostages." CNN. 11 Feb. 2015. <http://www.cnn.com/2015/02/11/world/isis-hostages/>.

Sabin, Laimat. "Abu Bakr Al-Baghdadi Profile: The Mysterious Leader of Isis – and Why He Is Called the 'Invisible Sheikh'." *Independent.* 10 Nov. 2014. <http://www.independent.co.uk/news/world/middle-east/abu-bakr-al-baghdadi-profile-the-mysterious-leader-of-isis-and-why-he-is-called-the-invisible-sheikh-9849413.html>.

Salih, Mohammed A., and Wladimir Van Wilgenburg. "Iraqi Yazidis: 'If We Move They Will Kill Us'." *Al Jazeera.* 5 Aug. 2014. <http://www.aljazeera.com/news/middleeast/2014/08/iraqi-yazidis-if-move-they-will-kill-us-20148513656188206.html>.

Smith, Samuel. "UN Report on ISIS: 24,000 Killed, Injured by Islamic State; Children Used as Soldiers, Women Sold as Sex Slaves." *The Christian Post.* 9 Oct. 2014. <http://m.christianpost.com/news/un-report-on-isis-24000-killed-injured-by-islamic-state-children-used-as-soldiers-women-sold-as-sex-slaves-127761/>.

Sydell, Laura. "Pro-ISIS Messages Create Dilemma for Social Media Companies." NPR. 18 Feb. 2015. <http://www.npr.org/blogs/alltechconsidered/2015/01/29/382435536/pro-isis-messages-create-dilemma-for-social-media-companies>.

Wing, Nick, and Carina Kolodny. "15 Shocking Numbers That Will Make You Pay Attention to What ISIS Is Doing in Iraq." The World Post, on Huffington Post website. 11 Aug. 2014. <http://www.huffingtonpost.com/2014/08/11/isis-iraq-numbers_n_5659239.html>.

Wood, Graeme. "What ISIS's Leader Really Wants." *New Republic*. 1 Sept. 2014. <http://www.newrepublic.com/article/119259/isis-history-islamic-states-new-caliphate-syria-and-iraq>.

JABHAT AL-NUSRA

"American and International Militants Drawn to Syria." Anti-Defamation League. 22 Nov. 2013. <http://www.adl.org/combating-hate/international-extremism-terrorism/c/syria-foreign-fighters.html?_ga=1.67398481.1388829510.1447814071#. VAjKnvldU1I?referrer=http://blog.adl.org/tags/jabhat-al-nusra>.

"Guide to the Syrian Opposition." BBC. 17 Oct. 2013. <http://www.bbc.com/news/world-middle-east-15798218>.

"ISIS+Al-Nusra Front? Islamists Reportedly Join Forces, New Threat Against West Issued." RT. 29 Sept. 2014. <http://rt.com/news/191396-nusra-qaeda-air-strikes-islamic/>.

Jabhat Al-Nusra section in Mapping Militant Organizations on Stanford University website. 1 Oct. 2015. <http://stanford.edu/group/mappingmilitants/cgi-bin/groups/view/493>.

"Profile: Syria's Al-Nusra Front." BBC. 10 Apr. 2013. <http://www.bbc.co.uk/news/world-middle-east-18048033>.

Abouzeid, Rania. "Interview with Official of Jabhat Al-Nusra, Syria's Islamist Militia Group." *Time*. 25 Dec. 2012. <http://world.time.com/2012/12/25/interview-with-a-newly-designated-syrias-jabhat-al-nusra/>.

Ahad, Abdul. "Syria's Al-Nusra Front – Ruthless, Organised and Taking Control." *The Guardian*. 10 July 2013. <http://www.theguardian.com/world/2013/jul/10/syria-al-nusra-front-jihadi>.

Bajoria, Jayshree. "Syria's Deepening Crisis." Council on Foreign Relations. 6 Feb. 2012. <http://www.cfr.org/syria/syrias-deepening-crisis/p27300>.

Cafarella, Jennifer. "Jabhat Al-Nusra in Syria." Institute for the Study of War. <http://www.understandingwar.org/report/jabhat-al-nusra-syria>.

Yan, Holly. "What's the Difference between ISIS, Al-Nusra and the Khorasan Group?" CNN. 24 Sept. 2014. <http://www.cnn.com/2014/09/24/world/meast/isis-al-nusra-khorasan-difference/>.

JAISH-E-MUHAMMED

"Jaish-e-Mohammad: A Profile." BBC. 6 Feb. 2002. <http://news.bbc. co.uk/2/hi/south_asia/1804228.stm>.

Jaish-e-Mohammad section in Mapping Militant Organizations on Stanford University website. 25 June 2015. <http://stanford.edu/ group/mappingmilitants/cgi-bin/groups/view/95>.

Jaish-e-Mohammad section on *Global Security* website. <http://www. globalsecurity.org/military/world/para/jem.htm>.

Jaish-e-Mohammed (Army of the Prophet) section on South Asian Terrorism Portal. <http://www.satp.org/satporgtp/countries/india/ states/jandk/terrorist_outfits/jaish_e_mohammad_mujahideen_e_ tanzeem.htm>.

Jaish-e-Mohammed (JEM) section in The National Counterterrorism Center website. <http://www.nctc.gov/site/groups/jem.html>.

Egan, Mark. "Synagogue Targeted in NY Plot, Four Charged." Reuters. 20 May 2009. <http://www.reuters.com/article/2009/05/ 21/idUSN20523965>.

Sharma, Rajeev. "Pakistan Army Quietly Reviving Jaish-e Moham- mad." Diplomatic Courier. 13 Sept. 2011. <http://www. diplomaticourier.com/news/regions/central-asia/363-pakistan-army- quietly-reviving-jaish-e-mohammad>.

JEMAAH ISLAMIYAH

Jemaah Islamiyah (a.k.a. Jemaah Islamiah) section on Council on Foreign Relations website. 19 June 2009. <http://www.cfr.org/ indonesia/jemaah-islamiyah-k-jemaah-islamiah/p8948#>.

Jemaah Islamiyah (JI) section on Australian government web- site. 12 July 2013. <http://www.nationalsecurity.gov.au/ Listedterroristorganisations/Pages/JemaahIslamiyahJI.aspx>.

Jemaah Islamiyah (JI) section on GlobalSecurity.org. <http://www. globalsecurity.org/military/world/para/ji.htm>.

Jemaah Islamiyah (JI) section on National Counterterrorism Center website. Sept. 2013. <http://www.nctc.gov/site/groups/ji.html>.

Jemaah Islamiyah (JI) section on Terrorism Research and Analy- sis Consortium website. <http://www.trackingterrorism.org/group/ jemaah-islamiyah-ji>.

Jemaah Islamiyah section in Mapping Militant Organizations on Stanford University website. 8 July 2015. <http://stanford.edu/group/mappingmilitants/cgi-bin/groups/view/251>.

"Profile: Jemaah Islamiah." BBC. 2 Feb. 2012. <http://www.bbc.com/news/world-asia-16850706>.

QE.J.92.02 Jemaah Islamiyah. (Report). Security Council Committee Pursuant to Resolutions 1267 (1999) and 1989 (2011) Concerning Al-Qaida and Associated Individuals and Entities, United Nations. 28 Mar. 2011.

Abuza, Zachary. "Jemaah Islamiyah Adopts the Hezbollah Model: Assessing Hezbollah's Influence." *Middle East Quarterly*. Winter 2009. <http://www.meforum.org/2044/jemaah-islamiyah-adopts-the-hezbollah-model>.

Erikson, Marc. "The Osama Bin Laden and Al-Qaeda of Southeast Asia." *Asia Times*. 6 Feb. 2002. <http://atimes.com/se-asia/DB06Ae01.html>.

Golburt, Yanina. "An In-Depth Look at the Jemaah Islamiyah Network." *The Fletcher School Online Journal*. 2004. <http://fletcher.tufts.edu/Al-Nakhlah/Archives/~/media/Fletcher/Microsites/al%20Nakhlah/archives/pdfs/golburt.ashx>.

Gordon, David, and Samuel Lindo. Jemaah Islamiyah section on Center for Strategic & International Studies website. 1 Nov. 2011. <http://csis.org/publication/jemaah-islamiyah>.

Witular, Rendi A. "Sons, Top Aides Abandon Ba'asyir over ISIL." *The Jakarta Post*. 13 Aug. 2014. <http://www.thejakartapost.com/news/2014/08/13/sons-top-aides-abandon-ba-asyir-over-isil-form-new-jihadist-group.html>.

JUND AL-SHAM

"A Look at the Terror Group Jund Al-Sham." Associated Press, *The Washington Post*. 12 Sept. 2006. <http://www.washingtonpost.com/wp-dyn/content/article/2006/09/12/AR2006091200844.html>.

Jund Al-Sham section on Terrorism Watch and Warning website. <http://www.terrorism.com/2014/04/26/jund-al-sham/>.

KUMPULAN MUJAHIDIN MALAYSIA

Kumpulan Mujahidin Malaysia (KMM) Malaysian Mujahideen Movement section on GlobalSecurity.org. <http://www.globalsecurity.org/military/world/para/kmm.htm>.

Kumpulan Mujahidin Malaysia (KMM) section on Terrorism Research and Analysis Consortium website. <http://www.trackingterrorism.org/group/kumpulan-mujahidin-malaysia-kmm>.

Kumpulan Mujahidin Malaysia (KMM) section on Terrorism Watch and Warning website. 26 Apr. 2014. <http://www.terrorism.com/2014/04/26/kumpulan-mujahidin-malaysia-kmm/>.

Center for Strategic Intelligence Research. *A Muslim Archipelago: Islam and Politics in Southeast Asia.* Rep. Government Printing Office. p. 52

Hefner, Robert W. *Making Modern Muslims: The Politics of Islamic Education in Southeast Asia.* Honolulu: U of Hawaii, 2009. p. 109

McIntyre, Ian, and C.A. Zulkifle. "Nik Aziz's Son Freed with 10 Others." *The Star Online.* 19 Oct. 2006. <http://www.thestar.com.my/story/?file=%2f2006%2f10%2f19%2fnation%2f15771918&sec=nation>.

Pike, John. Kumpulan Mujahidin Malaysia (KMM) section on FAS Intelligence Research Program website. 1 May 2003. <http://fas.org/irp/world/para/kmm.htm>.

LASHKAR-E-JHANGVI

Lashkar-e-Jhangvi (LeJ) section on Terrorism Research and Analysis Consortium website. <http://www.trackingterrorism.org/group/lashkar-e-jhangvi-lej>.

Lashkar-e-Jhangvi section in Mapping Militant Organizations on Stanford University website. 7 July 2015. <http://stanford.edu/group/mappingmilitants/cgi-bin/groups/view/215>.

Lashkar-e Jhangvi section on Australian government website. 3 Mar. 2015. <http://www.nationalsecurity.gov.au/Listedterroristorganisations/Pages/Lashkar-e-Jhangvi.aspx>.

Lashkar-e-Jhangvi section on South Asian Terrorism Portal website. <http://www.satp.org/satporgtp/countries/pakistan/terroristoutfits/Lej.htm>.

LASHKAR-E-TAIBA

About Us section on Jamat ud Dawah official blog. <https:// judofficial.wordpress.com/about/>.

"Lashkar-e-Taiba: From 9/11 to Mumbai." ICSR, King's College London. 27 Apr. 2009. <http://icsr.info/2009/04/lashkar-e-taiba-from-911-to-mumbai/>.

"Lashkar-e-Taiba Plot to Attack PM Narendra Modi Unearthed; IB, Delhi Police in Joint Operation." Daily News Analysis. 6 Dec. 2015. <http://www.dnaindia.com/india/report-lashkar-e-taiba-plot-to-attack-pm-narendra-modi-discovered-ib-delhi-police-in-joint-operation-2152523>.

Lashkar-e Taiba section of the *World Almanac of Islam*. The American Foreign Policy Council. 2 Oct. 2013. <http://almanac.afpc.org/lashkar-e-taiba>.

"Profile: Lashkar-e-Taiba." BBC. 3 May 2010. <http://news.bbc.co.uk/2/hi/south_asia/3181925.stm>.

"The Rise of Lashkar-e-Taiba: A Look at One of South Asia's Largest Terrorist Organizations." International Security Program. New America. 22 Sept. 2014. <https://www.newamerica.org/international-security/the-rise-of-lashkar-e-taiba/>.

Bajoria, Jayshree. Lashkar-e-Taiba (Army of the Pure). Backgrounder section on Council on Foreign Relations website. 14 Jan. 2010. <http://www.cfr.org/pakistan/lashkar-e-taiba-army-pure-aka-lashkar-e-tayyiba-lashkar-e-toiba-lashkar--taiba/p17882>.

Hussain, Zahid. *Frontline Pakistan: The Struggle with Militant Islam.* New York: I.B. Tauris & Co., 2007.

Kambere, Geoffrey, Puay Hock Goh, Pranav Kumar, and Fulgence Msafir. "The Financing of Lashkar-e-Taiba." *Global ECCO* August Vol 1 No. 1 (2011). <https://globalecco.org/ctx-v1n1/lashkar-e-taiba>.

Padukone, Neil. "The Next Al-Qaeda? Lashkar-e-Taiba and the Future of Terrorism in South Asia." *World Affairs*. Nov./Dec. 2011. <http://www.worldaffairsjournal.org/article/next-al-qaeda-lashkar-e-taiba-and-future-terrorism-south-asia>.

Tellis, Ashley J. "The Menace That Is Lashkar-e-Taiba." *Policy Outlook*. Carnegie Endowment for International Peace. Mar. 2012. <http://carnegieendowment.org/files/let_menace.pdf>.

Upadhyay, Tarun. "I Came to Kill Indians, It's Fun: Captured Pak Militant Naved." *Hindustan Times*. 8 Aug. 2015. <http://www. hindustantimes.com/india/i-came-to-kill-indians-it-s-fun-captured-pak-militant-naved/story-cxxFxBAjvfdZ3wWAuxziON.html>.

LIBYAN ISLAMIC FIGHTING GROUP

"Al-Qaeda-Allied Libyan Islamic Fighting Group Retakes Benghazi." LaRouche PAC. 21 Feb. 2013. <http://archive.larouchepac.com/node/25572>.

Libyan Islamic Fighting Group (LIFG) section on GlobalSecurity.org. <http://www.globalsecurity.org/military/world/para/lifg.htm>.

Libyan Islamic Fighting Group (LIFG) section on Terrorism Research and Analysis Consortium website. <http://www.trackingterrorism.org/group/libyan-islamic-fighting-group-lifg>.

Libyan Islamic Fighting Group section on Terrorism Watch and Warning website. <http://www.terrorism.com/2014/04/26/libyan-islamic-fighting-group/>.

QE.L.11.01 Libyan Islamic Fighting Group. (Report). Security Council Committee Pursuant to Resolutions 1267 (1999) and 1989 (2011) concerning Al-Qaida and Associated Individuals and Entities, United Nations. 7 Nov. 2013.

Black, Ian. "The Libyan Islamic Fighting Group – from Al-Qaida to the Arab Spring." *The Guardian*. 5 Sept. 2011. <http://www.theguardian.com/world/2011/sep/05/libyan-islamic-fighting-group-leaders>.

Roggio, Bill. "Libyan Islamic Fighting Group Joins Al Qaeda." *The Long War Journal*. 3 Nov. 2007. <http://www.longwarjournal.org/archives/2007/11/libyan_islamic_fight.php>.

MOROCCAN ISLAMIC COMBATANT GROUP

Moroccan Islamic Combatant Group section in Mapping Militant Organizations on Stanford University website. 6 Aug. 2012. <https://stanford.edu/group/mappingmilitants/cgi-bin/groups/view/129>.

Moroccan Islamic Combatant Group (GICM) section on The Investigative Project on Terrorism website. <http://www.investigativeproject.org/profile/139/moroccan-islamic-combatant-group-gicm>.

Moroccan Islamic Combatant Group (GICM) section on Terrorism Research and Analysis Consortium website. <http://www.trackingterrorism.org/group/moroccan-islamic-combatant-group-gicm>.

Q.E.M.89.02. Moroccan Islamic Combatant Group. (Report). Security Council Committee Pursuant to Resolutions 1267 (1999) and 1989 (2011) concerning Al-Qaida and Associated Individuals and Entities, United Nations. 14 Dec. 2009.

Jesus, Carlos E. "The Current State of the Moroccan Islamic Combatant Group." Combating Terrorism Center. 15 Mar. 2009. <https://www.ctc.usma.edu/posts/the-current-state-of-the-moroccan-islamic-combatant-group>.

Pike, John. Moroccan Islamic Combatant Group (GICM) section on FAS Intelligence Research Program website. 1 May 2003. <http://fas.org/irp/world/para/gicm.htm>.

MORO ISLAMIC LIBERATION FRONT

Frequently Asked Questions on the Draft Bangsamoro Basic Law. Office of the President of the Philippines, Office of the Presidential Adviser on the Peace Process. 10 Sept. 2014. <http://www.opapp.gov.ph/milf/news/frequently-asked-questions-draft-bangsamoro-basic-law>.

Moro Islamic Liberation Front (MILF) section on Terrorism Research and Analysis Consortium website. <http://www.trackingterrorism.org/group/moro-islamic-liberation-front-0>.

Moro Islamic Liberation Front section in Mapping Militant Organizations on Stanford University website. 24 Aug. 2015. <http://stanford.edu/group/mappingmilitants/cgi-bin/groups/view/309>.

Moro Islamic Liberation Front section on GlobalSecurity.org. <http://www.globalsecurity.org/military/world/para/milf.htm>.

"Perhaps the Moro Struggle for Freedom and Self-Determination Is the Longest and Bloodiest in the Entire History of Mankind." FAS Intelligence Research Program. <http://fas.org/irp/world/para/docs/ph2.htm>.

Mogato, Manny. "Factbox: The Philippines' Moro Islamic Liberation Front." Reuters. 5 Feb. 2011. <http://www.reuters.

com/article/2011/02/05/us-philippines-rebels-factbox-idUS-
TRE7140PP20110205>.

Republic of the Philippines, Congress of the Philippines, Eighth
Congress. *An Act Providing for an Organic Act for the Autonomous
Region in Muslim Mindanao.* 1989. Republic Act No. 6734. Available online at: http://www.lawphil.net/statutes/repacts/ra1989/
ra_6734_1989.html.

Whaley, Floyd. "Philippine Bill Would Give Muslims Autonomy." *The New York Times.* 10 Sept. 2014. <http://www.nytimes.
com/2014/09/11/world/asia/philippine-bill-would-set-up-autonomous-region-in-muslim-dominated-south.html>.

MUSLIM BROTHERHOOD

"Profile: Egypt's Muslim Brotherhood." BBC. 23 Dec. 2013. <http://
www.bbc.com/news/world-middle-east-12313405>.

Aminoff, Gary. "Islamic Fascism: The Nazi Connection." American Thinker. 11 Dec. 2012. <http://www.americanthinker.com/
articles/2012/12/islamic_fascism_the_nazi_connection.html>.

Laub, Zachary. Egypt's Muslim Brotherhood. Backgrounder section
on Council on Foreign Relations website. 15 Jan. 2014. <http://
www.cfr.org/egypt/egypts-muslim-brotherhood/p23991>.

Zalman, Amy. "Muslim Brotherhood: Roots of Modern Jihad?" About
News. <http://terrorism.about.com/od/politicalislamterrorism/a/
MuslimBrothers.htm>.

Wright, Lawrence. *The Looming Tower: Al-Qaeda and the Road to
9/11.* New York: Knopf, 2006. p. 25.

PALESTINIAN ISLAMIC JIHAD

Palestinian Islamic Jihad (PIJ) section on GlobalSecurity.org. <http://
www.globalsecurity.org/military/world/para/pij.htm>.

Palestinian Islamic Jihad section on Australian government website.
<http://www.nationalsecurity.gov.au/Listedterroristorganisations/
Pages/PalestinianIslamicJihad.aspx>.

Palestine Islamic Jihad section on Jewish Virtual Library website.
<http://www.jewishvirtuallibrary.org/jsource/Terrorism/PIJ.html>.

Fletcher, Holly. Palestinian Islamic Jihad. Backgrounder section on Council on Foreign Relations website. 10 Apr. 2008. <http://www.cfr.org/israel/palestinian-islamic-jihad/p15984>.

POPULAR FRONT FOR THE LIBERATION OF PALESTINE

Popular Front for the Liberation of Palestine (PFLP) section on GlobalSecurity.org. <http://www.globalsecurity.org/military/world/para/pflp.htm>.

Popular Front for the Liberation of Palestine (PFLP) section on Jewish Virtual Library website. <http://www.jewishvirtuallibrary.org/jsource/Terrorism/pflp.html>.

"Profile: Popular Front for the Liberation of Palestine (PFLP)." BBC. 18 Nov. 2014. <http://www.bbc.com/news/world-middle-east-30099510>.

Badger, Sam, and Giorgio Cafiero. "Assad and the Palestinians." Foreign Policy in Focus. 3 Apr. 2014. <http://fpif.org/assad-palestinians/>.

Volodarsky, Boris. "Terror's KGB Roots." The Wall Street Journal. 23 Nov. 2007. <http://www.wsj.com/articles/SB119578738628401849>.

SALAFIA JIHADIA

"Salafia-Jihadia: A Militant Movement Supporting Violent Struggle." Israeli Security Agency. <http://www.shabak.gov.il/English/EnTerrorData/Reviews/Pages/Salafia-Jihadiaa.aspx>.

Salafia Jihadia section on National Consortium for the Study of Terrorism and Responses to Terrorism (START) website of University of Maryland. <http://www.start.umd.edu/tops/terrorist_organization_profile.asp?id=4257>.

Salafia Jihadia section on Terrorism Research and Analysis Consortium website. <http://www.trackingterrorism.org/group/salafia-jihadia>.

Cherkaoui, Naoufel. "Morocco Dismantles Salafia Jihadia Cell." Magharebia. 1 July 2009. <http://magharebia.com/en_GB/articles/awi/features/2009/07/01/feature-01>.

SIPAH-E-SAHABA PAKISTAN

Sipah-e-Sahaba Pakistan section in Mapping Militant Organizations on Stanford University website. 15 Feb. 2012. <http://stanford.edu/group/mappingmilitants/cgi-bin/groups/view/147>.

Sipah-e-Sahaba Pakistan section on South Asian Terrorism Portal website. <http://www.satp.org/satporgtp/countries/pakistan/terroristoutfits/Ssp.htm>.

Sipah-e-Sahaba Pakistan (SSP) section on Terrorism Research and Analysis Consortium website. <http://www.trackingterrorism.org/group/sipah-e-sahaba-pakistan-ssp>.

THE TALIBAN

"A Divided Afghan Taliban Has Finally Accepted Its New Leader, Reports Say." *Time*. 17 Sept. 2015. <http://time.com/4037785/taliban-mullah-omar-new-leader-akhtar-mansour/>.

"Afghan Militant Leader Jalaluddin Haqqani 'Has Died'" BBC. 31 July 2015. <http://www.bbc.com/news/world-asia-33740337>.

The Taliban section in Mapping Militant Organizations on Stanford University website. 20 July 2014. <http://stanford.edu/group/mappingmilitants/cgi-bin/groups/view/367>.

"Who Are the Taliban?" BBC. 29 Sept. 2015. <http://www.bbc.com/news/world-south-asia-11451718>.

Farmer, Ben. "Mullah Mohammad Omar: Profile of the One-Eyed Taliban Leader." *The Telegraph*. 23 May 2011. <http://www.telegraph.co.uk/news/worldnews/al-qaeda/8531476/Mullah-Mohammad-Omar-profile-of-the-one-eyed-Taliban-leader.html>.

Goldstein, Joseph. "Taliban's New Leader Strengthens His Hold With Intrigue and Battlefield Victory." *The New York Times*. 4 Oct. 2015. <http://www.nytimes.com/2015/10/05/world/asia/kunduz-fall-validates-mullah-akhtar-muhammad-mansour-talibans-new-leader.html?_r=1>.

Hairan, Abdulhadi. "A Profile of the Taliban's Propaganda Tactics." The World Post, on Huffington Post website. 3 Apr. 2010. <http://www.huffingtonpost.com/abdulhadi-hairan/a-profile-of-the-talibans_b_442857.html>.

Laub, Zachary. The Taliban in Afghanistan. Backgrounder section on Council on Foreign Relations website. 4 July 2014. <http://www.cfr.org/afghanistan/taliban-afghanistan/p10551>.

Rashid, Ahmed. *Taliban: Militant Islam, Oil and Fundamentalism in Central Asia.* New Haven, CT: Yale University Press, 2010.

TEHRIK-E-TALIBAN PAKISTAN

Harris, Sarah Ann. "Who Is Maulana Fazlullah? A Look at the 'Radio Mullah' behind Pakistan School Attack." *Express.*18 Dec. 2014. <http://www.express.co.uk/news/world/547652/Maulana-Fazlullah-Radio-Mullah-Pakistani-Taliban-leader>.

Rehman, Zia Ur. "TTP Is Crumbling." *The Friday Times.* 14 Nov. 2014. <http://www.thefridaytimes.com/tft/ttp-is-crumbling/>.

Tehreek-e-Taliban Islami Pakistan (TTIP / TTP) section on Terrorism Research and Analysis Consortium website. <http://www.tracking-terrorism.org/group/tehreek-e-taliban-islami-pakistan-ttip-ttp>.

Tehrik Taliban-i Pakistan (TTiP) section on GlobalSecurity.org. <http://www.globalsecurity.org/military/world/para/ttp.htm>.

Tehreek-e-Taliban Pakistan section in Mapping Militant Organizations on Stanford University website. 7 Aug. 2012. <http://stanford.edu/group/mappingmilitants/cgi-bin/groups/view/105>.

Saifi, Sophia, and Greg Botelho. "In Pakistan School Attack, Taliban Terrorists Kill 145, Mostly Children." CNN. 17 Dec. 2014. <http://www.cnn.com/2014/12/16/world/asia/pakistan-peshawar-school-attack/>.

Yusufzai, Mushtaq. "Taliban Chief Behind Pakistan School Massacre Promises More Attacks." NBC News. 16 Jan. 2015. <http://www.nbcnews.com/storyline/pakistan-school-massacre/taliban-chief-behind-pakistan-school-massacre-promises-more-attacks-n280786>.

Yusufzai, Mushtaq, Wajahat S. Khan, F. Brinley Bruton, and Alastair Jamieson. "Death 'All Around Me': Victims Relive Pakistan School Massacre." NBC News. 16 Dec. 2014. <http://www.nbcnews.com/storyline/pakistan-school-massacre/death-all-around-me-victims-relive-pakistan-school-massacre-n269011>.

TUNISIAN COMBATANT GROUP

"Assets of Tunisia Group Are Frozen." *The New York Times.* 11 Oct. 2002. <http://www.nytimes.com/2002/10/11/world/threats-and-responses-assets-of-tunisia-group-are-frozen.html>.

Terrorist Organization Profile: Tunisian Combatant Group (TCG) section on National Consortium for the Study of Terrorism and Responses to Terrorism (START) website of University of Maryland. <http://www.start.umd.edu/tops/terrorist_organization_profile.asp?id=4346>.

Tunisian Combatant Group section on GlobalSecurity.org. <http://www.globalsecurity.org/security/profiles/tunisian_combatant_group.htm>.

The Tunisian Combatant Group (TCG) section on FAS Intelligence Resource Program website. <http://fas.org/irp/world/para/tcg.htm>.

Tunisian Combatant Group (TCG) section on The Investigative Project on Terrorism website. 2 Nov. 2006. <http://www.investigativeproject.org/profile/162>.

Tunisian Combatant Group (TCG) section on Terrorism Research and Analysis Consortium website. <http://www.trackingterrorism.org/group/tunisian-combatant-group-tcg>.

Joscelyn, Thomas. "Tunisian Government: Ansar Al Sharia Is a Terrorist Organization." *The Long War Journal.* 29 Aug. 2013. <http://www.longwarjournal.org/archives/2013/08/tunisian_government_1.php>.